**Andrew Edwards** is a writer and the translator of two books set in Sicily by the Spanish author Alejandro Luque. **Suzanne Edwards** is a linguistics graduate and dyslexia specialist. Between them, they have written widely on Sicily, its culture, literature and history.

# Sicily

## A LITERARY GUIDE FOR TRAVELLERS

*Andrew and Suzanne Edwards*

I.B. TAURIS

LONDON · NEW YORK

*To Adrian, Alfred, Irene and Patricia*

Published in 2014 by I.B.Tauris & Co. Ltd
6 Salem Road, London W2 4BU
175 Fifth Avenue, New York NY 10010
www.ibtauris.com

Distributed in the United States and Canada
Exclusively by Palgrave Macmillan
175 Fifth Avenue, New York NY 10010

ISBN: 978 1 78076 794 9
eISBN: 978 0 85773 487 7

A full CIP record for this book is available from the British Library
A full CIP record is available from the Library of Congress

Library of Congress Catalog Card Number: available

Typeset by JCS Publishing Services Ltd, www.jcs-publishing.co.uk

Printed and bound in Sweden by ScandBook AB

# CONTENTS

# ILLUSTRATIONS

All images were taken by Andrew Edwards or Suzanne Edwards and
edited by Nik Guyatt.

# ACKNOWLEDGEMENTS

When writing a literary guide such as this you are essentially standing on the shoulders of giants and it is to their thoughts and ideas that our first debt of gratitude must inevitably go. We are also indebted to all those biographers and researchers who have preceded us; their work has been informative, lively and always thought-provoking. Our own Sicilian journey in space and time would never have started without the good auspices of Franco Leone and Franca Canzone – so to both of them and their respective families we offer the most profound thanks. Giovanni Morreale, the instigator of the Times of Sicily website, has also been instrumental in encouraging our enthusiasm and interest in the island's literary landscapes. His infectious passion for his homeland and wish to inspire like-minded souls has been a constant reassurance. We would also like to thank the authors Frank Viviano, Gaia Servadio and Simonetta Agnello Hornby, who agreed to personal interviews and correspondence. Whilst travelling the island in pursuit of our writers, we have also had immense help from the staff of various museums and foundations: particular mention must go to the Fondazione Famiglia Piccolo di Calanovella at Capo d'Orlando and the Fondazione Leonardo Sciascia in Racalmuto. Regarding the photography, we have had the very knowledgeable technical services of Nik Guyatt (www.nikguyattphotography.co.uk), whose creative eye and work have been indispensable. Amongst friends, colleagues and family, we have met with nothing but help and further encouragement. Thanks to Jean and Simon Berriman and their family for showing such interest and to Anna Bricoli for her willingness to listen to all the details. Further gratitude must go to Tony and Pam Sanders, as well as Brian and Lili Sanders and their respective families, as it also must to Ron and Barbara

Baker. For sowing the initial seed, we have to thank the Spanish author, Alejandro Luque, whom we hope knows that he was part of the inspiration behind the whole project.

Additionally, we would like to specifically thank the following for permission to use quoted material: *Palermo*, Alajmo, R., translator, Waldman, G., Haus Publishing Ltd (The Armchair Traveller); Drinkwater, C., *The Olive Tree*, reproduce with permission of Curtis Brown Group Ltd, London on behalf of Carol Drinkwater copyright © Carol Drinkwater, 2008; *Notebooks* by Tennessee Williams, copyright © 2006 by the University of the South. Reprinted by permission of Georges Borchardt, Inc. for the University of the South; by Tennessee Williams (T), from *The Rose Tattoo*, copyright © 1950 by the University of the South. Reprinted by permission of New Directions Publishing Corp.; from *The Passionate Sightseer* by Bernard Berenson © 1960 and 1988 Thames & Hudson Ltd., London, text © 1960 by Estate of Bernard Berenson. Reprinted by kind permission of Thames & Hudson; © Robb, P., *M: The Caravaggio Enigma*, Bloomsbury Publishing Plc, 2000; *Whicker's War*, reprinted by permission of HarperCollins Publishers Ltd © (2006) (Whicker, A.); *Bagheria*, Maraini, D., translators, Kitto, D. and Spottiswood, E., Peter Owen Ltd, London; *Conversations in Sicily*, Vittorini, E., © Copyright Elio Vittorini Estate. All rights reserved handled by Agenzia Letteraria Internazionale, Milano, Italy; *The Wine Dark Sea*, Sciascia, L., translator, Bardoni, A., Carcanet Press Ltd, London, 1987; *Sicilian Uncles*, Sciascia, L., translator, Thompson, N. S., Carcanet Press Ltd, London, 1988; *God Protect Me From My Friends*, Maxwell, G., by permission of The Marsh Agency Ltd on behalf of Gavin Maxwell Enterprises; *The Ten Pains of Death*, Maxwell, G., by permission of The Marsh Agency Ltd on behalf of Gavin Maxwell Enterprises; extract taken from *The Ruby in Her Navel* by Barry Unsworth, published by Penguin Books. © Barry Usworth 2006. Reproduced by permission of Sheila Land Associates Ltd; *Once There Was A War*, Steinbeck, J., 2001, London, pp. 165 and 169, copyright © John Steinbeck, reproduced by permission of Penguin Books Ltd; excerpt from 'Syracuse' and 'Noto' from *Eternal Enemies: Poems* by Adam Zagajewski, translated by Clare Cavanagh. Copyright © 2008 by Adam Zagajewski. Translation copyright © 2008 by Clare Cavanagh. Reprinted by permission of Farrar, Straus and Giroux, LLC.; Abba, C., OUP Material: *The Diary of one of Garibaldi's Thousand* translated by Vincent (1962) 87w from pp. 23, 25; copyright © 2002 by Theresa Maggio from *The Stone Boudoir*: Reprinted

by permission of Counterpoint; excerpt from *Timebends: A Life*, copyright ©
1987 by Arthur Miller. Used by permission of Grove/Atlantic, Inc. Any third
party use of this material, outside of this publication, is prohibited; *The Letters
of D H Lawrence: Volume III, Part 1, 1916–1921*, Boulton, J. T., & Robertson,
A., (eds), Cambridge University Press, reproduced by permission of Pollinger
Limited and the Estate of Frieda Lawrence Ravagli; *The Sicilian* by Mario
Puzo, published by Arrow Books. Reprinted by permission of The Random
House Group Limited; *The Godfather* by Mario Puzo, published by Arrow
Books. Reprinted by permission of The Random House Group Limited;
*Midnight in Sicily* by Peter Robb, published by Harvill Press. Reprinted by
permission of The Random House Group Limited; *Cervantes: A Biography*,
Byron, W., The Orion Publishing Group, all attempts at tracing the copyright
holder were unsuccessful, but we would be happy to rectify any omissions in
future editions should the copyright holder come forward; extracts from *The
Dark Heart of Italy*, Jones, T., *Blood Rain*, Dibdin, M. and *A Sicilian Carousel*,
Durrell, L. by permission of the publishers, Faber and Faber Ltd; *Princes Under
the Volcano* by Raleigh Trevelyan (Copyright © Raleigh Trevelyan) reprinted
by permission of A. M. Heath & Co Ltd; *The Villa Diana*, Moorehead, A.,
original publisher, H. Hamilton, reproduced by permission of Pollinger
Limited and John Moorehead; Portraits & Observations, Capote, T., Modern
Library, an imprint of The Random House Publishing Group; *The Golden
Honeycomb: A Sicilian Quest* by Vincent Cronin, published by Harvill Press,
reprinted by permission of The Random House Group Limited; *The Leopard*
by Giuseppe Tomasi di Lampedusa, published by Harvill Secker, reprinted
by permission of The Random House Group Limited, translation copyright
© 1960 by William Collins & Co Ltd and Random House, renewed 1988.
Used by permission of Pantheon books. All rights reserved; *Happy Summer
Days* by Fulco de Verdura, The Orion Publishing Group, London, copyright
© 1976 Fulco de Verdura; 'In Sicily', from *Collected Poems of Siegfried Sassoon*
by Siegfried Sassoon, copyright 1918, 1920 by E. P. Dutton. Copyright
1936, 1946, 1947, 1948 by Siegfried Sassoon. Used by permission of Viking
Penguin, a division of Penguin Group (USA) LLC and George Sassoon; *La
forma dell'acqua (The Shape of Water), Il cane di terracotta (The Terracotta Dog),
La gita a Tindari (Excursion to Tindari), Il giro di boa (Rounding the Mark)*
by Andrea Camilleri, © Sellerio editore via Siracusa 50 Palermo; *The Nun*
by Simonetta Agnello Hornby, Europa Editions, copyright © Giangiacomo
Feltrinelli Editore; *Sometimes the Soul* by Gioia Timpanelli, reproduced with
the permission of W.W. Norton & Company. Gratitude is also due to all those
other publishers and authors whose full details are listed in the bibliography.

# Literary Sicily

1. Palermo and Surroundings
2. The Tyrrhenian Coast
3. Messina, Taormina and the North-East
4. Catania and Mount Etna
5. Syracuse and the South-East
6. Agrigento and the South Coast
7. Enna and the Interior
8. Trapani and the West

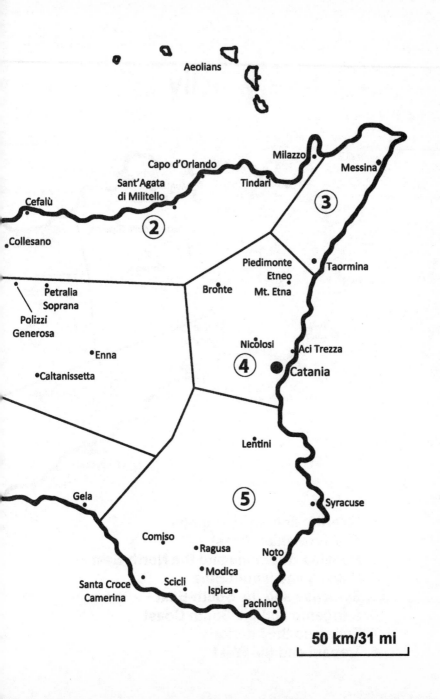

50 km/31 mi

# INTRODUCTION

As the largest island in the Mediterranean, with a central location, Sicily has often had the misfortune of being in the eye of the historical storm. Over 16 invading forces have trodden its sun-drenched soil. In the tracks of these military footsteps have come those bringing more cultural influences: the architects, bureaucrats, politicians, painters and, of course, writers. In many ways, a literary journey along the autostrade and byways of Sicily is a journey through these historical layers. Each invader brought a new perspective, a new vision with which to view the island, whilst the indigenous voice struggled to be heard above such constant commotion.

Any literary guide would be remiss in omitting the Greeks and Romans. At the height of Grecian power, the great cities of Agrigento and Syracuse attracted poets and playwrights to laud their rulers and fill their theatres. Stand where the actors stood in Taormina or Neapolis and you cannot help but feel the years slip away, as you imagine the sandal-clad audience shuffling to their stony seats. The plays of Aeschylus would have echoed around the auditorium, his ground-breaking theatre a novelty to the assembled spectators. Time your visit to coincide with the classical theatre festivals and you can still hear him today.

The Romans saw Sicily as a granary, a possession worth struggling for against others with similar intent. The Greeks and Carthaginians eventually bowed to Roman military might. As elsewhere, the empire needed to administer its resources as efficiently as possible – a task not always fulfilled with the utmost proficiency. Step forward Cicero, orator, legal eagle and writer who has left us some marvellous descriptions of the island under Roman rule. He was also a keen observer of Greek culture, a Grecophile who paid homage to its philosophy and mythology. Many of these legends of gods and goddesses in love or conflict belong to Sicily. Their impact has reverberated through the generations, influencing Renaissance writers, Romantic poets or Victorians steeped in a classical education.

In common with Spain, a power that would later dominate Sicily for centuries, its coasts and mountains were eventually overrun by the Moors, commonly known as the *Saraceni*. They brought those fruit so associated with the island, oranges and lemons, in the process revolutionising agriculture and the use of sparse water resources. Their true literary flowering became apparent to a wider world with the arrival of the Normans. As William was conquering England, Robert Guiscard and his younger brother Roger crossed the straits of Messina. The Norman court was happy to adapt to Arab practices and employ Moorish scholars. In this atmosphere of semi-benign tolerance, poets and geographers flourished. Al-Idrisi produced his famous annotated map known as the *Book of Roger* and Ibn Jubayr left his travel impressions for posterity.

The Norman rule was not to last, but under the auspices of Frederick II, the Hohenstaufen Holy Roman Emperor, Sicily continued to encourage its authors. Known as 'Stupor Mundi' (Wonder of the World), Frederick was himself a poet who brought to the fore a school of poetry, the Sicilian School. One of its principal exponents was Jacopo da Lentini, the supposed originator of the sonnet verse form, used to such brilliance by Shakespeare centuries later.

The Shakespearean connection is not just based on the adoption of a poetic style. He set two plays on the island, *A Winter's Tale* and *Much Ado About Nothing*, with a further one, *The Tempest*, supposedly on an islet in the seas between Naples and Sicily. If you're not a Stratfordian – i.e. if you doubt that a man from Stratford wrote these masterworks – then the city of Messina is fertile ground for an alternative take on the authorship debate. If some of the greats of world literature have Sicilian connections, why not make a case for Shakespeare as well? Those prone to flights of fancy could even imagine a meeting between the Bard and that other literary hero of the age, Miguel de Cervantes.

Cervantes was a soldier long before he wrote *Don Quixote*. Stationed in Messina and involved in the Battle of Lepanto, he returned to the town injured and war weary. His later work, particularly one of the *Exemplary Novels*, harks back to Sicilian memories; even *Don Quixote* contains the occasional vignette. As Spanish power on the island waned, the Neapolitan Bourbons of the Kingdom of the Two Sicilies started their inexorable decline, fading to a decadent twilight. This era coincided with increased travel and the consideration of Sicily as a Grand Tour destination. Patrick Brydone, who published his letters in book form, struck a chord with a Europe hungry for new destinations. Translations of his Sicilian journey soon appeared in French and German. Subsequent travellers such as Henry Swinburne found that Brydone had paved the way but also muddied the waters. The local aristocracy were somewhat less fulsome in divulging their experiences, fearing their appearance in print.

The Garibaldian invasion in 1860 was pivotal in unifying Sicily with northern Italy, creating one state. Galvanised by this vision, journalists and writers reported from the front – the most eminent of whom was Alexandre Dumas, who was a personal friend of the General. Aboard his yacht, he coasted from Palermo along the Tyrrhenian shore, putting into port at the scenes of battles or celebrations. His accounts bring to life this bloody struggle for a new start in Italian politics. The aftermath, with such high expectations, could only fall short, provoking an inevitable wistfulness and an open wound that authors continued to jab with their satirical pens. Years later, Giuseppe Tomasi di Lampedusa returned to this era and the weakening aristocracy to write his one and only classic, *The Leopard*. The fatalistic novel with its note of melancholic beauty and resistance to change has provoked and inspired ever since.

Certain Sicilian destinations rose to popularity on the back of artistic and literary recommendation, especially Taormina on the eastern coast. Its sublime setting with Mount Etna rising above a blue Ionian Sea washed in a motley selection of monied northern Europeans and artistic bohemians searching for the freedom to exercise their eccentricities or lifestyles that diverged from the strictly accepted Victorian norm. The town developed to accommodate these visitors in a degree of luxury hitherto missing from many other Sicilian destinations – a fact so often highlighted by writers venturing through the interior and complaining about the state of the inns. An exiled Oscar Wilde came down from Naples to lick his wounds; his friend, André Gide, visited more often, and was to stay for longer – his presence fascinating writers from a newer generation, notably Truman Capote.

These golden years of luxury and indulgence were not to last, disrupted by the Great War and its cataclysmic sequel. Sicily was at the heart of this second conflict, its beaches the point at which the Allies decided to land and liberate Italy from Mussolini and the Germans. In a bid to turn literary skills to a useful end, John Steinbeck followed in the footsteps of what was known as Operation Husky. Poetry was the outlet for many a soldier facing the horrors of war; others were able to look back and pen nostalgic memoirs. In a confused attempt at dampening resistance, the Americans enlisted the help of Sicilian immigrants to the States, not all of whom had the most impeccable of reputations. These connections with organised crime may have facilitated the American passage to Palermo and subsequent occupied governance, but it had the side-effect of strengthening the Mafia, once suppressed by Mussolini.

It is impossible to write a literary guide to Sicily without touching on the subject of the Mafia; although it has provoked strong reaction, it should be noted that it is just one aspect of the society and should be balanced by the weight of output on other subjects. *The* crime novel is *The Godfather* and its success has been responsible for numerous copycats. The majority of the action actually takes place in the United States. Puzo's real island novel was *The Sicilian*, a partially fictionalised account of Salvatore Giuliano, the bandit who robbed to help his community but became synonymous with a massacre that still remains largely unexplained. Giuliano's fame encouraged writers to investigate this seamier side of life, including the otter-loving naturalist, Gavin Maxwell.

Native Sicilian authors are uniquely placed to examine the phenomenon of criminality and corruption; one such is Leonardo Sciascia, whose clear and condemnatory vision refused to shy away from controversial subjects. Writers in the latter half of the twentieth century and the beginnings of the twenty-first tend to fall into two camps: those with an eye to the past and those intent on confronting the present. They are not mutually exclusive, though, as Sicilian history inevitably informs current reality.

Scholarly travellers have written eloquently on everything from the Greek ruins to eighteenth-century palazzi – none more so than Vincent Cronin, whose *Golden Honeycomb* still stands as a prime example of its genre. Andrea Camilleri turned to the police procedural to delineate his corner of the island. The Inspector Montalbano series now enjoys considerable popularity in book and film format, reaching across the Atlantic. A generation after poverty forced mass emigration from Sicily, second- and third-generation immigrants living in countries such as the United States have delved into their roots to unearth stories hidden by the years and further obscured by familial reticence or myth. The likes of Frank Viviano and Theresa Maggio have produced works that lift the veil on less well-known destinations.

Sicilian cuisine quite rightly has an international reputation for quality. It is not all pasta and pizza – its variation caters for many palates. The same could be said for literature written in or about the island. Not all aspects of this cultural output will appeal to every taste but there is always another choice from the menu: classical texts, Muslim cartography, pre-Renaissance poetry, Golden Age drama, the travel tales of Grand Tourists, Romantic poets, louche expatriate lives, gritty crime, investigative journalism, novels from every era or the wry eye of modern satire. Take your pick.

# 1

# PALERMO
# AND SURROUNDINGS
## Peeling the Onion

### *Palermo*

Any visitor approaching Palermo for the first time, be it from air, land or sea, will be struck by the magnificence of its setting at the heart of a wide sweeping bay known as the Conca d'Oro, or Golden Shell. Seen from the air, it appears that one of the Greco-Roman gods has taken a bite from the coastline. At the western end of the bay, presiding over Sicily's capital, is the brooding presence of Monte Pellegrino. On 2 April 1787, Johann Wolfgang Goethe, the German writer, poet and intellectual sailed into Palermo harbour and was so overcome by the view on offer he was reluctant to leave the deck of his ship, writing that 'It might be long before we could again enjoy such a treat for the eyes from such a vantage point.'

Palermo's fortunes have waxed and waned with the centuries, but the natural splendour of its setting has continued to evoke purple prose from the world's literary elite. In the same balmy month of April, during the Sicilian spring of 1900, another author of world renown was equally awed. In a letter to his close confidant, Robert Ross, a world-weary Oscar Wilde wrote that Palermo was 'The most beautifully situated town in the world, it dreams away its life in the Conca d'Oro, the exquisite valley that lies between two seas.' Palermo's dreams, however, have not always reflected the angelic sleep of the just. For every Baroque aristocratic palace with jasmine-filled gardens, there are streets of graffiti-strewn boarded-up or bomb-damaged housing, a constant reminder of World War II. First impressions will soon fade to something more realistic and raw.

A complicated city, it takes time to learn how to embrace its finery whilst forgiving its flaws. Roberto Alajmo, a native Palermitan, writer and television journalist, wrote a siren song to his birthplace entitled *Palermo è una cipolla*, simply translated as *Palermo* in its English version: a title which drops the Italian metaphor. A *cipolla* is an onion and it is precisely this layer-like quality which makes Palermo so fascinating, yet so hard to understand. A visitor may be forgiven for feeling trepidatious when ready to set out into the semi-organised chaos. Alajmo understands these feelings: 'you shilly-shally over something to keep you busy so that everything in the room is perfectly sorted. Let's be honest: you're a trifle nervous.'

The nerves soon begin to dissipate as you take your first glimpse at the inner layers of the onion. Palermo's aristocratic palazzi still survive in sufficient number to paint a recognisable picture of life under the Bourbon monarchy in the nineteenth century. The documenter par excellence of this era was himself a Sicilian aristocrat and the author of just one novel, which was published posthumously, *The Leopard* (*Il Gattopardo*). Giuseppe Tomasi di Lampedusa, Duke of Palma and Prince of Lampedusa, was born in 1896 and lived the privileged life of a literary dilettante. Contrary to the Mediterranean stereotype, Lampedusa had an introverted character and during his trips to London it took him months to enter into literary conversation – despite his more-than-adequate English. His biographer, David Gilmour, discovered that one of his favourite pastimes was rummaging through the second-hand bookstalls on Charing Cross Road.

Giuseppe grew up in the heart of Palermo in the eponymously named Palazzo di Lampedusa, next to the Oratorio di Santa Zita with its richly decorated stucco work by Giacomo Serpotta. Mercifully, the World War II bomb that was to destroy Giuseppe's home left this Rococo masterpiece largely intact; the allegorical figurines surrounding a depiction of the Battle of Lepanto still glisten with marble-flecked whiteness. The loss of the family's principal residence, however, had a significant impact on his life; one more nail in the coffin of a dying era. In *Places of my Infancy* (*Infanzia*) – the jottings that should have formed part of his planned autobiography – it is easy to see the indelibly happy mark left by his childhood home:

> At no point on earth, I'm sure, has sky ever stretched more violently blue than it did above our enclosed terrace, never has sun thrown gentler rays than those penetrating the half-closed shutters of the 'green drawing-room', never have damp-marks on a courtyard's outer walls presented shapes more stimulating to the imagination than those at my home.

After years of allowing the structure to crumble into the surrounding weeds, the planning authorities have finally given permission for restoration work. Walking to the corner of Via Lampedusa and Via Bara all'Olivella, there are modern breeze blocks rising from the ruins of the old structure. Little remains of the palace's white and yellow façade arranged around three patios. At the time of writing, the modern additions are not sufficiently advanced to see how sympathetic the finished product will be to the original design.

Despite parallels with Lampedusa's own life, the central character of *The Leopard*, Don Fabrizio, is based on his great-uncle, Giulio Tomasi. The book is set during the Garibaldian invasion of Sicily in 1860. Fabrizio, the Prince of Salina, is iconic of the *ancien régime* – a Bourbon prince with villas in Palermo and landed estates in the countryside. His nephew, Tancredi, is involved in the movement to unify Sicily with the rest of Italy, led by Giuseppe Garibaldi's Red Shirts. The book's beauty, and its frustration, lies in the Prince of Salina's time-worn observations of Sicilian society, expressed in Lampedusa's limpid prose.

Giuseppe Tomasi di Lampedusa did not start writing *The Leopard* until he had long been resident in the eighteenth-century Palazzo Lanza Tomasi at 28 Via Butera, now marked with a green plaque. The residence overlooks the Italico Umberto I, which is Palermo's rather far from the sea seafront promenade. He spent his days passing on his literary knowledge to a chosen few pupils – one of whom would become his adopted son.

In moments of idleness, he amused himself by watching Palermitan life in all its vitality unfold amongst the Italico's shadows. If you walk along the Mura Catene today, the wall that once housed the fifteenth-century chains that closed the harbour, there is a good view of the crisply rendered yellow and white plaster of the author's final home. Bougainvillea and other Mediterranean shrubs spill over the garden wall, softening the lines of this impressive terrace. Next to the palazzo is the former Hotel Trinacria where Lampedusa has the Leopard breathe his last.

Sitting in an arm-chair, his long legs wrapped in a blanket, on the balcony of the Hotel Trinacria, he felt life flowing from him in great pressing waves with a spiritual roar like that of the Rhine Falls. It was noon on a Monday at the end of July, and away in front of him spread the sea of Palermo, compact, oily, inert, improbably motionless, crouching like a dog trying to make itself invisible at his master's threats.

1 *Palazzo Lanza Tomasi with the former Hotel Trinacria in the background, Palermo*

It is just a short walk from what was the Trinacria to the old fishing port known as the Cala. Now a yachting marina, it is the westward extension of the Italico promenade. Rubble deposited after World War II accounts for the Italico's distance from the sea. It was not always this way. One of the first British travellers to include Sicily and Malta as Grand Tour destinations was the Scottish writer and future Royal Society member, Patrick Brydone. His book – compiled from letters written home to William Beckford, uncle of the identically named author of *Vathek* – was to become one of the first travel classics written about Sicily, simply entitled *Travels in Sicily and Malta*. He enthused about this seafront walk, then known as La Marina, describing it as one of the 'great pleasures of the nobility of Palermo'. He details the flamboyant summer night-time concerts held in temporary 'temples' of music. From midnight onwards, the late eighteenth-century revellers in carriages or on foot were subject to an order forbidding torch lights as, Brydone hinted, this was all the 'better to favour pleasure and intrigue'.

Such aristocratic intrigue was often carried on within the confines of the carriage. Washington Irving was another visitor who shared Brydone's experience of Palermo's idle rich. He would go on to be an accomplished traveller, diplomat and the legendary author of *The Legend of Sleepy Hollow* and *Rip Van Winkle*. His taste for the exotic would lead him to set up camp in Andalucía's then semi-ruined Alhambra, whose stories he recounted in *Tales of the Alhambra* published in 1832. Contrary to many other writers of the age, Irving's journey finished rather than started in Palermo, where he was happy to indulge in a bit of luxury after a tortuous journey across the centre of the island. He wryly noted the Palermitan nobility's obsession with the carriage: 'As the use of one's limbs is determined here to be vulgar and plebeian we resolved to set up our equipage also.' On his first jaunt down the Marina in his 'handsome chariot', Irving was keen to see and be seen, having a sharp eye for the attractive debutantes and a politically astute view towards the powers that be. He was more than happy to be honoured with two polite bows from the viceroy.

Not far from the Marina, the visitor is plunged into the twists and turns of the city's backstreets. It is through this maze of alleyways that Lampedusa's Leopard has to walk in order to visit his mistress. As he strides out, the Prince of Salina carries on an internal dialogue regarding the moral dilemma of such an assignation. Justifying his actions, he reflects on never having so much as seen his wife's navel despite their seven children together. The city is in ferment, Bourbon troops are stationed in the squares and potential skirmishes lie around every corner. Lampedusa captures the tension in the air as Don Fabrizio heads for the lady's door:

> Sinister-looking youths in wide trousers were quarrelling in the guttural grunts Sicilians use in anger. In the distance echoed shots from nervous sentries. Once past this district his route skirted the Cala; in the old fishing port decaying boats bobbed up and down, desolate as mangy dogs.

The 'mangy dogs' may have been replaced by sleek yachts and the industrial shipping moved along to the modern port, but a contradictory air still hangs over today's Cala. Roberto Alajmo, chronicler of Palermo, warts and all, does not shy away from the potential environmental disaster awaiting these murky coastal waters. He describes the colour of the sea as washed-out white with an oily consistency. Alajmo's urban myth, perpetuated amongst the city's residents, is that you would be more likely to catch a mouse than a fish if you were ever tempted to go angling here.

So far, we have been teetering on the edge of the city proper. Just to the east of the Cala lies the Porta Felice, one of the old city gates which is mirrored at the other end of the Corso Vittorio Emanuele by the Porta Nuova. The Felice was by far and away Brydone's favourite gate with its contrasting architectural styles, from Renaissance to Baroque, and its stone carved eagles displaying the Hispanic heraldry of the royal family. Once through the gate, the Corso opens on to Piazza Marina. Nature provides the most stunning architectural feature in this square. The centre is dominated by the strangling limbs of a Moreton Bay fig (*ficus macrophylla*), giving an eerie atmosphere to the surroundings. Indeed, the tortuous root system is an apt metaphor for an institution that was housed in the piazza's other dominant structure.

The Palazzo Chiaramonte, otherwise known as the Steri, was home to the Office of the Inquisition. From the war of the Sicilian Vespers in 1282 until Sicily's unification in 1860, the Spanish played a significant colonial role. Whether as a separate Aragonese kingdom, as part of the Spanish empire or under the Bourbons of the Kingdom of the Two Sicilies, Spain was the overarching power. One of its most insidious influences came in the shape of the Holy Office whose tentacles even reached into the more obscure corners of Sicilian society. The palazzo, once the feudal seat of the Chiaramonte family, was ceded to the Inquisition in 1601. It is an imposing square structure with a roofline edged in fishtail crenellations. The interior, now part of the university complex, still hides dungeons – their walls scrawled with the desperate graffiti of Sicily's supposed heretics.

The dark legend of the Inquisition has inspired several writers. One of Sicily's most famous literary sons, Leonardo Sciascia, was moved to write an essay entitled *The Death of the Inquisitor* (*Morte dell'Inquisitore*). Sciascia was from Racalmuto in the south, but his works have a pan-Sicilian outlook and have touched an international audience with their sincere, yet condemnatory, depictions of the island's difficulties. His wider literary output will appear later but this work, in particular, centres on an historical incident that actually took place in the Steri Palace. Brother Diego La Matina, incarcerated in the dungeons, broke his manacles and killed the Inquisitor General, Señor Don Juan Lopez de Cisneros. He had already been an escapee, which was no mean feat, as Sciascia indicates:

> But his spirit was invincibly sustained by a gigantic body and by tremendous force, of which we get an idea simply by taking a look at the Steri Palace, where the Holy Office had its seat and its prisons. It was a fortress within the city for the Chiaramontes who had built it, no less massive than their castle at Racalmuto and all the others they had disseminated throughout Sicily to watch and defend the towns huddled at their feet. And from the Steri Palace Fra Diego escaped in 1656.

Brother Diego was burned at the stake in an infamous *auto da fé*, the showy end product of the Inquisition's torture chambers. Dacia Maraini, another local author who grew up in the neighbouring town of Bagheria and now internationally acclaimed, describes just such an ostentatious display in her book, *The Silent Duchess* (*La lunga vita di Marianna Ucrìa*). The Duke Signoretto di Fontanasalsa has taken his deaf-mute daughter, Marianna, to witness the hanging of a brigand: 'A splendid blood-red flag flaunts itself; from there, from the Palazzo Chiaramonte, the Noble Fathers of the Inquisition are emerging, two by two, preceded and followed by a swarm of altar boys [. . .] The air reverberates to the beat of a big drum.'

A foreign visitor who would have had a psychological field day with the inner workings of such a sadistic organisation was Sigmund Freud. He stayed in a three-roomed suite in the Hotel de France in Piazza Marina. The iron-balustraded frontage is still in place next to the Steri. Recently refurbished and reopened by the university as a residential hall for foreign research students, its façade maintains part of its former grandeur. Back in 1910, Freud was accompanied by the Hungarian follower of psychoanalysis, Sándor Ferenczi. The principal aim of Freud's extended visit was to indulge his passion for Magna Graecia – in particular, its archaeological remains.

Before quitting Palermo in search of temples and telamones, he was moved to describe the capital: 'Such a splendour of colours, smells, views – and wellness I've never had all at once.' In fact, as Rosalba Galvagno points out in her work, 'Freud and Greater Greece', Sicily pops up in two important footnotes in his books: *The Psychopathology of Everyday Life* and *The Interpretation of Dreams*. The latter relates to his final destination of Syracuse in the south-east – an important Freudian location, both physically and mentally.

Further along the Corso Vittorio Emanuele, the street is intersected by two of Palermo's great thoroughfares: Via Roma and Via Maqueda, the latter further testament to Spain's influence, being pronounced in Spanish style. The Bourbons of the Two Sicilies were finally overthrown in 1860 with the invasion of Garibaldi and his 'Thousand' – the red-shirted soldiers who were with him when he landed at the western port of Marsala. On their way to Palermo, they picked up many Sicilian irregulars, known as *picciotti*, everyone from exuberant young aristocrats of a liberal persuasion to proto-mafiosi and bandits. Travelling with this assorted band of warriors was the French writer Alexandre Dumas.

Dumas was a natural adventurer, most famed for his novels, *The Count of Monte Cristo* and *The Three Musketeers*. The son of a well-travelled general, it was his mother's stories of such military escapades that prompted his own spirited imagination. Dumas's early adult life was spent in Paris and he participated in the revolution which dethroned Charles X. His desire to travel was fulfilled when he hit upon the idea of chronicling southern Europe, which he realised in his Sicilian travelogue *Impressions of Travel in Sicily* (*Le speronare*). Parisians styled him as the 'discoverer of the Mediterranean'. Twenty-six years later he would be back in Palermo and, given his youthful politics, it is easy to see how his allegiance would lie with Garibaldi.

The red blouses worn by the revolutionary soldiers became a badge of honour for all those in sympathy with the cause of unifying Italy. Together with the remaining green and white of the new Italian *tricolore* flag, Palermo was bedecked with colour. Dumas paints an exotic picture of post-revolutionary fervour along the city's central boulevards:

> In the evening, at every window are displayed two lanterns, by the side of the national colours of red, white, and green. This has a very curious effect when seen from the Square of the Four Nations, where the Strada di Toledo and the Strada di Maqueda intersect each other. It presents the appearance of four rivers of flame flowing from the same source.

At the heart of Baroque Palermo is Piazza Vigliena, a meeting of the Corso and Via Maqueda. The four angles, mentioned above by Dumas, create the crossroads which gives rise to the four distinct districts of Palermo and the nickname given to the square, 'Quattro Canti' (the Four Corners). Each corner has its own façade designed by Giuseppe Lasso in 1609, and a fountain topped by a statue depicting one of the four seasons. Spanish monarchs of the country's Golden Age stare down from centrally located niches.

Adjacent to the Quattro Canti, a short distance along Via Maqueda, are a cluster of the city's most well-known churches. The churches of San Cataldo and Santa Maria dell'Ammiraglio, in particular, are perfect examples of the intercultural mix of Norman Palermo. Both commissioned in the twelfth century, their vivid interweaving of the Byzantine, Arabic and Norman has been the living embodiment of many writers' historical imagination. Two who have captured this era in their work are Barry Unsworth and Tariq Ali.

Unsworth was born into a mining family in the north of England. His father left the mines, securing a career in insurance, and was able to provide a more comfortable lifestyle for his family. After Barry left university, his peripatetic academic travels led to inspiration for his writing career. With an eye to the past, novels like *Pascali's Island* and *The Songs of the Kings* have recreated Greco-Turkish history. In his later years, Unsworth moved with his second wife, Aira Pohjanvaara-Buffa, to Umbria in central Italy. A former Booker Prize winner, he was also long-listed for his novel on Norman Sicily, *The Ruby in her Navel*. The zenith of Norman colonisation on the island provided a fascinating context for Unsworth's novelistic treatment of the complicated multiculturalism of twelfth-century Sicily.

The book's narrator and central character is Thurstan Beauchamp, an Anglo-Norman working in the island's civil service, which at the time was still known by the Arabic name, *Diwan*, and was run by the sage-like Yusuf. Thurstan is a frustrated would-be knight, longing to serve his king, Roger II – the thoroughly orientalised monarch who presides over a court where Latin, French, Greek and Arabic all have official status. The Muslim domination of the island is a recent memory and the Palermo skyline is still full of minarets. He has to walk a tightrope between the competing cultures in order to fulfil his royal duties and find love.

As Thurston walks through the city, he hears the muezzins calling the faithful to prayer, their 'veils of sound' fading into the response from the Christian monastery and church bells:

With this I was swept by a familiar love for this city of Palermo, where I had spent most of my years, for the diversity these sounds expressed, the different faiths that live together here, the different races that jostled in the markets and laboured on the buildings that were rising everywhere.

Tariq Ali's evocation of Norman Palermo forms part of his Islam Quintet – the recreations of places and times that have played a central role in Muslim history. As a British Pakistani, Ali brought the full weight of his political and historical leanings to the series. The first book, *Shadows of the Pomegranate Tree*, takes a novelistic look at the fall of Muslim Spain through the eyes of one family. *A Sultan in Palermo* is his portrait of the medieval cartographer Muhammad al-Idrisi and his relationship with Roger II of Sicily, with whom he shared a love of classical literature and geography. Roger commissioned him to produce an accurate map of the known world, leading al-Idrisi to get caught up in the factional machinations that became Muslim resistance to Norman rule.

After swimming together in a cove near Palermo, then pausing on the beach to discuss astronomy and the maps of Ptolemy, the King and his geographer return to the city by sea. Rujari (the Muslim name for Roger) turns to Idrisi and asks, 'whether differences between their two peoples were rocks that could not be shifted, or might their faiths become intertwined in the years ahead?' Al-Idrisi is not the only Muslim from this historical period to have left accurate impressions of Sicily. On a return journey from Mecca, Ibn Jubayr from al-Andalus, the Arab-dominated part of Spain, visited the island and noted down his impressions, which would later appear in his book, *The Travels*.

He was particularly struck by the Church of Santa Maria dell'Ammiraglio, now known colloquially as the Martorana after the nun who formed a nearby convent. Completely entranced, he referred to it as 'the most wonderful edifice in the world'. Despite numerous alterations over the centuries, the beautiful golden mosaic work and intricate inlay are still as they would have been in the days of Norman rule.

The inner walls are all embellished with gold. There are slabs of coloured marble, the like of which we have never seen, inlaid throughout with gold mosaic and surrounded by branches (formed from) green mosaic. In its upper parts are well-placed windows of gilded glass which steal all looks by the brilliance of their rays, and bewitch the soul.

Mindful of his Islamic heritage, he finishes this passage with 'God protect us (from their allurement).' The modern historian and chronicler of this epoch, John Julius Norwich, has written two masterly histories entitled *The Normans in the South: 1016–1130* and *The Kingdom in the Sun: 1130–1194*. He is careful to remind the casual visitor that the church also includes a mosaic portrait of King Roger on the southern wall. Above his head is a Latin inscription written in Greek letters which is accompanied by an Arabic inscription on a nearby pillar. Julius Norwich points out that it 'seems to diffuse the whole spirit of Norman Sicily'.

Continuing along the Corso Vittorio Emanuele, you pass through the Porta Nuova with its turbaned giants, where the street opens out onto the Piazza del Parlamento in front of the Palazzo Normanni. Now the regional parliament, this royal palace was built by the Arabs and truly embellished by the Normans, before passing through the hands of every ruler since. Its confines, particularly the Palatine Chapel, have been a honey-pot for illustrious writers throughout recent centuries. The metaphor is well chosen when one considers Oscar Wilde's comments in another letter to Robert Ross: 'In the Cappella Palatina, which from pavement to domed ceilings is all gold, one really feels as if one was sitting in the heart of a great honeycomb *looking* at angels singing.'

The Frenchman Guy de Maupassant was another writer galvanised by the unique nature of these churches. After the publication of his classic, *Bel Ami*, in 1885, Maupassant set off with his friends, Amic, Legrand and Gervex, in search of Italy. Perversely, he was not enamoured of Venice and Rome but drawn to Sicily. On the island he found the exotic, earthy and macabre elements that appealed to his character and found their way into his works. Maupassant serialised his Sicilian travels in the newspapers *Le Figaro* and *Gil Blas*, eventually compiling them into a larger travel compendium called *La vie errante*. They are available to the English-speaking reader simply as *Sicily*.

It was the Palatine Chapel's 'jewel of a basilica' that aroused his sensualist nature:

> Upon entering our Gothic cathedrals, we experience a severe, almost sad, sensation. Their grandeur is imposing, their majesty astonishes, but does not seduce. Here, we are conquered, moved by that something, almost sensual, that color adds to the beauty of forms.

The chapel leads off from one of the courtyards which form the integral structure of the building, an edifice with a mongrel architecture testament to Sicily's procession of rulers. The Swabian power of Frederick II and his enlightened court added their mark, as did the Spanish – even leaving behind impressive tapestries depicting Don Quixote and Sancho Panza, whose author Miguel de Cervantes will also have his own Sicilian tales to tell, as we will subsequently see. Nineteenth-century salons mingle with vice-regal escutcheons and Gothic arches.

Anatole France, the future Nobel laureate and French academician, based some of the novel that made him famous in Sicily. Entitled *The Crime of Sylvestre Bonnard* (*Le Crime de Sylvestre Bonnard*) and published in 1881, it tells the story of an aged bachelor immersed in his books. Upon finding the mistreated daughter of a former love, he resorts to abduction, spiriting her away to a new life. Many critics have supposed the central character to be a partial reflection of France's true personality. It may be that he was thinking of his own impressions when he wrote the following in *Le Crime* about Palermo harbour: 'the view inspired me with such admiration that I resolved to travel a little in this island, so ennobled by historic memories.' It is these historic memories that are so eloquently explained in his *Letter from Sicily*, where he compares Palermo to a slavegirl weighted down with adornments bestowed by a succession of masters.

Further traces of Norman Palermo slumber under the meridional sun in the district surrounding the royal palace. The Church of San Giovanni degli Eremiti, in common with San Cataldo, sports the quintessential pink domes so favoured by these orientalised Vikings. It is an unequivocal example of King Roger's desire for different faiths to live side by side, as a mosque adjoined the church. This attitude of manifest acceptance is echoed perfectly in the thoughts of Barry Unsworth's central character, Thurston: 'in this he had shown the wisdom and spirit of tolerance that made me proud to serve him.' Little remains of the interior, but the mosque's courtyard and church's proud cupolas are enough to feed the imagination. On a more secular level, the nearby twelfth-century pleasure palaces of the Zisa and the Cuba still retain enough of their Arab-Norman style to conjure up visions of sybaritic royal feasts after a day's hunting.

A more macabre destination has been immortalised in print by a morbidly fascinated Maupassant, a factually detached Patrick Brydone and a startled Harold Acton. The Convento dei Cappuccini in Piazza Cappuccini, an unremarkable monastery from the outside, houses a crypt that brought these three writers, among others, within touching distance of their own mortality. Today's visitor is provided with a leaflet that quotes from the Italian poet Ippolito Pindemonte's *Sepulchres* (*I sepolcri*), in which he explains that in these catacombs never have life and death been so united. The compelling truth is that the mummified cadavers are not individually entombed but are simply on display: a ghastly museum of gaping-mouthed citizenry dressed in their Sunday best, crammed in row upon row, floor to ceiling.

The catacombs were originally intended for the Capuchin friars; the great and good of Palermo also decided that they wanted to follow suit. The dead bodies were dried on racks, where the fluid could drip away, and were then often washed in vinegar to help the mummification; later corpses were actually embalmed. Maupassant details this truly hideous ensemble, being particularly taken aback by the women:

> Here are the women, yet more ludicrous than the men, for they have been decked out coquettishly. Their heads face towards you, clasped in lace- and ribbon-trimmed bonnets, a snow-like whiteness around these black, rotten faces, wasted by the strange workings of the earth. The hands, similar to the cut roots of trees, emerge from the sleeves of new robes.

The saddest sight is the children – something which brought tears to his eyes as they were dressed in the 'little costumes' that clothed them moments before their death. He was spared the image of Rosalia Lombardo, one of the last children to be placed in the catacombs, in 1920. Unlike the shrivelled guffawing of her slack-jawed neighbours, she was embalmed using a radical new process which has left her in a seemingly perfect sleep.

Harold Acton, the English aesthete, writer and historian, visited in 1952, accompanied by Evelyn Waugh of *Brideshead Revisited* fame. In his autobiography, *More Memoirs of an Aesthete*, he recounts their visit, which had a surprising outcome. At this stage in Waugh's life, he was on his way to a breakdown, partially aided by a considerable drug intake, which included the mixture of bromide, chloral, brandy and crème de menthe. He was also taking pills for severe rheumatism. This chemical cocktail must have left the author feeling almost as pickled as the mummies. Acton was worried by his increasing paranoia and a visit to the crypt was probably not the best idea, especially as Harold describes the shrunken bodies as being 'like the victims of a famine or a Goya caricature'.

Seemingly his concerns were confirmed when a very cantankerous Waugh abruptly dismissed the monk guiding them around. Things took an unusual turn, however, when Evelyn started to praise the stifling atmosphere. Contrary to all prior warnings, he loved the smell and was convinced that either the dry ambience or the mummies' presence had cured his rheumatism. So sure was he, that he left his trusty walking stick in the taxi after their visit and praised the catacombs as a sure-fire cure for years afterwards.

Over 100 years before Maupassant and some 160 years before Acton and Waugh, Brydone would have seen the corpses in a slightly better state of repair; his British sang-froid did not permit the emotional heights of the Frenchman's response. Indeed, he supposed that visits to these dead relatives would be a lesson in humility and not as horrific as could be imagined. He compares the corpses to a gallery of portraits drawn from life. However, he is not so impervious as to escape the feelings of humbleness and reverence that such visions of death evoke.

He admits the 'portraits' are faded and that the hand that drew them was not the most flattering in the world, but 'it is the pencil of truth, and not of a mercenary, who only wants to please.'

Maupassant could escape the horrors of the Capuchin monastery by returning to his accommodation, the luxurious Grand Hotel et des Palmes, often known by its Italian name the *Delle Palme*. Originally home to the illustrious Ingham–Whitaker Marsala wine barons, it became a hotel in 1874 and has since hosted many notable writers, artists and musicians. In a casual conversation at the entrance, Maupassant was astonished to find that the composer Richard Wagner had been a long-term guest. During his stay, he completed the opera *Parsifal* – based on Chrétien de Troyes's *Perceval, the Story of the Grail*. The Des Palmes seems a strange location to inspire the sombre tones of his last opera. The day after its completion, Pierre-Auguste Renoir came to pay his respects and agreed to produce a swift portrait of the composer which Wagner later likened to that of a 'Protestant minister'. Apparently Wagner was a taciturn guest, with Maupassant learning of his 'insufferable character' and 'extraordinary pride'. Nonetheless, the Palermitani named an adjoining street after their famous German visitor.

Despite such negativity, Maupassant wanted to see Wagner's suite in a search for 'his strong personality' that 'must still remain' there. For those who have the wherewithal, the composer's suite is still available today. At first, Maupassant was disappointed to discover a well-appointed hotel apartment with little of the maestro's individuality. It was only when he opened the door of a mirrored closet that he was rewarded. The manager explained that it had once contained Wagner's bed linen, which he was in the habit of steeping in rose essence: 'A delicious and strong perfume flew out, like the caress of a breeze that had passed over a field of rose bushes.'

For an interesting, *fin de siècle* description of the Des Palmes, we turn to the English author Douglas Brooke Wheelton Sladen. This splendid Victorian name, appearing on his four books with Sicilian themes, was usually shortened to Douglas Sladen. From 1896 to 1900, he spent much time in Sicily, often as a guest of the powerful Anglo-Sicilian Whitaker family. His novel, *The Sicilian Lovers*, sometimes retitled as *The Sicilian Marriage*, contains a description of the hotel's smoking rooms.

2  *The Grand Hotel et des Palmes, Palermo*

The book's narrator accompanies his friend, Tommy Cust, on a recuperative journey around Sicily after an accident to Tommy's eyes. Cust foolishly flirts with an aristocratic lady; misinterpreting the signals, the tide of Sicilian courtship sweeps him along to a potential, unwanted, marriage. Two years after extricating himself from this predicament, the gentlemen find themselves at a ball in the Des Palmes where they bump into the same woman and her father. Papà, convinced the courtship is still alive, awaits Cust in one of the rooms adjoining the grand salon. 'The Hotel des Palmes is full of fascinating little rooms hung with old prints and old pictures, worked in sewing silks and pieces of fabrics, where one can smoke in peace.' We can only wince at the damage they were doing to the delicate material. Torn, but agreeing to the marriage, Tommy makes a success of his Sicilian liaison.

Not all sojourns in the hotel have ended so well. Nearly 50 years after Maupassant, fellow Frenchman and author Raymond Roussel checked in to the Albergo with the weight of the world on his shoulders. Sadly, he was to leave room 224 in a coffin. The surrealist author and poet of *Locus Solus* and *Impressions of Africa* had suffered a mental breakdown and, by 1933, was a serious drug addict. Before arriving in Palermo, he had already put his Parisian affairs in order – a possible clue to his intentions. Complicating his life still further was the addition of a hired mistress, Charlotte Dufrène. Ashamed of his homosexuality, his parents had hired her, supposing that an unwed liaison in the Des Palmes was more socially acceptable than any hint of 'the love that dare not speak its name'.

Roussel's 'mistress' kept a list of his intake of barbiturates and their subsequent effects, which mostly consist of euphoric highs and confusion. He paid lip-service to kicking his habit but essentially refused to imagine a life without chemical consumption. Twice during his stay he nearly died (once through overdose, and a second time through slashing his wrists), finally achieving his supposed aim with a massive ingestion of barbiturates. This tale of desperation and loneliness has inspired three other writers: the Sicilian Leonardo Sciascia, Jean-René Selva, who produced a 1985 novel called the *Grand Hôtel et des Palmes*, and Jochen Beyse in a recent work entitled *Palermo 1933* – none of which is yet available in English translation.

Other visitors of note have included the playwright Arthur Miller, accompanied by the campaigning lawyer Vincent Longhi and Aleister Crowley, the self-styled occultist author who took trips to Palermo from his home in Cefalù. Crowley would come in search of supplies, drugs and prostitutes for use in acts of sexual ritual. Both of these characters and their Sicilian sojourns will resurface at a later date. As a final flourish to this alternative history, the hotel was even the location for a 1957 meeting of organised crime families from both sides of the Atlantic, building on links forged by expatriate Mafiosi implanted by the American occupation force.

The rarefied atmosphere of this belle époque establishment is but a short walk from the earthier climes of the Vucciria, the district which plays host to Palermo's most famous market. Once the stalls have been packed away, the narrow dark alleys, graffiti and decay inevitably bring more readily to mind the city's associations with the Mafia. Roberto Alajmo, seeing his city from a visitor's perspective, is well aware of the subtext underlying the mere mention of Sicily's capital. Hollywood has played its part in cementing these attitudes with *The Godfather* trilogy based on Mario Puzo's book of the same name. However, it is his fictionalised account of the bandit Salvatore Guiliano which is completely set in Sicily, specifically many of the hill towns surrounding Palermo.

The author Norman Lewis, well known for his in-depth study of the Mafia, *The Honoured Society,* is perhaps more traditionally considered a travel writer and has produced some of the most insightful works on Sicily in this genre. It is less appreciated, however, that he wrote two novels at least partially set on the island: *The Sicilian Specialist* and *The March of the Long Shadows*. Lewis' understanding and perception came from familial links through his first marriage to Ernestina Corvaja, the daughter of a Sicilian aristocrat. Signor Ernesto Corvaja had fled Sicily in slightly mysterious circumstances; rumours were whispered with regard to his Mafia connections and the reasons behind his hasty relocation to Bloomsbury. Norman was able to draw on Ernesto's name to gain an entrée into the Sicilian world that so interested him. He was to become great friends with the campaigning journalist Marcello Cimino, who wrote for the left-wing *L'Ora* newspaper. Lewis compared the effect of Cimino's death from liver cancer to that of losing a family member.

In *The Sicilian Specialist*, Marco Riccone is responsible for arranging the 'disappearance' of those that the Mafia bosses deem inconvenient. The first third of the book takes place on the island, and one of the initial acts of barbarity rocks the very foundations of the buildings in Piazza Caracciolo, the heart of the Vucciria. Having been deported from the United States as an undesirable, the hoodlum Johnny La Barbera turns up in Palermo, only to have his body parts scattered to the four winds:

La Barbera angrily opened the door of the intrusive Alfa Romeo, there was an explosion that illuminated the whole piazza with a greenish flash, broke windows a quarter of a mile away and caused several midnight strollers to fall to their knees in the belief that the end of the world had come.

Another author who deals with the seedier side of Palermitan life is Peter Robb. Robb spent 14 years travelling southern Italy and Sicily. The fruits of his extensive research were published as *Midnight in Sicily*: a journey into the labyrinthine byways of Mafia crime and political intrigue. To this day, the book has never found a publisher in Italy; even its Australian and English publishers received veiled threats. It is not all dark, though; there are some glimpses of light, particularly when describing that very Sicilian obsession with food. He brilliantly captures the market in its hey-day before its slow decline into a pseudo-tourist attraction.

> The swordfish and tuna were flanked by many smaller fish, striped mackerel and fat sardines, and squid and prawn and octopus and cuttlefish. I don't remember seeing shellfish. I remember how the diffused red light of the market enhanced the translucent red of the big fishes' flesh and the silver glitter of the smaller ones' skins.

Robb's eatery of choice is in the same piazza as Lewis' fictional explosion. Like so many of Palermo's best restaurants, it is pretty unprepossessing from the outside – an alleyway, creaky door and narrow stairs lead to a small canopied terrace where Robb was happy to dine on the stuffed squid whilst the proprietor declaimed his hand-written poetry.

Food is a key to understanding Palermo and its inhabitants. Whether it is street food, a humble restaurant or fine dining, each will have passion, history and artistry. The café also has a long and venerable tradition, playing host to itinerant and resident writers, affording them the opportunity to observe the stream of passing street-life. One writer in particular is associated with two of Palermo's best-known coffee shops. It was at the Caffè Mazzara just off Via Ruggero Settimo that Giuseppe Tomasi di Lampedusa wrote much of *The Leopard*. There is a ceramic plaque opposite the café celebrating its famous customer. Lampedusa would sit with an exercise book and pen, scribbling the lines of his classic work in his meticulous, cramped hand. He always carried Shakespeare with him to leaf through at idle moments or to distract his attention from something he considered unpleasant.

The Mazzara is in a twentieth-century concrete block, its beautifully laid-out counter and smartly attired staff betrayed by such a bland exterior. Lampedusa's favourite café, however, has far more character. The Pasticceria del Massimo, as the name suggests, is a stone's throw from Palermo's magnificent opera house, the Teatro Massimo, whose grandiose stairway and Greco-Roman columns dominate the piazza. Always with a book, he is once said to have read an entire Balzac novel without moving from his seat at the café. The opera house was opened in 1897, decades too late for the Irish tenor Michael O'Kelly – charmingly known as Signor Ochelli to the Sicilians. As a protégé of Sir William Hamilton, he performed in Palermo on more than one occasion, hobnobbing with the aristocracy. In his memoir, entitled *Reminiscences of Michael Kelly*, he paints a picture of the city's music scene in the late eighteenth century: 'The Palermitans are all fond of music and every evening there was an Accademia di Musica held at some private house.'

Under the tutelage of the male soprano Giuseppe Aprile, he performed at the houses of the rich and famous. His memoir is not short of admiring descriptions of black-eyed vivacious women and evening soirées:

> The best suppers were given by the Princess Villa Franca, and the Prince her husband, an old man, he was good tempered and affable, while his consort was young and perfectly beautiful; their palace at the Seven Hills, a short distance from Palermo, was magnificent, and always crowded with visitors during the vintage when all is life and pleasure.

The majority of Palermitan nobility kept grand houses on the city's outskirts. One of the most celebrated is the Villa Malfitano at the end of Via Dante, where Joseph and Tina Whitaker set up home. Joseph, known as Pip, was the inheritor of the family business originally based on Marsala wine but swiftly diversified into shipping, banking and many other areas of commerce. Tina Whitaker, née Scalia, was the daughter of General Alfonso Scalia, a supporter of Garibaldi's in the Risorgimento. Having bought some land, they had the Malfitano constructed with an ostentatious ballroom and reception rooms which were decorated in Louis Quinze style. The house was embraced by a landscaped garden full of luxuriant exotica.

Tina loved to socialise and the family millions attracted the great and the good. Having taken singing lessons to perfect her voice, she was confident enough to give a recital of Wagner's music in front of the man himself, who seemingly showed great appreciation. She was host to Queen Mary, Empress Eugénie and other crowned heads of Europe, not to mention people of less savoury reputation, including Mussolini and those connected with the scandal of the Irish crown jewels theft. Tina was also happy to play the grand dame in literary salons as she herself had published a novel entitled *Love in the Sunny South* and, on a far more serious and substantial note, *Sicily and England: Political and Social Reminiscences 1848–1870*. In the latter book, she recounts her meetings with the novelist, essayist and first paid female journalist, Eliza Lynn Linton.

Never would one have suspected the burning fire hidden by the complacent, indulgent manner of the kindly old lady, as I knew Mrs Linton when she came to Palermo in 1881, and again in 1883; but when roused, then all the fire of youth flashed forth in a moment with amazing vigour. This was the moment when she was at the zenith of her literary career.

Linton, despite her ground-breaking journalism, was opposed to the suffragettes and considered politics a male endeavour. Luckily for Tina, dabbling with writing was not so taboo, as it was Eliza who encouraged her to pen the *Sunny South* – a novel that Mrs Whitaker was happy to distance herself from in later years. The title was probably inspired by a similarly named chapter in Linton's 1884 novel *Ione*, which was dedicated to that great Italianophile, Algernon Charles Swinburne.

Raleigh Trevelyan's book on the Whitakers, *Princes under the Volcano*, reveals a good deal about Tina's remarkable life, including the fact that one of her nieces inferred that Tina 'always attracted people with bad reputations, like Ronny Gower'. Gower was an aristocratic artist who had been given the honour of creating the Shakespeare memorial at Stratford, which was unveiled by his friend Oscar Wilde in 1888. Gower was used by Wilde as a model for Lord Henry in Wilde's novel *The Picture of Dorian Gray*. It is no surprise that Tina also attracted this Irish poet and playwright who turned up unannounced in March 1900. In a letter, she refers to Gower and his friend Frank Hird as having left 'in good time before the embarrassing arrival of Oscar Wilde'. At this stage of his life, seven months before he died, Oscar was on a downward spiral and his reputation, following his incarceration for gross indecency, unfortunately preceded him to all corners of Anglo-influenced society.

At this time, Tina was inundated with British visitors. In addition to the literati, some doctors turned up to visit the Villa Igiea: a flamboyant property acquired by another Sicilian magnet, Ignazio Florio. He had commissioned Ernesto Basile to build a vast tuberculosis sanatorium – hence the visiting British medics. Their suggestion to Tina was that he would be better off turning it into a casino instead.

Like the Des Palmes, it was eventually converted into that other cash-cow, a luxury hotel. Its guest list rivals that of its illustrious contemporary but remains less indecorous. In 1984, the Argentinian writer, Jorge Luis Borges, stayed in its sumptuous surroundings. His presence on the terrace and in Basile's grand salon were immortalised by the Magnum photographer Ferdinando Scianna, in his book which follows the blind author around Sicily. On receiving this slim red volume as a present, the Andalucian journalist Alejandro Luque was compelled to make his own self-confessed fetishistic pilgrimage in the footsteps of his beloved Borges. The result of his travels are documented in *Journey to Sicily with a Blind Guide* (*Viaje a la Sicilia con un guía ciego*). Borges came away from his trip with an honorary doctorate and the special award of a Silver Rose; Luque was equally satisfied with his reward – a profound love of Sicily.

In the small world of Palermitan nobility, family connections and friendships were commonplace. In his memoir of a Sicilian childhood, Fulco de Verdura mentions both the Whitakers and the Florios.

He left the island in the 1930s to become a jewellery designer in America, connected with both Coco Chanel and Cole Porter, but his reminiscences in *The Happy Summer Days* are fondly rose-tinted. He grew up in the Villa Niscemi near the Favorita Park on the outskirts of the city. The residence still sits in its own landscaped garden, a fact that pleased Fulco: 'The house is still there, thank God, the same dear old villa, smothered in bougainvillaea, bulging with balconies and protrusive terraces, sunbaked and tired . . .' Today, the gardens are easily accessible with well-kept box-lined paths, brightly coloured flowers spilling from urns, a citrus grove and a duck-filled pond. Fulco describes it as 'a semi-tropical English garden', which is as accurate today as it was when the memoir was published.

The most famous floral accompaniment to the Villa Niscemi was the bougainvillea – a fact not lost on Fulco's cousin and author of *The Leopard*, Giuseppe Tomasi di Lampedusa. We have already seen the Prince striding through the streets of Palermo in anticipation of the forthcoming sexual liaison with his mistress. To get to Palermo, Prince Fabrizio takes his carriage, which slips by his nephew Tancredi's own villa, its decay masked by the flora: 'they drove past villa Falconeri, whose huge bougainvillea cascaded over the gates like swags of episcopal silk, lending a deceptive air of gaiety to the dark.' Despite the fact that the Niscemi never fell into ruin, it is not difficult to identify the inspiration for Tancredi's ancestral pile.

These villas to the west of Palermo give way to the Piano dei Colli where the architecture is smaller but laden with Sicilian Baroque. A prime example is the Villa de Cordova, beautifully described by Mary Taylor Simeti in her Sicilian journal, *On Persephone's Island*. Taylor Simeti is an expatriate American who, in the spirit of early 1960s freedom, came to Sicily after university, expecting to take in a bit of culture whilst avoiding the dangers lurking in every shadow – or so she was led to believe by her wary friends. Planning to stay a year, she is still there, having married a local. Her insights come from that curious position of being both foreigner and insider.

The Cordova is known for its wisteria, which wraps itself around the curved balustrades of the double staircase leading to the front entrance:

In the central bed a hibiscus bush, unpruned and shapeless, is surrounded by spikes of deep-purple iris and the pale violet flowers of a rambling scented geranium, thus stating in the foreground the range of hue to be admitted within the curve of the staircase, where the thick gray trunk of the wisteria vine echoes exactly the arc of the broad stone banister, swirling up like a spiral of smoke to lose itself in the cloud of lavender flowers suspended in the stairs' embrace, a watery cascade of purples and violets laced with the first tiny leaves of green.

The villa is now an events venue where well-heeled guests tread the red carpet up to the terraced entrance.

Presiding over all this floral opulence is the rocky outcrop of Monte Pellegrino. Depending on the time of day, the mountain can display a range of emotions: the dappled sunlight giving rise to a beneficence which feels wholly missing when its outline darkens into the brooding Palermitan night. The German Johann Wolfgang Goethe, a lover of geology, was obsessed by the rock's many facets, not least of which were its artistic merits: 'The delicate contours of Monte Pellegrino to the right were in full sunshine [. . .] For an artist, there was an inexhaustible wealth of vistas to be seen, and we studied them one by one with an eye to painting them all.'

Goethe wrote up his diaries into the volume *Italian Journey* (*Italienische Reise*) published in 1816, some 30 years after his trip. He left for Italy after a stressful time at Weimar in order to reawaken his recalcitrant muse. Of all the Italian stones he unturned, Sicily's mountainous landscape left the biggest impression, along with its cities and mythology. When talking about Goethe's visit to the island, it is hard to avoid the massively overused quote that has become as ubiquitous as a famous Shakespeare line. However, he did manage to bottle the island's essence in one succinct phrase, and who are we to deny the reader now? 'To have seen Italy without having seen Sicily is to not have seen Italy at all, for Sicily is the clue to everything.'

Goethe was a great admirer of the classical world and it would seem less likely to find a similar heart beating in the green khaki of a North American captain in World War II. During the battle for Sicily, John

Steinbeck, in his role as war reporter for the *New York Herald Tribune*, followed the Americans through the island on Operation Husky. Already respected as the author of *The Grapes of Wrath*, he collated his reports into the book *Once There Was a War*. After the Seventh Army took Palermo, Steinbeck interviewed the captain of a patrol torpedo boat who was moved in a similar way to Goethe by Monte Pellegrino:

> You know what Palermo looks like. That great, big, strong mountain right beside the city and the crazy lights that get on it and then the city spilled down there at the base. It looks like Ulysses has just left there. You can really get the sense of Vergil from that mountain, from the whole northern coast of Sicily, for that matter. It just stinks of the classics.

The spiritual charm of Pellegrino does not only lie with its classical associations. In the twelfth century a Norman Sicilian woman called Rosalia left her comfortable existence in the city to take up residence in a cave on the mountain, where she lived her life as a religious hermit. For years her bones remained undiscovered. Her story forms an interesting aside in Gioia Timpanelli's book of two Sicilian novellas, *Sometimes the Soul*. Timpanelli is a Sicilian American who has been lauded for reinvigorating the oral tradition in North America. In the story, 'A Knot of Tears', she draws heavily on the stylistic traditions of her ancestors' island as evidenced by Rosalia's story:

> But in all the years since then, no one had found her remains, until one night the shoemaker dreamt that Santa Rosalia had shown him where he could find her holy bones, and then and there she had promised him she would save the people from the plague.

And so it proved. As the patron saint of Palermo, Rosalia is celebrated in a festino every July, her silver statue paraded through the streets. Many of the travelling literati have documented the procession, but it is to Patrick Brydone that future generations of writers have often turned for a quote full of insight, including his observations of Rosalia's 'triumphal car [. . .] already higher than most houses in Palermo'.

## *Terrasini*

The hills and mountains surrounding the city have not always hidden such a benign presence; the area was once bandit country. To the west of Punta Raisi, the airport now christened Falcone-Borsellino in remembrance of the two assassinated anti-Mafia judges, lies the small town of Terrasini. This seaside settlement was the ancestral home of the Viviano family and the place where Frank Viviano, journalist and author, came in search of the bandit Francesco 'the monk', his great-great-grandfather. His research led to the book, *Blood Washes Blood*.

Viviano is an American foreign correspondent and author who felt compelled to investigate the story of his long-buried ancestor. Rather than take his secret to the grave, on his death-bed Frank's grandfather whispered to him the name of the monk's killer. With this oral evidence and little more, Frank relocated to Terrasini, setting up home in a small villa borrowed from a local with American connections whom he had already befriended. The house is located in the nearby suburb of Paternella and is near to a former palazzo of the Duke d'Aumale, the son of King Louis-Philippe of France. The Duke employed Frank's great-great-grandfather in his stable block. During the 1990s, when Viviano wrote the book, the palazzo was in disrepair; its distinctive terracotta and yellow stripes now have the pristine signs of renovation.

The monk's story takes place against the backdrop of Garibaldian insurrection and even after so many years, the investigating author still encountered that very Sicilian precautionary behaviour of hearing nothing, seeing nothing and saying nothing when he asked the locals about his ancestor's legend. He managed to discover that Francesco Viviano took to the hills as part of the *picciotti* – irregulars fighting in the 1860 uprising – and that he continued to wander the countryside from Monte Palmeto onwards: a Robin Hood figure dressed in the robes of a friar. This pseudo-monk fell foul of a nascent Mafia boss, a local strong-arm whose tactics resembled those that later came to be employed by this criminal brotherhood.

Here, Frank Viviano recreates the scene his ancestor saw when leaving his wife and son behind in their Paternella cottage:

The lemon groves are in full fruit, and as the April sun breaks over Punta Raisi, the spring is ripe with the odours of salt water, lemon blossom and wild fennel. From the trail that coils up the face of Monte Palmeto, Francesco Viviano can see the villa of the French duke [. . .] But night still clings to the face of the ridge, and although he can sometimes hear the laboured breathing and footfalls of other men on the trail, they are invisible.

The monk disappears into the hills, leaving his American namesake to trawl through parish records, archive files and newspaper clippings to recreate his story. The modern mayhem of 1990s Sicily even encroached on the assiduous author in his Paternella retreat. Away on assignment in Turkey, he returned to his cottage only to find a mysterious burglary had taken place. Nothing of note had been taken and nothing ransacked. The locals were full of theories with regard to the culprit, the most plausible being one of mistaken identity. On the run at the time was Giovanni Brusca, the crime boss who oversaw the explosion that destroyed the lives of Giovanni Falcone and his wife. Everybody supposed that Brusca had grown a big curly black beard – one identical to that of the author. The locals were convinced that the police had staged the robbery in search of the mysterious stranger who was living near to the Paternella coastline.

Today's Terrasini shows little outward sign of these skirmishes in either epoque. Its parochial church, where Viviano rustled through the records of births and deaths, rises over the central square, with cafés and small shops cascading down either side towards the sea. Its harbour is an inlet with a wharf of limestone carved from Monte Palmeto. Seen from the sea, Viviano describes it as a 'cubist jumble of pastel houses, set on a cliff'. Its long tradition of emigrant returners is summed up by the epithet, 'Meddicani' (Americans) – a term applied to anyone who has sought a life overseas to return home or, simply, to anyone from elsewhere. Your authors were sitting in a seaside restaurant chatting to the owner who had spent 20 years in Boston, only to overhear him use the same term with regard to us.

Frank is now a habitual returnee, ensuring he visits once a year if possible. His abiding memories of the town are summed up in these words from an interview about his writing of the book: 'Arancini di riso in the morning at a caffè on Piazza del Duomo, the fishing fleet sailing into port, sunset on the Gulf of Castellammare. And above all, the people, among the most generous on Earth, who treated me as a son and a brother.'

## Montelepre

Not far from Terrasini is the town of Montelepre, a name seared into the heart of twentieth-century Sicilian history. This seemingly unimportant little town, nestled in the mountains behind Terrasini, has been a magnet for writers and journalists since the 1940s – the reason: Salvatore Giuliano. Giuliano was that very Sicilian figure, a latter-day bandit born of necessity, driven by loyalty and a misplaced faith in others, whose story would eventually end in tragedy. It was Giuliano's charisma and looks, articulate responses to publicity, as well as his sense of mission that set him apart from your run-of-the-mill outlaw. His fiefdom was centred on Montelepre, a place that Norman Lewis features in his book on the Mafia, *The Honoured Society*; Lewis mentions how its then poor dwellings almost infected the mountainside with their meagre, dark appearance.

Giuliano was not a Mafioso, but his tale is inextricably linked to the Cosa Nostra. It was this subliminal link to the deeper underworld, the idea of a Robin Hood figure moving within the quagmire of this dirty milieu of criminal association that led many authors to scrutinise his complicated life, whether as investigative reportage or fictionalised spectacle. The most notable include the aforementioned Lewis; the decorated Australian writer and correspondent Alan Moorehead; the writer of *The Godfather*, Mario Puzo; and the seemingly incongruous author of *Ring of Bright Water*, Gavin Maxwell.

Maxwell's pursuit of the bandit's story is a tale in itself, which he implicitly includes in his book on the case, *God Protect Me from My Friends*. Maxwell was the product of a military family and a public school education. He had spent the war as part of the Special Operations Executive and in the postwar early 1950s was casting around for a suitably exciting direction in which to take his nascent writing career.

Attracted by Sicily, he threw himself wholeheartedly into uncovering the secrets behind the Giuliano affair.

Montelepre was a poor place, downtrodden by the effects of conflict and rationing, a place where the black market naturally flourished. Maxwell describes the town's brooding presence at night in poetic terms: 'The lights shine on the Norman castle so that it is floodlit against the dark encircling mountains, and the close confines of the town are picked out hard and sharp by other lamps, giving the appearance of a walled and embattled fortress.'

By day the harsh southern sun would reveal the patchwork nature of the town, with its single street 'capable of carrying wheeled traffic'. Today, this is lamentably not the case as twenty-first-century vehicles wheel ferociously along its seventeenth-century Spanish alleyways. But it is churlish to deny such progress to the Monteleprans, a form of development so conspicuous by its absence in the late 1940s and early 1950s.

Maxwell arrived in Sicily during 1953, three years after the death of Giuliano: a wound still festering under the infection of conspiracy and lies. With very little money, the author pitched his tent outside the town's cemetery where the bandit was buried. Existing on a diet of bread, cheese, tomatoes and tinned beans with garlic, he was regularly visited by curious locals who would either simply stare in disbelief at the strange Englishman, or attempt to converse whilst taking advantage of his English cigarettes. Maxwell adapted his linguistic skills to the local dialect and was quickly able to form a connection. However, the constant intrusion on his privacy, not to mention the lack of shade, led him to seek, rather bizarrely, the silent cool marble of Giuliano's sarcophagus.

Eventually moving his tent to a tree-shaded terrace with a view of the town, he established relationships with the local farmers who would bring him gifts of their produce. His magpie journalism was able to piece together a cogent and coherent version of Salvatore's story from the nuggets of half-buried information he managed to extract from those close to the case. In many respects, the whole town was a witness to unfolding events. As Maxwell points out, the nearest thing Giuliano had to a headquarters was the Grotto Bianco cave on the slopes of Monte d'Oro just above the town. People knew he was often there, as did the carabinieri, but their attacks never proved fruitful, as we can see from Maxwell's description of the fortifications in place: 'Across the mouth of the cave they planted a row of sisal cactus, and from the cover of these they shot at any carabinieri who approached them from below.'

The official story had Giuliano shot by Captain Antonio Perenze, but Gaspare Pisciotta, the outlaw's 'lieutenant' and cousin, later claimed he had shot Salvatore in exchange for leniency. Maxwell had the benefit of hindsight, but even as he was investigating the case and waiting for an interview with Pisciotta, he was shocked to hear that Gaspare had been poisoned in gaol on the eve of his testimony. This turn of events meant that the author had some serious editing to do and some tweaks to the conclusions that he had initially drawn.

One writer who followed events as they happened was the Australian Alan Moorehead. From his base at the Villa Diana in Tuscany, he came down to Sicily in the late 1940s to research the bandit's story. Moorehead was a war correspondent, novelist and biographer very used to extracting the clear picture from a mirage of falsehoods. He quickly grasped the political situation and the special position of Sicilian culture; comparing the fate of former partisans in northern Italy to those on the island, he noted: 'Like the Irish in Eire and the Jews in Israel, the Sicilians simply wanted the right to govern themselves.' This fight for Sicilian freedom from Rome was naively supported by Giuliano, who wrote to President Truman asking the Americans to annex the island.

The Monteleprans saw the carabinieri and the forces of the state as just one more occupier – an attitude Moorehead pinpoints when he likens the town to 'village scenes in Sicily during the Allied invasion [. . .] machine guns stacked against the wall, and military vehicles waiting outside'. Giuliano started his campaign with the desire to clear his name – manifesting distinctly Robin Hood tendencies – with his largesse from kidnappings distributed amongst the poor. However, as we shall see when Maxwell picks up the story in Portella della Ginestra, the outlook would become obscured by the darkening clouds of mistrust, manipulation and violence.

This very real story was also fictionalised by the author of *The Godfather*, Mario Puzo. In many ways, his novel based on the Giuliano affair, *The Sicilian*, is the off-screen sequel to this classic of Mafia literature. In addition to his retelling of events, the fictional history of Michael Corleone's exile in Sicily is woven through the tale. Puzo did a fair amount of leg-work in southern Italy, ensuring his descriptions were accurate. He corroborates Maxwell's impressions of Giuliano from his Grotto Bianco hideout, imagining 'he could hear the music coming from the loudspeakers in the square, which always played Rome radio station broadcasts to serenade the town's strollers.'

Puzo was an Italian American whose family hailed from the region of Campania, not Sicily, and, contrary to popular belief, he claimed never to have met a real gangster in his life. Such was his legend that, on research trips to Italy, the locals would talk to him in Italian, not knowing that he barely understood them and spoke not a word himself. As recounted by his long-time partner, Carol Gino, he would nod sagely whilst rolling a cigar around his mouth, leaving the interlocutor with the impression that he was carefully ruminating on the opinions expressed.

He is famously quoted as saying: 'I have written three novels. *The Godfather* is not as good as the preceding two; I wrote it to make money.' His experience of writing the sequel seems to have been more pleasurable: '*The Sicilian* was a fun book to write. A reprise of the Mafia, but in Sicily.' The novel has an operatic scale and an edge-of-the-seat suspense. Whatever the literary merits of these Mafiosi on paper, it is undeniably true that his works have contributed to a worldwide stereotyping of the island's culture, whether you have read his novels or not; a fact helped along by a considerable trade in tourist souvenirs – from Godfather T-shirts to little ceramic figurines and lighters with the image of Marlon Brando emblazoned on their shiny plastic.

### From Partinico to Portella della Ginestra

Some six miles to the south-west of Montelepre lies the regional hub of Partinico, where many of the carabinieri chasing Giuliano were stationed. It was also the base for the social crusader Danilo Dolci in the 1950s. To this day, it has the air of a struggling regional market town whose tarmacked connections spiral into the surrounding mountains. This area of western Sicily was the location for Norman Lewis' novel, *The March of the Long Shadows*. As we have seen, Lewis was passionately affiliated to the island's landscape and its people. The novel is set in 1947, when the central character, a British intelligence agent, has been sent to report on the growing separatist movement – a movement well noted by Moorehouse. The mountainous scenery in the vicinity of Montelepre and Partinico is beautifully described at its spring best when the coastal regions have already set their gaze towards summer: 'the interior could have been the highlands of Scotland, an emerald landscape of rolling mountains and glens, and there were foxes bobbing up their heads in the heather and eagles spiralling in the sky.'

A pastoral idyll soon to be shattered by the fiery blasts of African summer heat. In his memoir, *Places of my Infancy*, Giuseppe Tomasi di Lampedusa describes the journey his family have to make from Palermo to their country palace in Santa Margherita Belice far to the south. The first part of the trip taken by train passes through this region.

> For hours then we crossed the lovely, desperately sad landscape of western Sicily; it must have been I think just exactly the same as Garibaldi's Thousand had found it on landing – Carini, Cinisi, Zucco, Partinico; then the line went along the sea, the rails seemingly laid on the sand itself; the sun, already hot, was broiling us in our iron box.

The trains have greatly improved but the same experience can be had by travelling through the countryside in a car without any air-conditioning. Not to be recommended.

It was not only the sun that had such a devastating effect on the people. To the east of Partinico is the unusually named town of Piana degli Albanesi, which reflects its Greek Orthodox worshipping inhabitants of Albanian extraction who established a settlement here in 1488, fleeing Turkish invasion of their country. Road signs as you enter the town are still written in both Italian and Albanian. In 1947, for the May Day labour celebration, workers from here and neighbouring San Giuseppe Jato gathered at the halfway house of Portella della Ginestra.

Portella is a saddle between the mountains that joins the two towns. Rocky outcrops embrace the plain and the land falls away to what is now the reservoir below Piana. The area has a solitary beauty that was shattered on that day in 1947. Salvatore Giuliano was a fervent anti-Communist and intended to break up the May Day gathering. He claimed to have only intended to assassinate Li Causi, the Communist senator. Instead, his men fired into the picnicking throng, killing women and children in the process. Reading the inscriptions on the modern standing stones, erected in memory, it is chilling to imagine the snipers positioned on the rocky ridge above waiting for the moment when nothing would be the same again.

This haunting memory must have been even more tangible when Maxwell visited during his two-year sojourn in the early 1950s. Overwhelmed by the brutal poetry of the surroundings, he was sure that 'It would be hard to devise a more savage setting for a massacre.' Gavin was not alone in finding it difficult to unravel what exactly happened. Mouths would not open easily to his questions; publishing deadlines came and went – being stretched even further with the killing of Pisciotta in gaol. Maxwell was looking for the *éminence grise* who may, or may not, have lurked behind the tortuous machinations of the case. His putative publisher, Burns and Oates, grew restless with these explanations and demanded a book or a refunded advance. Until now, he felt he had been playing at the career of a writer and decided he needed an agent and a new publisher. Luckily, he was placed with Longman, who threw their weight behind the project to such an extent that he was able to go on and write a second Sicilian book, *The Ten Pains of Death*, about the tuna-fishing community in Scopello.

An interesting footnote to the Salvatore Giuliano story involves the American playwright Arthur Miller and his travelling companion on his trip to Sicily, the lawyer Vincent Longhi. We already know that they stayed in the Hotel des Palmes. You would expect such an illustrious establishment to have a fine restaurant but the impositions of postwar rationing and indiscriminate Allied bombing meant that the two men had to go in search of a decent meal. Crossing town, they came across a nondescript but reconstructed building on a 'shattered little square'.

Seated and ready to eat, they were horrified to discover that the gangster Lucky Luciano was behind them. Luciano, after a commuted sentence, had been deported by the Americans in a misguided thank you for supposed intelligence efforts during the war. He had been born in Lercara Friddi, a town in central Sicily, and so it was an easy decision to return to his homeland.

Miller and Longhi fell into a reluctant conversation with the gangster. In his autobiography, *Timebends*, Miller describes Luciano's physiognomy:

> I had a chance now to realize that I had never seen a face so sharply divided down the center. The right side was hooded, the mouth downturned and the cheek drawn flat. This was the side he killed with. The left, however, had an eye not at all cold but rather interested and intelligent and inquisitive, his social eye fit for a family dentist.

During their stilted chat, the gangster discovered they wanted to tour the island and in finding out that they were staying at the Des Palmes, he insisted they be driven to the hotel. Further horror ensued when they realised Lucky was in the adjoining room. Longhi convinced himself that Luciano thought they were hired hitmen. A knock on their door had the pair riveted with fear then convulsed in nervous laughter. Relieved, Miller saw 'A tall, marvellously handsome young man stood there in a blue navy watch cap and neat plaid mackinaw'. He knew of their desire to see Sicily and assured them that petrol and cars could be found if needed.

Ten years after this encounter, Miller was on a plane with the director Peter Brook, who was showing him newspaper articles about the bandit Giuliano, the subject of a possible film. On seeing a close-up photograph of the dead Salvatore, Miller was convinced that 'in the grainy blowup' he saw 'our friend in the mackinaw'. This was not the only imprint left by Sicily: Miller also went on to write *A View from the Bridge*, a play set in the New York docklands with a cast of Sicilian immigrants, characters he saw gathered in the dusty piazzas of rural villages waiting for work that would never come.

## *Corleone*

South from Portella della Ginestra, centrally located between the north and south coasts, is the town of Corleone. It would be impossible to write a literary guide to Sicily without mention of this unassuming little settlement. The name is, of course, synonymous with *The Godfather*. The central character, Vito Andolini, changes his name on emigration to the New World in remembrance of his Sicilian home town, Corleone. Puzo's don is fictional but Corleone has had its own share of real-life Mafiosi, the most notable (or should that be infamous?) being Totò Riina, linked to the assassinations of the judges Falcone and Borsellino in the 1990s, and his successor, Bernardo Provenzano, known as 'the Tractor'. Puzo wrote *The Godfather* back in the 1960s and set part of the book in Vito's birthplace.

The protagonist's son, Michael, is dragged into the family business following an attempt on his father's life. After killing a rival and a corrupt police officer, he flees to Sicily. Puzo's investigations imbue the Sicilian sections of the book with a real sense of place. On Michael's long walks through the Corleone countryside, he is struck by the Mediterranean abundance of the citrus groves and the early irrigation systems 'with their ancient conduits splashing water out of the fanged mouths of great snake stones carved before Christ'.

Just as Puzo's eye was also drawn to the crumbling misfortune of a once-magnificent classical past, Michael too gazes over vaulted Roman villas plastered with weeds and home to wandering sheep. The future inheritor of the Corleone empire would sometimes stroll into town, a town as noticeable for its precipitous outlook today as it was when Puzo carried out his research. Some of the houses and buildings are perched precariously on rocky outcrops, including the former prison. The author of *The Godfather* describes the inhabitants as living in 'dwellings that pitted the side of the nearest mountain, the mean hovels built out of the black rock'. Corleone is not as 'mean' as this suggests. The central piazza, named after the two assassinated Mafia judges, is ornamentally tiled, surrounded by shops and a tidy, well-maintained park. At its edge, the tourist office advertises an anti-

Mafia museum which is sporadically open, its displays a reminder of the absence of any glamour in the real world of organised crime.

## *Monreale*

Arching back towards Palermo, after our u-shaped sweep through the city's hinterland, it is impossible to miss the spectacular cathedral suburb of Monreale. Signposted from the majority of outerlying towns, Monreale has long been on the obligatory must-see list of the visitor to Sicily. Some 52 kilometres (32 miles) from Corleone, the cathedral and its environs lie only six miles from the centre of the capital on one of nature's most stunning balconies overlooking the Conca d'Oro, the shell-like bay embracing Palermo.

The cathedral building was begun in 1174 by William II with the architects and stonemasons drawing heavily on the Arab-Norman influence. From the outside, apart from the intersecting arches on the eastern apses, the structure is relatively plain; but as we have seen with the Palatine Chapel, the real glory is hidden within. The art of golden mosaic, based on the Byzantine tradition, reached ethereal levels in William II's magnum opus. Writers came in their dozens to witness one of the island's great sites.

Authors with a leaning towards artistic scholarship, such as the historical biographer Vincent Cronin, were carried away in descriptive detail on entering the cathedral. In viewing the brilliant mosaic vignettes of Christian history, Cronin's flowing prose reached poetic heights: 'To cross the threshold is to throw a golden light forward over the rest of one's life.' This Renaissance scholar and travel writer, whose book, *The Golden Honeycomb*, is a classic of the genre, extends the shining metaphor to the whole island. The title aptly encompasses not only the classical myth of Daedalus' honeycomb gift to Aphrodite, but also the golden stone of Sicilian architecture and its shimmering wheat fields. The revered traveller Patrick Leigh Fermor described Cronin's text as 'Honey from Hybla' – praise indeed from this illustrious Grecophile. Fermor himself spent a period of months in Sicily, but sadly left little written trace for posterity.

Guy de Maupassant was more taken with the building's cloister, an example he compares favourably with those of his native France, which he considered to be 'a bit too monkish, a bit too sad'. The pillars in Monreale's courtyard continue the Byzantine theme with barley-sugar twisted columns encrusted with the same mosaic tiles. Each pillar is a masterpiece of individualistic talent, no two being the same and each with its own story to tell. Maupassant was moved to quote Victor Hugo recalling the work of a Greek artist capable of 'Something beautiful like a human smile/On the profile of the Propylaea'.

One of the more lasting, yet oblique, references to Monreale can be found in W. B. Yeats' poem 'Sailing to Byzantium'. Yeats accompanied the American poet, Ezra Pound, on a recuperative trip around Sicily in 1924, many references to which are found in the postcards sent home by Dorothy Shakespear, Pound's wife. Four years later, Yeats published the poem, a paean to an idealised Byzantium in contrast to the decline felt in old age – something with which he was all too familiar. With mortality in mind, his muse faces the magnificent interior of the cathedral:

> Once out of nature I shall never take
> My bodily form from any natural thing,
> But such a form as Grecian goldsmiths make
> Of hammered gold and gold enamelling
> To keep a drowsy Emperor awake [. . .]

Not every author responded with enduring passion. Oscar Wilde, who 'often drove there' during his second visit to the island in 1900, mentioned the locale in passing when writing to Robert Ross, but penned more lines on the 'most dainty, finely-carved boys' whose pedigree he thought outshone the famous Sicilian horses, particularly one fine young man by the name of Manuele. It is also no surprise, given the nature of the subject matter in Norman Lewis' novel, *The Sicilian Specialist*, that Monreale takes a darker turn. The assassin, Marco, is described as having eyes like 'those enormous vacant mosaic faces' found tessellated onto the walls of Monreale. Lewis describes them as oriental, having little to do with the serenity ascribed to such features by Sicilians.

## *Bagheria*

When the Palermitan nobility were tired of city life, many of them would retire to their landed estates in the surrounding countryside of Bagheria, just to the east of Palermo. The Bagheria of today is unrecognisable as a country retreat, the town being described by the Spanish author Alejandro Luque as a 'turbulent Scalextric'. This whirl of traffic and systematic architectural violation has only left a few of the aristocratic villas of yesteryear – the most famous and notorious being the Villa Palagonia.

The villa itself was commissioned in 1715 by the fifth Prince of Palagonia, Don Ferdinando Gravina y Crujillas, a Sicilian noble and Spanish grandee, but it is thanks to the seventh prince, Francesco Ferdinando Gravina e Alliata, that the villa became a place of curiosity and fear. He embellished the garden and interiors with a series of fantastical statuary and quirky decoration, leading to the epithet, the Villa of the Monsters. The gruesome twosome at the entrance are only a hint of what lies beyond. The flower-covered gatehouse and gravel drive open out to reveal a mythological Frankenstein – lining the top of the villa's garden walls are periwigged aristocrats bidding music from courtiers faced by horse-headed gargoyles and hunch-backed gnomes, whilst scaled dragons snarl towards cherubs enveloped in the dubious caress of winged demons.

What phantoms of the mind could have led to the creation of such a menagerie? Rumours abound. The most salacious involves Francesco Ferdinando's promiscuous wife so taunting the aesthetically challenged Prince with her many lovers that he decided to immortalise their caricatures in stone. Visiting writers fell into two camps, the villa virulently dividing opinion in equal measure. Johann Wolfgang Goethe, wedded to his eighteenth-century idea of classical beauty, found the statues repellent and was convinced that they were born of insanity. The Argentinian Jorge Luis Borges was right at home – perhaps no surprise given the fact he had written *The Book of Imaginary Beings*, a modern bestiary full of gryphons and Minotaurs.

3 *The Villa Palagonia statues, Bagheria*

Patrick Brydone, ever the British pragmatist, was one of the few to straddle the fence. Taking a detached view, he simply described the scene that confronted him:

> He puts the head of a lion to the neck of a goose, the body of a lizard, the legs of a goat, the tail of a fox. On the back of this monster, he puts another, if possible still more hideous, with five or six heads, and a bush of horns, that beats the beast of the Revelations all to nothing. There is no kind of horn in the world that he has not collected; and his pleasure is to see them all flourishing upon the same head.

However, both Goethe and Brydone noted the Prince's charitable contributions and extravagant payments to workers. A strange madness indeed. The surreal theme continues inside the villa. The beautiful mirrored ballroom, whose glass is now sadly mottled and faded, is reached through a doorway topped with this startling warning written in Italian: 'See your reflection in the glass and contemplate in its magnificent splendour the image of mortal fragility that it expresses.' Mortal fragility was not the only surprise that the Prince had in store for his guests – hiding in the plush cushions of the opulent furniture were little spikes for the unwary aristocratic bottom.

The eighteenth-century travel writer Henry Swinburne – whose quotes on the Villa Palagonia have so often been wrongly attributed to his great-nephew, the poet Algernon Charles Swinburne – could not wait to leave 'this world of monsters', feeling giddy from the experience. It is difficult not to have an opinion on Gravina's eccentric commission and writers, being what they are, have supplied more descriptions than it would be possible to include. Other luminaries to this height of folly include Washington Irving, Harold Acton and his travelling companion Evelyn Waugh (who christened the town 'Buggery'), Tobias Jones and Dacia Maraini.

The modern eye, with its more forgiving attitude to difference, is inclined to indulge the Prince's fantasy, but the locals contemporary to Palagonia's construction were convinced there was a curse. Pregnant women avoided eye contact with the monsters' stony glare, fearful of the consequences to unborn offspring. Deformities at birth were blamed on Francesco Ferdinando's creations. For many of a superstitious nature, the curse struck again in 1948 when bandits from Salvatore Giuliano's band fired shots into the darkness of the villa's garden. Daylight revealed a dead policeman at the foot of the five-eyed statue at the entrance.

One of the most astute chroniclers of a rapidly changing Bagheria is the Italian author Dacia Maraini. In her memoir, appropriately entitled *Bagheria*, which outsold everything else in Italy in 1993, she recounts the years of her childhood spent in her family's ancestral villa, the Valguarnera. It is a warts-and-all portrait of a town and society in decline, but on the cusp of something new. Despite the at-times bleak references to encroaching urbanisation, she still sees a glimmer of hope:

Something still remains of the old greatness of Bagheria, but only in isolated fragments between the vestiges of abandoned villas, amidst the obscenity of new motorways that have forced a way right into the centre of the town, savagely destroying gardens, fountains, and everything that exists beneath one's feet.

Dacia's former home, the Valguarnera, at the very heart of the town and opposite the Palagonia, was and still is one of Bagheria's most sumptuous residences. Its long drive leads to a building with two wings and an enclosed courtyard, the centre with a graceful staircase. A sign at the grandiose entrance gate informs the reader that one of the many illustrious guests was that well-known Italianophile, the French writer Stendhal, otherwise known as Marie Henri Beyle. It would have been easy for Maraini to wax lyrical about her ancestors and their complex past, alive with riches and scandal. Her memoir rejects this approach to confront an altogether less palatable truth: the weight of a past laden with exploitative nobles whose origins explain some of Sicily's problems.

She compares the elderly aristocracy of nineteenth- and early twentieth-century Sicily to closed oysters, 'long since dead and dried up inside their precious shells'. She wants to know what is left of all the magnificence and what will be the fate of the children's children: 'People who struggled between old debts and new debts, overwhelmed by suicidal depression or mad delusions of grandeur – enough to make one wash one's hands of them forever.'

It was only after eight novels that she finally decided to make a heart-searching literary return to Sicily, with her book based on an ancestor, *The Silent Duchess*, closely followed by this memoir. They all leave, but they eventually return, pulled back by a scent, an image, a memory or a flavour. This could be the mantra for so many of Bagheria's famous sons and daughters, whether we are talking about Maraini herself, or the film-maker Giuseppe Tornatore, the photographer Ferdinando Scianna or the artist Renato Guttuso, who lies buried in the grounds of Villa Cattolica, the museum dedicated to his work. Dacia Maraini's olfactory link to home soil is the 'almost painful intensity of the jasmine in Bagheria'. She says that if she were allowed to remain alive for a few days before death visited, she would choose the town's jasmine as her comfort.

# 2

# The Tyrrhenian Coast

## Castles in the Air

### *Termini Imerese*

The coastal road east from Palermo hugs the Tyrrhenian coastline, weaving through small villages such as Santa Flavia and Trabia. The first settlement of any size is the town of Termini Imerese. The double-barrelled name has a two-fold connotation: Termini refers to the natural spring whose curative powers can still be experienced at the spa in the Grand Hotel delle Terme; whereas Imerese is the Italianised adjective referring to the nearby Ancient Greek settlement of Himera. The Arabs knew the town as Thirmah and even 800 years ago Ibn Jubayr, in his book of travels, praised the springs which aided 'an extreme fertility and abundance of victuals'.

Termini has a split personality – its older, historical self sits contentedly on an outcrop overlooking the gulf; its *belvedere* is a pleasant place to stroll away the late afternoon. Its modern identity has the usual attractions of a twentieth century that was in far too much of a hurry. The speed theme is contagious – in many ways Termini is a place to pass through, a place to stop and restock before setting off for somewhere else, whether by train or the autostrada that hurtles by the town's suburbs.

In 1906, the famous Targa Florio road race was instituted, created by the wealthy aristocrat Vincenzo Florio, a car fanatic. Such was the popularity of the race that over-eager crowds spilled onto the roads, anxious to get a glimpse of the cars – fatalities inevitably ensued. The author Gesualdo Bufalino, from Comiso in south-eastern Sicily, took the

Targa tradition and combined it with the Sicilian legend of Giufà to produce his short story 'The Death of Giufà' ('Morte di Giufà'). Bufalino was a friend of Leonardo Sciascia and it is thanks to his more well-known colleague that Gesualdo's talents were recognised in the wider world.

Giufà is central to Sicilian folklore, a simpleton or village idiot who often comes up smelling of roses due to his naivety or cunning. In Bufalino's story, Giufà's vagrant life sees him snatch his food and drink from the animals of the field, napping amongst the hay and wandering with the sheep. He is attached to the verbal instructions of his fellows, 'he trusts completely in the face-value and guilelessness of words.' After years of sneaking into fields, avoiding the watchful gaze of farmers, he is unaware that they are turning a blind eye to his pilfering, particularly when there is something better to do:

> Like tonight, when all have stayed up to wait for the Big Race to go by, the race that anyone who can read has seen billed on every stuccoed wall from Termini to Buonfornello. Along with the most thunderous warnings not to allow stray calves or unattended children on the highway [. . .]

Needless to say, Giufà cannot read and the story has a sad inevitability. With a stolen hen, he dives into the full glare of the headlights belonging to an oncoming motor car – a contraption which will be, as the narrator notes for our village simpleton, the 'ruin of your pastoral contentment'. As a poignant footnote, the author himself was to die in a car accident before the full breadth of his artistic talent could be realised.

After arduous travel of a less mechanised nature, the American Washington Irving was much relieved to reach Termini, which had some 3,000 inhabitants at the time of his visit at the beginning of the nineteenth century. It was after dark and a very tired Washington collapsed on the bed in his room at the inn. He was awoken by voices; his travelling companion, Captain Hall, was chatting with a man dressed as a Turk. In an opportunity that so rarely happens to the modern traveller, the masked Ottoman invited them to a carnival ball. A fatigued Irving had to be persuaded to don one of the Captain's finest marine uniforms.

The nameless Turk returned to conduct them to what the pair supposed would be a modest affair. They were taken to a mansion whose stairway was lined with liveried servants and glowing torches. The mask was to take place at Baron Palmeria's residence, with its salons luxuriously decorated for the occasion. An embarrassed Irving thought he had gate-crashed this sumptuous private party and so, with Frenchified Italian, did his best to explain their role as interlopers. The gracious host asked them to explain who had been so kind as to invite them. Neither Irving nor the Captain had the name of the man dressed in Eastern robes, but their blushes were spared by the marine's dress uniform that Washington had been so reluctant to wear. The Turk appeared from nowhere to whisper an explanation in the ear of the Baron: it transpired he was an English teacher employed to instruct the aristocrat's daughters and was keen to find native speakers of such a stately bearing. The rest of the evening went off so well, a Sicilian noble was heard to praise their dancing with the back-handed compliment: 'What devils!' The romance of the evening prompted the Baron to offer an extended welcome to the pair.

Douglas Sladen, another author whose prolonged stays in Sicily were abundantly aided by the wealth of aristocratic patrons, was fond of delving through the layers of the island's history whilst pampering himself in its luxuries. Whilst making use of the spa waters in Termini, he searched the surrounding countryside for classical ruins. Having read a thesis written by Luigi Mauceri, he was convinced of the existence of a Cyclopean acropolis near to town. 'Cyclopean' is the lovely adjective applied to any vestiges of early ancient civilisation, in other words those that date from the time of Homer. These belle époque treasure hunters were also fascinated with the medieval, and one of Sicily's best preserved medieval centres lies some seven miles inland from Termini.

## Caccamo

The road to Caccamo hairpins its way up a mountainside through olive groves and prickly pears. From the road, a steep drop to the valley floor gives rise to the equally vertiginous face of Monte San Calogero.

Caccamo sits in the lee of this paternalistic mountain – its fortress-like structure making the town an ideal location for a defensive castle. Carlo Levi took this exact same road in the 1950s whilst writing his book about Sicily, *Words Are Stones* (*Le parole sono pietre*): 'The road runs up from the coast along slopes dripping with oil, then you enter the mountains and the gaze ranges among the light-blue expanses of the large landholdings, and then, solemn and enormous, the Castle of Caccamo rears up from its rocky cliff.'

Levi, a qualified doctor, chose not to follow a career in medicine. His family wealth enabled him to dabble in art and politics. It was his left-leaning anti-Fascist sympathies that saw him removed to a remote hill village in the Italian province of Matera. His experiences of the local characters, social injustice and poverty were set down in the book *Christ Stopped at Eboli* (*Cristo si è fermato ad Eboli*). His unfortunate exile from cosmopolitan Turin was turned into one of the postwar world's best-selling books.

Driven by a passion for the problems he encountered in the south, the debate started by Carlo was widened on the publication of his Sicily book. It is a text that focuses on inequality but also paints a vibrant portrait of the island struggling free from the chains of conflict. His Sicilians are gentle, courteous and cheerful in the face of an unbearable load. In the course of his travels, he often returned to a house in Sciara, a village on the opposing side of Monte San Calogero from Caccamo. One of the access roads is via the town: 'We stopped to gaze at it from the roadside; it was as compact as a single body of a thousand houses, with the shape of a great bird or a dove with folded wings set on the mountain.' Levi did not come for the fortifications, but it is the castle that drew historians, travellers and authors inspired by the Middle Ages. Henry Gally Knight was one such writer.

Knight, an English MP and author, was from the northern vales of Yorkshire. Perhaps because of these septentrional climes, he was drawn to the heat of oriental folklore and penned three books full of Eastern tales: *Ilderim*, *Phrosyne* and *Alashtar*. However, it was his work on *The Normans in Sicily* that would bring him much greater acclaim and led him to delve into the history of Caccamo. He recounts the story of

Maio and Bonel. Maio was the son of a Barese oil baron – that is to say, olive oil – who, in search of more wealth, relocated to the Norman court of William the Bad. His obsequious nature soon saw him appointed as prime minister, one of the few westerners allowed access to William's inner sanctum.

With the Sicilian barons breaking into open rebellion, Maio eventually persuaded the indolent William to action, only to see him quickly retreat to the comforts of his Arabicised court. Maio was free to exercise his Machiavellian nature and to form any deals he saw fit. One such alliance was made with the wealthy and handsome Matthew Bonel, to whom he had promised the hand of his daughter. Eventually, Bonel's eyes were opened to the cruel schemes of William's prime minister which culminated in the poisoning of the Archbishop of Palermo. Avowing revenge, Bonel was to plunge his sword into Maio's chest, ending his tyranny. Gally Knight picks up the story: 'When the deed was accomplished, Bonel, with his followers, left the city, and

*4 Caccamo Castle, guarding the entrance to the town*

withdrew to the castle of Caccamo, which was one of his possessions,' where 'the people were in a tumult of joy at the death of Maio.'

A visit to the castle, which often floats on a haze of early morning mist, pitches the visitor back into the heart of medieval Sicily; its fishtail ramparts still frame the heart-stopping drop to the fields below. The castle's reconstructed grand salon displays the escutcheons of past barons, a visual representation of all those who have conquered the island. The steep cobbled stairway to the castle affords spectacular views to the coast and over the maze of alleyways that form the heart of Caccamo.

At the centre is the Chiesa Madre, the cathedral church of San Giorgio. The building, partly dating from 1090, with Baroque additions, is the magnet for the town's medieval labyrinth. Stone archways attach themselves to the lower structure, outlining paved streets, barely wide enough for a car. These lanes trickle over the steep hillside, surmounting the defensive walls of Caccamo's historical bastion. Street signs – Via Ruggero, Via Enriquez and Via Spuches – are ample evidence of baronial interference from within the castle walls.

Henry Gally Knight, in tune with the rhythm of courtly revenge, lets his factual prose flow with the same abandon he enjoyed in his oriental tales. Perversely, though, Knight may well go down in history for a work that was written by a far more famous contemporary, Lord Byron. In Byron's poem 'Ballad' rendered to the tune of 'Salley in our Alley', Henry felt the full force of Byron's satirical tongue: he referred to the Yorkshireman as a 'poetic dandy'. His verse even goes on to spew more vitriol: 'His rhymes are of the costive kind/And barren as each valley.' Unfortunately, there is no evidence to suggest that Byron spent any significant time on Sicilian soil. He appears to have briefly disembarked at Porto Empedocle on the south coast in 1809 and could have taken a moonlit stroll along the Valley of the Temples. His other close encounter with the island was from the deck of the frigate *Salsette*, from where he saw Mount Etna. It was a sight that reappears in stanza 74 of the fourth canto in *Childe Harold*: 'I've looked on Ida with a Trojan's eye;/Athos, Olympus, Ætna, Atlas, made/These hills seem things of lesser dignity.'

A more temperate but no less interesting account of Bonel's dash to Caccamo can be found in John Julius Norwich's *The Kingdom in the Sun*. This self-confessed historical reporter gives a very readable description of the Baron's revolt. He speculates on the general morale in Palermo if Matthew Bonel had decided to remain firm in his Caccamese fortress which 'was commandingly situated and strongly defended'. As it was, Bonel, tempted back to court, ended his days 'in a particularly revolting dungeon'.

## Collesano

As with Caccamo, the coastal road frequently affords a turn inland, and a few miles to the east of Termini, just such a road points towards a mountain range known as the Madonie, a regional park with protected tree species. The steep escarpments are a stark contrast to the lush coastal plain; near the tree-line, bare pastures are exposed to the full force of Sicilian weather – blistering sun in the height of August and heavy snowfall during the short winter months. Surprisingly, there is a ski resort at Piano Battaglia, complete with lifts and alpine-style chalets. The road to Battaglia passes the pretty hilltown of Collesano. Turning once again to Carlo Levi for an emotive description of the area, we find his words echo the Targa Florio race and the travails of Giufà: 'As the road gradually climbs along the course of the Circuito delle Madonie where Sicilian aristocrats like to kill themselves – and one another – racing cars, nature begins to don the serious, noble, desolate appearance of the Italian interior, the Italy of the peasants.'

When Levi arrived in Collesano, he was met by a gaggle of excited country boys used to hanging around in the main square and by Armando, described by Carlo as the 'village lunatic', an already elderly man who 'greets us with a hurrah and then stretches out on the pavement at our feet'. The mountains are nature's fortress protecting a fragile population from the marauders who came from an altogether more bohemian coast. In times of trouble, Sicilians have retreated to their rocky home, battening down the hatches and protecting themselves from the very real physical danger of invasion and the more esoteric difficulties of invading ideas and ideals. One of these points of contact with a grasping wider world is the nearby coastal town of Cefalù.

## Cefalù

> It looked like a great whale basking in the blueness – a mythological ruminant of a fish, dreaming of some oceanic Eden, its eyes shut.

Such was Lawrence Durrell's first impression of Cefalù, the seaside town a 30-minute car ride away from Caccamo eastwards along the coast. After years of indulging his islomania on the Greek islands, the author of the *Alexandria Quartet* finally got around to discovering Sicily in the 1970s. His whale refers to the bullnosed rock that towers above the town giving a distinctive outline to all postcards sold in the vicinity, and a clue to the origin of Cefalù's name – *kephale* comes from the Greek, meaning 'head'.

Both Roberto Alajmo and Lawrence Durrell approached the town from the Palermo direction. Alajmo, in his journey around Sicily, *L'arte di annacarsi*, notes how the famous Norman cathedral seems out of scale from this angle. Indeed, it dominates the town. Lawrence's visit to Sicily was a somewhat unusual choice for a continentally astute French resident; in short, his mode of transport was a charabanc full of tourists, a miscellaneous bunch he shrewdly satirises in the book he christened *Sicilian Carousel*. Roberto, their university-educated guide, was insistent that 'it was no place to treat with tourist disrespect'. The narrow alleys still teem with visitors of all nations, but the town has managed to keep its street plan and soul intact.

Deep within the lanes, the basilica, so apparent from the approach, disappears from view. Only an experienced driver such as Durrell's Mario would attempt to drive his bus through the eye of such a needle. The cathedral, known as a *duomo* in Italian, sits appropriately enough in Piazza Duomo. An often scathing Durrell is, as Roberto suggested he should be, very respectful of this supreme example of Norman-Byzantine church architecture.

The cathedral was started in 1131 by the Norman King Roger. In an apocryphal account often circulated as the letter of truth, the King was blown to Cefalù in a storm that shipwrecked his vessel. At the height of the tempest, he vowed to build a church in thanks should he make landfall – that location was the little town sitting under its enormous Greek rock. The mosaicists' art is once again prevalent inside the building with a large *Cristo Redentore* in gold above the altar.

Not far from the square is the Mandralisca Museum in the street of the same name. Among its homely exhibits of Sicilian life is a far more iconic piece, an enigmatic painting by the Renaissance master Antonello da Messina, known as the *Unknown Mariner*. It was one of the inspirations for Vincenzo Consolo's complex narrative, *The Smile of the Unknown Mariner* (*Il sorriso dell'ignoto marinaio*), whose title reflects the Mona Lisa-like features on the sailor in question.

Consolo, who was born in Sant'Agata di Militello further along the Tyrrhenian coast, was known for his experiments with historical memory and linguistic research. His narratives are often deliberately sketch-based and fragmentary. The *Mariner* begins with Baron Mandralisca shipping the eponymous painting to Cefalù from the Aeolian Islands. A sailor on board the vessel displays the essence of the painting's smile – so much so, that Mandralisca calls him the unknown mariner. From this point, the narrative splinters into an oblique look at the liberation politics of the Risorgimento and the snails of Sicily! The island's molluscs are the Baron's real passion and may be an extended metaphor for the changes taking place. Joseph Farrell, the translator of the novel, believes the text is 'free from all suggestion that there exists an eternal, mythical Sicily outside history'. Instead of a static monolithic structure, the plot weaves and twists like the helicoidal swirl of the Baron's favourite shells, as each episode builds to create an ever-decreasing historical circle which Mandralisca has to break. Knowing political events are overtaking him, he finds no further comfort in malacology, even destroying some of his manuscripts.

This is sadly Vincenzo's only work to be translated into English, but not the only one with Cefalù as part of the scenery. *Nottetempo, casa per casa* picks up the story of the English occultist and writer, Aleister Crowley, once a resident of the town. In the 1920s, driven by a reading of the Chinese *I Ching*, Crowley moved to the hills of the Santa Barbara district, renting a modest Sicilian country villa in the hope of setting up the self-styled Abbey of Thelema.

Aleister Crowley was the only son of strictly religious parents who followed the doctrines of the Plymouth Brethren. His entire adult life appears to have been an attempt to reject the stifling atmosphere of his childhood. After the death of his father, his mother retreated into an ever more bellicose religiosity. She was convinced her son was the Antichrist of the Apocalypse and started to refer to him as 'the beast' – a name he would later willingly adopt. Rather than rejecting all religion, it was the hypocrisy surrounding it that he found unbearable, saying, 'I did not hate God or Christ, but merely the God and Christ of the people whom I hate.'

Cambridge educated, a writer and poet, he began to dabble in occultism during a trip to Sweden and eventually joined the Hermetic Order of the Golden Dawn, whose alumni include Arthur Edward Waite and W. B. Yeats. Yeats, considerably the better poet, had been critical of Crowley's work *Jephthat*, a fact that led to a personal feud and a mutual dislike. Schisms in the order enabled Crowley to follow his own path. A 1904 trip to Egypt with his new wife gave Crowley a series of visions and rituals evoking the Egyptian gods Thoth and Horus. Believing he had heard disembodied voices, he scribed what would become his *Book of the Law*, the basis for his thelemic philosophy – its central tenet being: 'Do what thou wilt shall be the whole of the law.'

This central tenet enabled him to do what he wanted with many women and a fair share of men, 'sexual magick' being part of his philosophy. The years leading up to 1920 saw his increasing involvement with drugs and occult organisations such as the Ordo Templi Orientis. By the turn of the new decade, Crowley and his wife Leah needed to find somewhere to practise their thelemic rituals in a setting that would be remote and private. A journal entry, later appearing in his novel *The Diary of a Drug Fiend*, describes the idyllic location they found in the hills of Cefalù:

We are high on the neck of the peninsula, and can see West to Palermo, East over the sea. North is the mighty rock of Cephaloedium and behind us to the South rise hills, green with trees and grass. My garden is full of flowers and the promise of fruit.

The house, however, was less idyllic, rather like a superior farm dwelling with no amenities. Crowley set about adorning the walls with his own frescoes and murals, sometimes lurid pictures of his sex magic, one example showing a man sodomised by the god Pan. The theory behind the murals was to ease visitors into a setting where sex was 'studied scientifically without shame or subterfuge'. The reality was somewhat less idealistic. Crowley would occasionally travel to Palermo, another visitor to the Hotel des Palmes, in order to pick up supplies, drugs and visit prostitutes or sail to Naples to sample the whores there. It was his escape from the jealous arguing of the two main women in his life: Leah and Ninette, referred to by Crowley as the 'first concubine' and 'second concubine' respectively.

Seriously addicted to heroin, Crowley experienced a literary high as well. Following the rejection of a novel and his memoirs, he was given an advance for the semi-fictionalised *The Diary of a Drug Fiend*, a novel he wrote in 27 days fuelled by a narcotic diet designed to keep him working. The figure of King Lamus, a thinly disguised Crowley, helps the addicted central characters to shake their drug habit through his philosophical teachings in the self-same town of Cefalù. Critics have argued that the book portrays the Abbey of Thelema as Crowley had hoped it would be rather than as it was – a flawed experiment that seriously damaged people's mental state.

The central characters of *The Diary* are based on Mary Butts and Cecil Maitland, an English author and her friend. Ritual events in the villa reached new heights and shocked these fresh recruits. As Mary herself pointed out, 'It was one thing to partake in the rite of preparing the Cakes of Light, in which Crowley, in a scarlet-and-black robe, sacrificed a cockerel for its blood, but quite another to participate in bestiality.' They left without their health and addicted to drugs – an enlightenment of an altogether different kind.

Crowley's own descent into terminal addiction continued, not helped by the notoriety he was achieving, which ran contrary to his supposed desire for privacy: a contradiction for a man who was always seen as a great self-publicist. He was reported libelously in the British press, notoriously by the *Sunday Express*, who dubbed him 'The Wickedest Man in the World'. His partial literary rehabilitation would only come in the 1960s when the counter-cultural revolution identified with some of his ideology and recognised the graphic portrayal of addiction described in *The Diary of a Drug Fiend*. Earlier, in the mid-1950s, the film director Kenneth Anger, accompanied by the American sexologist Alfred Kinsey, came to the villa and uncovered some of the whitewashed art. Crowley also made an appearance as Oliver Haddo in Somerset Maugham's novel *The Magician* long before his stay in Sicily.

The shenanigans in the villa eventually came to the notice of Benito Mussolini and his local administrators in 1923, when the Fascists gave Crowley a week to leave the island. At this distance in time, it is difficult to decipher who, exactly, was responsible for his expulsion but it seems that the locals, despite crossing themselves when passing his property, were not overly happy to see their source of gossip go.

One last literary link of note occurred after Crowley's expulsion. In a visit to Lisbon in Portugal, his translator, the subsequently famous writer Fernando Pessoa, helped him fake his own suicide at a spot near the city, appropriately named Boca do Inferno (the Mouth of Hell). During the war, he was recruited for special operations disinformation, with little success, by the future writer of James Bond, Ian Fleming. Crowley died in 1947, a broken man, riddled to the core by his addiction to opiates.

Today, the villa just about remains standing in the hills of Cefalù's hinterland. Its entrances are boarded, its decayed roof exposing gaps in the ceiling, allowing the elements to penetrate the vestiges of 'the beast's' art. The occultist's colourful legacy still provokes conflicting opinions. He had wanted to be buried in the Temple of Diana, the ruins on the rock overlooking the town. Unsurprisingly, the town council refused this request. Debate still rages over the fate of the house, as the owners seek to sell the property. There is reluctant talk of a museum dedicated to his curious life and works, but as yet its fate remains in the balance.

## *Capo d'Orlando*

Of all the small Tyrrhenian coastal towns, Capo d'Orlando is the most prosperous. Fifty miles to the east of Cefalù, its well-tended streets are pedestrianised and landscaped with lush vegetation. A long strip of pale blond sand is cooled by the rhythmic exhalations of a sapphire sea. In the heat-haze, the Aeolian Islands melt mysteriously into the horizon. The evening *passeggiata*, or stroll, is a convivial experience, a fitting place for another writer with well-bred connections.

Lucio Piccolo was the cousin of Giuseppe Tomasi di Lampedusa and the first of his extended family to achieve literary fame. The ancestral villa, a country retreat to Lucio and his siblings, is an aristocratic distance from the centre of town. Now surrounded by surburban development, its location has still enabled it to hide away from the twenty-first century. The house and gardens are administered by the Fondazione Famiglia Piccolo di Calanovella, a foundation dedicated to preserving the memory and works of this most artistic of families. The property in Contrada Vina has a gladed cedar-lined entrance drive leading to a gravelled forecourt that opens to the gardens on the left and the house on the right. Lampedusa, a frequent visitor, was always captivated by its bucolic charm.

The Piccolos completely relocated to Capo d'Orlando when Lucio's spendthrift father frittered the family fortune in card games and on his Spanish mistress. They took as much of the fine furniture from their Palermo home as they could possibly fit into the comparatively smaller villa, which was still far from a beach hut. The lower floor is now given over to an exhibition space where the Foundation promotes Sicilian creativity. The first floor, where the family lived, is preserved intact and can be visited with a guide. Divided in half by a corridor that runs from front to back, the rooms are an intimate portrait of the Piccolos' rarified existence.

The right-hand side was reserved for guests and includes a dining room; the left contained the bedrooms. The most unusual room is to be found at the end of the corridor – a large drawing room with French windows that open onto a balconied garden with spectacular views over the Capo coastline. The room was essentially divided into two. Casimiro, Lucio's artist brother, had the left-hand section – his armchair carefully positioned in just the right spot. He suffered from obsessive–compulsive disorder and required his side of the room to be exactly as he wanted. Gioacchino Lanza, Lampedusa's adopted son, recalls how his hands often showed the marks of obsessive cleanliness.

Lucio's side was more disorganised and informal, his upright piano still remains. Further to the right is the library with shelves of books reflecting the family's disparate interests. One theme commonly shared between the brothers was an interest in spiritualism; in particular, it was Casimiro who collected a library of texts on the subject. His art reflects his reading and the walls of the villa are adorned with representations of woodland sprites and nymphs imagined from his wanderings in the garden during the dead of night.

Lucio's literary fame comes from his poetry. He was introduced to the world of letters by the talented and respected Italian poet, Eugenio Montale. It was Montale who invited Piccolo to a literary function in the Lombard town of San Pellegrino Terme and presented him to the Italian literati. Shy of this colourful world, he took along his as-yet-unpublished cousin, Lampedusa, for moral support.

The two Sicilian aristocrats were a rare spectacle – both timid, overdressed in an unfashionable style but gracious to all. The result of Piccolo's initial poetic efforts was the volume *Baroque Songs* (*Canti barocchi*); as described by his English translator, it was written in a language that, despite solid anchors, 'almost floats away'. He went on to produce two more works: *Hide and Seek* (*Gioco a nascondere*) in 1960 and *Plumelia* in 1967. Piccolo received a prize and it was this award that prompted Lampedusa's wife to tease her husband, saying that if his cousin, whom she considered intellectually inferior, was worthy of literary recognition then he, who was a genius, could well achieve something more. Driven onward, Giuseppe wrote *The Leopard*.

Piccolo's poetry has a distinctly nuance-driven, lyrically cultivated feel, running against the tide of much avant-garde poetry of the time.

His verses on the sirocco, the pestilential Arabian wind that occasionally torments the Sicilian summer, are a beautiful example of his work:

> And over the mountains, far above horizons
> a long strip of saffron:
> the Moorish wind-swarm breaks through,
> takes the main portals by force
> the lookout-turrets on the enamel roofs,
> batters façades from the south,
> tosses scarlet hangings, blood-red pennants, kites,
> opens blue clearings, cupolas, dream-forms,
> jolts pergolas, vivid roof-tiles
> where spring-water stands in opalescent jars [. . .]

To hear his voice in its Baroque Italian metre, it is worth quoting the first three lines of the above in the original:

> E sovra i monti, lontano sugli orizzonti
> è lunga striscia color zafferano:
> irrompe la torma moresca dei venti

The sirocco has ignited the passion of more than one author. The dog days of late summer, where the hot wind renders all listless, is a theme explored by Lampedusa himself. It must be remembered that this aristocratic pairing were at least used to the phenomenon, whereas Patrick Brydone, more accustomed to the light zephyrs of a Home Counties spring or the squall of a Scottish moor, was overcome by the transformation in weather: 'I opened the door without having any suspicion of such a change; and indeed I never was more astonished in my life. – The first blast of it on my face felt like the burning stream from the mouth of an oven.'

Alexandre Dumas, in a break from writing about the escapades of Garibaldi's Thousand, wrote a novel of Sicilian brigandage entitled *Pascal Bruno*. The narrative waxes lyrical about the sublime climate to be found on the island, only to pummel the reader with the full force of siroccan power: 'A drift of clouds to the northward announces the approach of the sirocco, the Khamsin of Arabia; a burning mist, rising from the Libyan sands, and wafted to Europe upon the south-eastern wind.'

Giuseppe Tomasi and Lucio, along with Casimiro, created their very own private literary salon within the confines of Calanovella. It is a fair bet that the works of Alexandre Dumas, among many others, would have been discussed long into the velvety Sicilian night. The erudition of the trio was considerable, spanning the full panoply of European literature, and led to a mutually enjoyable mock antagonism where each intellect would try to outdo the other. The relationship between Piccolo and Lampedusa was particularly strong in this respect: each relying on the other for lasting cerebral stimulation. Visitors were often dumbfounded by the interchanges of wordplay.

It is the reader's fortune that much of Giuseppe's correspondence to his cousins remains and has recently been published in book form. The letters were commonly written from locations throughout Europe, especially during Lampedusa's extended stays in London, along with visits to locales in France and the Italian peninsula. In the letters, the author of *The Leopard* refers to himself as 'the Monster', a voracious devourer of culture. A sample of their wicked interchanges can be seen in this letter, dated 6 September 1927, sent from Collalbo:

Dear Lucio,

Your pen, so accustomed to sketching azure seraphim among woods of golden trees, has suddenly adopted the very harsh style in which those chapters in Genesis on the last days of Sodom were composed [. . .]

Their correspondence is full of these teasing literary allusions which reflect the closeness of their friendship and interests. Lucio was as avid a letter writer as his cousin and, in his youth, started to correspond with W. B. Yeats. One imagines the main topic of their exchanges would have been poetry, but it seems Piccolo was more interested in discussing the 'little people' – the differences between the elves and spirits of Irish myth in comparison with their Sicilian counterparts.

The association was not flippant, as he admired Yeats' *Celtic Twilight* in which the Irishman used local mythology with sensitivity. These nostalgic musings and folkloric stories ended with a poem of the same name. Piccolo was keen to emulate such an achievement for the Sicilian equivalent, but was not supported in his goals by his more sceptical cousin. Yeats and Ezra Pound, on their tour of Sicily in 1924/5, received some guidance from an enthusiastic Lucio.

The library at the villa is testament to the rarified literary atmosphere. Bookcases line the walls of this neat and tranquil space, with the venerable old reading desk as a centre point resting on the terracotta honeycombed floor. Dumas takes his place on the shelves along with Byron, Wilde, Shakespeare, Kafka, Borges, Calvino, Moravia, the Russian greats and the full flowering of French nineteenth-century literature. The family leanings to the esoteric are also not forgotten: witness the copies of *Magic and Mystery in Tibet* by David-Neel and *Il senso delle cose e la magia* by Campanella. The family must have spent many contented hours in the company of these silent friends.

The other-worldly atmosphere extends to the garden – Casmiro's midnight muse and the pride and joy of his sister Giovanna. The garden rises from the courtyard, its pergolas leading to the hillside, which contains a pet cemetery. The little outlined graves, capped with headstones, house the remains of the much-loved family dogs. The visitor today is likely to be greeted and accompanied around the garden by a good-natured and friendly canine descendant.

Lucio, happily tied to the garden and villa of Calanovella, was less inclined to travel than his cousin, although both belonged to the illustrious Bellini Club in Palermo. Despite the conviviality and intellectual curiosity of the Capo d'Orlando villa, it seems that the pair were more socially hamstrung in a wider society. Franceso da Mosto – the architect, author and film-maker with partial Sicilian ancestry – remembers his grandfather observing Lampedusa at his club and the extravagant parties thrown by contemporaries. Giuseppe Tomasi would lean against the door 'like a spectator rather than an actor in that magical comedy'.

## *Tyndaris*

Leaving the belle époque to its inevitable decline, we move along the coast in the Messina direction to the ruins and shrine of Tyndaris, known in modern Italian as Tindari. The area is notable for three things: the natural balcony that overlooks a golden spit of sand curling with feline grace into the Tyrrhenian; a partially excavated Greek ruin complete with theatre; and a Catholic shrine. The legend behind the shrine of the black Madonna suggests that she unfurled the sandy arm to enfold a falling baby in her careful embrace. The faithful believe the remaining headland resembles her profile.

The importance of the site attracted a visit from Pope John Paul II and a contemporary metallic sculpture was erected to celebrate the occasion. It sits rather incongruously to the side of the road that winds its way up the hillside to the church. On first sight, you would be forgiven for thinking it was part of an electrical sub-station. The writer Alejandro Luque, on his Sicilian odyssey in the footsteps of Borges, was equally unimpressed, suggesting it was 'a copy of a scrapped space capsule lying abandoned on the grass at the entrance to the grounds'.

The tarmacked forecourt in front of the shrine overlooks the spit; providing you look in the right direction, it is easy to see how the panorama would have stirred the imagination of the poet Quasimodo. Salvatore Quasimodo, born in the south-eastern Sicilian town of Modica, looked to more than just his birthplace for inspiration. He received the Nobel Prize for Literature in 1959 and was cited for his poetry, 'which with classical fire expresses the tragic experience of life in our own times'. His poem entitled 'Wind at Tindari' ('Vento a Tindari') captures these classical allusions, ending in a bitter plea for tranquillity:

> Tindari, return serene;
> rouse me mild friend
> to thrust me to the sky from a rock,
> pretending fear to those who do not
> know what deep wind has sought me out.

Salvatore also translated the Greek and Latin poets and playwrights, including Aeschylus. It is fun to speculate if the Ancient Greek's trilogy, the *Oresteia*, which he wrote on the island of Sicily, was ever performed in the small but beautifully situated Tindarian theatre. There is no doubt, however, that the classics have returned today: there is a theatrical festival held at the site every June.

Given the combined delights of archaeology, natural beauty and religious contemplation, it is no surprise that Tindari is a popular outing for both islanders and foreigners alike. Busloads of tourists are disgorged at regular intervals throughout the year. Far from his usual terrain of the southern Agrigentine coast, the author and crime thriller writer Andrea Camilleri decided to christen one of his books, *Excursion to Tindari* (*La gita a Tindari*). Inspector Montalbano, his often taciturn yet endearing detective, whom we will meet fully later, is asked to investigate the disappearance of an old couple en route to the shrine. The book never reaches these environs, but is imbued with the humour and resignation often witnessed when groups of septuagenarian Sicilians gather together. The story revolves around the disturbing theme of human organ trafficking, and a troubled Inspector consoles himself at the end with what he remembers of the area: 'the small, mysterious Greek theatre and the beach shaped like a pink-fingered hand [. . .] if Livia stayed a few days, an excursion to Tindari might not be a bad idea.'

## Milazzo

Of all the fingers pointing upwards from Sicily to the neighbouring island of Sardinia, Capo Milazzo is the longest. The promontory, hooked to the left, and gently facing Tyndaris across the Patti Gulf was the site for one of Sicily's most famous battles and, given that it concerned Garibaldi, inevitably drew the attention of that avid follower, Alexandre Dumas. Retracing many of the coastal footsteps he took whilst on board *Le Speronare* (the boat whose name became a book), Alexandre returned with Garibaldi's men during the unification of Italy.

Milazzo Castle was a key strategic point in their fight against the Bourbons. It is a 20-minute walk from the port and dominates the peninsula. Originally Norman, on the site of a Greek acropolis, it was extended by the Spanish in the sixteenth century. Garibaldi's aim was to take the castle. Dumas recounts the whole story in his book, *The Garibaldians in Sicily* (*Les Garibaldiens: révolution de Sicile et de Naples*). As the Genoese General approached Milazzo, Dumas found himself in the port of Alicata, miles from the action. After picking up forwarded letters and money in Malta, he returned to the city of Catania. He had dispatched a letter to Garibaldi, who anxiously requested his return.

Racing to the front, Dumas, who had promised French money to aid with musket purchase, came upon Milazzo as the Neapolitan army began to retreat with the Garibaldians in hot pursuit. His description of the General in action may be rose tinted with hero-worshipping fervour, but it does portray the urgency of the action and Garibaldi's leadership:

> Milazzo is built on a peninsula, on high ground, sloping on each side. The battle, which had begun on the east bay, gradually turned to the western side. In the Gulf of Milazzo was the *Tuckery* frigate (formerly the *Veloce*). Garibaldi, calling to mind his old vocation, that of a sailor, got quickly on board the frigate, climbed up into the rigging, and from that point watched the progress of the battle.

The Bourbons advanced from the fort and the General drew their gunfire by aiming cannon at the forces. With this action in progress, the leader himself, with 20 men, took to the fight in the streets of the town. House-to-house combat saw every last Neapolitan withdraw to the confines of the castle walls. Dumas witnessed this entire exchange from the deck of his yacht – presumably without a gin and tonic. He picks up the story as his feet touch *terra firma*: 'I accordingly proceeded to land, and in the midst of the last musket-shots entered Milazzo.' At this stage, the seriousness of the situation hit home with full force:

> It is difficult to give any idea of the disorder and terror which prevailed in the town, never very patriotic in feeling, it is said. The dead and the

wounded were lying in the streets, and the house of the French consul was full of dying men.

On finally meeting up with the Genoese, Dumas was flattered to find the General wished his company for the following day, but realising he would have to bed down on cold flagstones, decided to pitch his tent with four of his crew on the sandy shore of the western bay. The western side of the cape still preserves the gently shelving sands, whereas the eastern flank drops more precipitously from the heights with the road carved into the reinforced hillside.

The gates leading from the castle were supposedly well guarded by Garibaldini in order to prevent a sortie from within the walls, but a curious Dumas found one soldier 'almost dead with fatigue', with 15 of his comrades asleep. The shore, which these days resounds to games of beach volleyball and the enjoyment of day-trippers, had the appearance of a refugee camp, some even taking cover on their small boats anchored in the bay. Small caves on the eastern side also housed the scared populace. A wary Dumas sailed past all these sights, taking the precaution of hoisting his own flag in place of the newly stencilled tricolour.

Summoned to pull alongside Garibaldi's frigate, the *Tuckery*, he boarded it to find the General relaxed. Quoting Dante, he thought that 'it is difficult to imagine a composure of countenance such as his; it is really that of the lion reposing.' It was this meeting that confirmed Dumas's desire to set up a pro-Risorgimento newspaper and it was Garibaldi who suggested the title, penning this very note:

The newspaper which my friend Dumas is about to establish, is to bear the appropriate title of 'The Independent': and it will be the more deserving of this title, if it be the first to deal a blow at me, should I deviate from my duties as a child of the people, and a soldier of humanity.

Flush with this news, Dumas left on his boat for Palermo. On landing, he learned of the surrender of the fort at Milazzo and the subsequent capture of the city of Messina. He kept his promise and, in 1860, launched the paper, *L'indipendente*, in Naples, at what was the very heart of the old regime.

## *The Aeolian Islands*

Milazzo is the modern point of departure for ferries to the nearby Aeolians, also known as the Lipari Islands. An archipelago of volcanic origin, it is formed of seven inhabited islets, namely: Lipari itself, Vulcano, Salina, Panarea, Stromboli (of pyroclastic fame), Filicudi and Alicudi. Each has its own charms and attracts worshippers of *la dolce vita* during the balmy summer months. It is through these wealthy inhabitants of the film world that the islands have achieved most fame, specifically through the eponymously titled movies, *Stromboli* and *Vulcano*; starring Ingrid Bergman and Anna Magnani respectively. Sometimes known as *The War of the Volcanoes*, the first film was more artistically acclaimed and popularly successful.

Salina also has cinematic claims to fame, being the location for many of the beach scenes shot in the film *Il Postino*. The movie was based on Antonio Skármeta's novel, *The Postman*, originally *El cartero de Neruda*. Michael Radford's film took locational liberties with the book and transposed the poet Neruda's Chilean island to the coasts of Italy. The atmosphere and characterisation remain faithful, with Massimo Troisi giving his last memorable performance.

The more curious literary traveller also went out of his way to visit the islands; one such writer to take an excursion on a 'filthy steamboat' to reach the archipelago was Guy de Maupassant. His principal destination was the island he christened the 'flower of sulphur', Vulcano, which, as the name suggests, is alive with sulphurous volcanic activity. His fascination was in stark contrast to the horrors he had experienced when visiting the sulphur mines on the mainland. He hired a rowing boat to take him from the steamboat's destination of Lipari across the waters to Vulcano.

The boat entered the bay which confronts the crater and Maupassant was surprised to be told that the house seemingly guarding access to the slopes belonged to an Englishman. During this period of Sicilian history, the British Victorian era was in full swing and the expansionist entrepreneurial spirit of Britain's businesses had cast an envious glance towards the riches on offer in Sicily. Some companies arrived to make a quick buck and move on, others were headed by Anglo-Sicilians such as the Whitakers who made the island their home and integrated with the local aristocracy. Marsala wine first attracted the investment of these men of trade, but this was soon followed by the exploitation of more earthy natural resources such as sulphur and salt. Those who stayed branched out into banking, shipping and other more profitable enterprises.

It is not clear which organisation Maupassant's Englishman represented, although he was relieved to discover that the *anglais* was sleeping – not through any desire to avoid conversation, but in order to avoid any prohibitions he might have placed on Maupassant's ascent to the summit of the volcano. The incongruous site of an isolated English guardian, whose house came complete with miniature market garden, was due to his company's rights to excavate the abundant sulphur deposits.

Negotiating gorse and lava rock, the Frenchman followed a steep and tortuous path to the top. His climb was punctuated with tiny fissures in the mountain wall, where the elements had spilled forth: 'you perceive an immobile cascade of sulphur that pours out through a crevice. You might think they were streams of fairyland, of congealed light, or fluid rays of the sun.' As visitors will still see today, Maupassant found a large natural platform circling the crater's edge, from where he was able to view the vents spitting steam and fire, their airborne deposits landing in small buttery lakes.

His description of the crater depths is a blizzard of yellow, which obviously left a deep impact on his senses and pen:

Everything is yellow around me, under my feet and over me, a blinding yellow, a maddening yellow. Everything is yellow: the ground, the high walls, and the sky itself. The yellow sun casts into that roaring gulf its intense light, which the heat of that pit of sulphur renders painful like a burn. And you see the yellow liquid boiling, flowing; you see strange crystals flowering, dazzling and strange acids frothing at the edge of the red rims of the furnace.

The journey back down ended in gasps for fresh air and a resolution to drink more of the Malvasia wine produced on neighbouring Salina. He called it the 'devil's wine', convinced as he was of the lingering taste of sulphur in this deep sweet dessert drink. Production methods have improved a great deal since then, but the flavour still has a very distinctive *terroir* – 'the wine of volcanoes' indeed.

Readers familiar with classical literature will find the name 'Aeolian' ringing bells. Those prolific sailors of the Mediterranean, the Greeks, named the archipelago after their god, Aeolus, the keeper of the winds. It is this name that has led to much speculation regarding their appearance in Homer's *Odyssey*. Some scholars, notably the Victorian Samuel Butler, who was convinced of the Sicilian origins and female authorship of the work, place Aeolus' seat elsewhere – in his case, to the west of the main island.

Book X of the *Odyssey* has Odysseus meeting the god of wind, having escaped the clutches of the Cyclops. With the sun rising 'when the child of morning, rosy-fingered Dawn appeared', the crew 'smote the grey sea' in the direction of the Aeolians. Homer describes their destination appearing as if floating on the sea, an apt description to anyone who has seen the island group from a distance.

The god, after much entertainment, agrees to hold the 'roaring winds' in a sealed ox-hide, only allowing the west wind to blow. If Odysseus is to head home to Ithaca through the Straits of Messina, this is the only direction the wind could reliably have come from. As with all things in the *Odyssey*, the path is not a smooth one and his mutinous crew loosened the leather sack, letting all hell break loose; a disgruntled ship was blown all the way back to Aeolus.

# ❈ 3 ❈

# MESSINA, TAORMINA
# AND THE
# NORTH-EAST COAST

## A Playground for the Literati

### *Messina*

In 1588, the 24-year-old Michelangelo Florio Crollalanza was a hunted man. One step ahead of the Inquisition, he fled its fiery embrace for the colder climes of Protestant England. His problems started back in Messina, when Michelangelo's father, Doctor Giovanni, published a few works that did not sit well with the doctrines of the Catholic faith. His son was well educated, a European traveller with trips to Denmark, Greece, Spain and Austria under his belt.

The family first moved to the Veneto from their island home where they rented the house of a merchant named Otello. The house, probably going cheap, had a sad history: said merchant had murdered his wife in a fit of jealousy. Moving on, Crollalanza was to meet a bewitchingly beautiful 16-year-old Milanese countess who went by the name of Giulietta. So begins a tale of star-crossed lovers, thwarted in their love by her family, who thought she would be marrying beneath her, not to mention the prospective son-in-law's religious leanings. The family decided she would be better off in Verona – a fatal mistake given the fact she was abducted by the double-dealing Inquisition, who were happy to frame Michelangelo for her disappearance. The inevitable ending has Giulietta committing suicide.

This is all beginning to sound very familiar – fodder for the imagination of a great playwright, one William Shakespeare. But who was Shakespeare and how did he know so much about contemporary Italy? If you believe many Messinese, as well as the retired literature professor Martino Iuvara, he was our hero, Michelangelo Florio Crollalanza. Of course, sizeable holes can be picked in the theory by Shakespearean scholars, but this romantic idea does explain some of the mystery behind the playwright's more intimate knowledge of things Italian.

The theory has Crollalanza taking letters of introduction from the philosopher Giordano Bruno to the Earls of Pembroke and Southampton, both linked to the Shakespeare story. Michelangelo already had relatives in England, including the renowned translator and dictionary writer, John Florio. He was put up by relatives of his mother, Guglielma Crollalanza. At this point, he decided it would be a good idea to anglicise his name. He took the male form of his mother's first name, making it the English 'William', and loosely translated his surname – 'Crolla' became 'Shake' and 'lanza' became 'speare'. This was also the name of a deceased cousin from Stratford, whose shoes he could happily fill, leaving his old identity behind.

The *pièce de résistance* behind this story is the fact that a no-longer-extant play, set in Messina and attributed to Michelangelo, is documented. The work went by the dialectal title of *Tanto traffico per niente*, known in standard Italian as *Molto rumore per nulla* and rendered into English as *Much Ado About Nothing*. The missing tale has been whimsically recreated by Andrea Camilleri of Inspector Montalbano fame. His book, *Troppu trafficu ppi nenti*, written in full-on Sicilian dialect, recreates the possible work of Signor Crollalanza. However, there is no need to look beyond the standard Shakespearean histories to find a connection between William and the city of Messina. The port city, set back from the narrow strait of the same name that separates Sicily from the mainland, is indeed the location for *Much Ado*.

It is well documented that William was a magpie-like pillager of sources, probably borrowing from the likes of Matteo Bandello, Baldassare Castiglione and his work *The Courtier* (*Il cortegiano*) and Ariosto's *Orlando Furioso* for this play. His geography is also more accurate than many people had previously thought. An interesting book by Richard Paul Roe, *The Shakespeare Guide to Italy: Then and Now*, looks at the minutiae of the plays and relates them to real and sometimes unexpected details on the ground.

Messina is, unfortunately, prone to natural disaster and has been rebuilt several times after serious earthquakes. This makes tracking Renaissance locations somewhat difficult but Roe is convinced that the opening scenes of this romantic comedy, set in the governor's palace, were based on the real royal palace which once stood to the side of Piazza del Governolo and overlooked the harbour. This is now the setting for the Prefettura, the offices of the central government's representative in Messina. The Messinese tradition of 'pleaching' vines, i.e. weaving them together to form a dense cover, also makes an appearance in *Much Ado* and Richard Roe cites the character Hero, who notes they 'forbid the sun to enter'. Pleaching also extends to trees bent into green tunnels for shade and our intrepid searcher for Sicilian truth behind William's words has a wonderful picture in his book of just such an alley at Messina University.

The play centres on Beatrice and Benedick, whose witty exchanges and wordplay show a supposed disdain for each other. The pair are tricked into believing that one is in love with the other and eventually love does, in fact, ensue. Technically, this is a subplot to the tale of Hero and Claudio, whose marriage is ruined by a wicked scheme against them; the plot is revealed, resulting in the wedding of Hero and Claudio. As usual, Shakespeare intersperses the main characters with a series of others who fill out the comedy and intrigue; one such is the drunkard Borachio, a nice Spanish reference to a bibulous Bacchus, who helps in the undoing of Hero's reputation. In Act III, he announces that the nuptials will take place in the 'Temple', which Roe is sure refers to Messina's once-famous Temple of Hercules Manticles which became a church dedicated to Saint Michael.

One other character, Don John, had much contemporary resonance for Elizabethans and much influence on another famous writer of the period who was to spend more time than he had planned in Messina: Miguel de Cervantes Saavedra, the author of *Don Quixote*. Historically,

Don John was in charge of the Christian fleets that went into battle at Lepanto with the Ottoman Turks. Known as the Holy League, the ships gathered at the port of Messina before heading off. Messina harbour is a natural sickle-shape and the perfect location for such a gathering of fire power. On 25 August 1571, Don John, the bastard brother of the Spanish king, Philip II, set foot on Messinese soil among much pomp and celebration including draped heraldry, Latin poetry lauding his best attributes and a cannonade of celebratory gunfire. In the crowd was a young man with literary ambition and the immediate future of a soldier's life: Cervantes.

For the time being, Miguel was happy to be in Messina as it gave him the opportunity to catch up with friends and relatives who had joined the expedition, including his cousins Alonso Cervantes and Gonzalo, who was himself a poet, albeit an unsuccessful one. The soldiers must have been an incredible sight, wearing the gaudy uniforms of the day which led to the locals christening them *pappagalli*, parrots. Given the papal sanction for the fleet, it is no surprise to discover that delegates from the Vatican were handing out largesse to all and sundry and it is more than likely that Miguel would have received a rosary and the promise to remit his sins. Ships came from all quarters, the Venetians, Genoese, Sicilians and Savoyards adding to the Spanish contingent, but the weather and choppy seas, notorious in the Straits of Messina, were to delay departure.

Miguel and his friends were huddled onboard incredibly cramped boats, over-stocked with the paraphernalia of display and war. The intemperate weather would have had a devastating effect on stomachs already tight with the anticipation of coming battle. William Byron, the writer of an excellent biography of Cervantes, plunges us into the fervour of the occasion as the ships leave the harbour:

> The noise must have been hallucinatory. Chains thundered, hulls creaked, sails boomed, skippers' mallets rhythmically thudded to give the stroke to the rowers. Orders were shouted in a dozen languages while an immense crowd cheered feverishly, as though the blood of all Christendom had rushed to its head there in the port of Messina.

Miguel was suffering from fever onboard a galley called the *Marquesa*. Battle was joined approaching Lepanto, now known by the Greek name Nafpaktos. Cervantes refused to stay below deck, despite his illness, and took full part in the action. Contemporary accounts praise his bravery in the face of incredible carnage. To say he stared death in the face is an understatement and it left an indelible mark. In a poem known as the 'Epistle to Mateo Vázquez' ('Epístola a Mateo Vázquez'), he describes the horrors of war:

> The cries confused, the horrid dine and dire,
> The mortal writhings of the desperate
> Who breathed their last 'mid water and 'mid fire,
> The deep-drawn sighs, the groanings loud and great
> That sped from wounded breasts, in many a throe
> Cursing their bitter and detested fate.

Miguel was injured three times, twice from a harquebus volley. It took weeks for the wounded writer to find himself back in Messina. He must have wished the raucous celebrations to be happening anywhere else given the extent of his injuries. Eventually, he was taken off the ship and transported the short distance to the Grand Hospital, a building which, given the city's seismic history, no longer exists – although the location was alongside the Church of Santa Maria degli Alemanni.

To the modern ear, the word 'hospital' ought to conjure up images of sterility, calm and recuperation. However, life at the Grand was far from matching this description, being a breeding ground for bacteria and infection; although the veneration given to soldiers of the great battle meant that conditions were not as bad as they could have been. The patients even received a visit from their commander, Don John. Amazingly, Cervantes survived but was left with a permanently impaired left hand. It put an end to his career as a soldier and steered him in the direction of letters.

It was still to be a long while before Miguel's talents would lead to worldwide recognition and his magnum opus, *The Quixote*, a book praised by writers as prominent as Dostoyevsky, Nabokov, Mann and

Fuentes. He would still have to endure captivity in Algeria, where he became friends with the Sicilian poet, Antonio Veneziano, and to undergo legal proceedings for debt and penury. Having lived a difficult life, Cervantes always held a place in his heart for time spent in Sicily, particularly before the action in Lepanto. Echoes of the island reverberate throughout his works, as can be seen in this idiosyncratic quote from Don Quixote, that righter of wrongs, slayer of giants and mad idealist: 'Likewise, in the island of Sicily, there have been found leg-bones and arm-bones so large that their size makes it plain that their owners were giants, and as tall as great towers; geometry puts this fact beyond a doubt.'

The impact of Cervantes' great book was felt throughout Europe within his lifetime, although he was to receive little benefit. Translations abounded, some better than others, and rogue sequels encouraged the author to complete his second part. This story of madness, knight errantry, romanticism and the eternal human condition has continued to have an influence even in the post-modern world of twenty-first-century letters. Dostoyevsky's work, *The Idiot*, owes a debt to Miguel, as does the work of Giovanni Meli who, in 1785, wrote *Don Chisciotti and Sanciu Panza*.

Meli was a philosopher, medic and poet who wrote in Sicilian dialect. His continuation of the story brings Sancho to centre stage, a role reversal which may have been influenced by Sicily's own subjugated situation with regard to its larger Spanish brother. The Sicilian perspective stalks the book like a third character. In this quote, Sanciu's reply to Hero could have reflected the political situation at the time: 'I saw and I still see some awful tangled labyrinths in which mendacity succeeds in every case and is more welcome than the truth itself.'

Shakespeare and Cervantes, these two giants of world literature, share Messina as a common location, but coincidentally, they also departed this life on the same day, 23 April, albeit under different calendars. To recognise this auspicious date, UNESCO has christened it the International Day of the Book. The two men never met, although Anthony Burgess imagined such a meeting in his compilation of short stories, *The Devil's Mode*. If we go back to Miguel's recuperation and squint a little, we may be able to see Dr Florio and his young son, Michelangelo Crollalanza, doing the rounds of the Grand Hospital. Perhaps Michelangelo stopped at Cervantes' bedside and listened to the young warrior's stories, or perhaps this is a romantic step too far.

Messina, with its coastal location a giant's stone's throw from the Italian mainland, was and to a degree still is, an *entrepôt* – a place where merchants gathered, goods were shipped and news exchanged. The town had a rapid turnover of people, a floating populace of incomers and outgoers. It is against this backdrop of trade and travel that the Anglo-Sicilian author Simonetta Agnello Hornby set her book, *The Nun* (*La monaca*). Agnello Hornby has only been published since the year 2000 but her works have become classics, particularly *The Almond Picker* (*La mennulara*), which won the Stresa, Forte and Alassio literary prizes. Born into a Palermitan family with an aristocratic background, she married an Englishman and settled in London. Trained as a lawyer, she has spent most of her working life in the field of family law with particular emphasis on child welfare.

A self-described 'vision' at an airport gave her the characters and plot of her first book, *La mennulara*. She has the ability to create fictional locations or people and intertwine them in the fabric of a real Sicily. *The Nun* was born of a desire to write about the problems of marriage, either enforced or denied. She originally intended the book to focus on the difficulties of a modern Muslim girl anticipating an enforced marriage and a nineteenth-century Sicilian girl who was forced into a convent. Agnello Hornby felt the presence of the Sicilian character to be so strong that she took over the book.

Don Peppino Padellani is a Messinese field marshal with a younger wife, Gesuela, who loves the local high society and is renowned for her evening soirées. One of their daughters is the nun-to-be, Agata. At the height of their family life, the city is back to its former glory after the plague, an earthquake and a flood:

Messina was enclosed by a ring of walls with seven gates, and it boasted a three-century-old university, numerous convents and monasteries, two theatres and four libraries, five piazzas, six fountains.

The list is impressive and the Messina of its day also boasted a burgeoning commercial sector led by foreign residents, often English. When times get hard for the family, this backdrop of mercantile wealth is small comfort, especially after the death of Don Peppino. Family interference leads to the failure of a possible marriage to Giacomo Lepre. Gesuela takes her daughter on a trip to Naples in search of a much-needed stipend. Agnello Hornby's English connections have helped her portrayal of Agata's next love, the English captain of the boat to Naples, James Garson.

Generally speaking, Simonetta sees a great deal of similarity between the two islands, with the island mindset demonstrating a shared fear of invasion – a distant experience in the case of Britain and a very real one in the case of Sicily. In interviews, she has highlighted a conceit inherent in both cultures that comes from the insular mentality, in addition to the shared experience of a vestigial aristocracy dominated by male inheritance. Clannish behaviour is something she sees in both these cultures sharing Norman roots. Simonetta is more forgiving of English humour, which she compares to the Sicilian use of sarcasm, a desire to laugh at others rather than at yourself. It is not for nothing that much of the trade seen in the Messina of *The Nun* is in the hands of foreigners; as Agnello Hornby admits, Sicilians have little tradition of business practices outside the confines of the family.

Returning to *The Nun*, the trip to Naples fails and the desperate Agata is sent to a convent, where she continues to receive messages from the outside world and books from her beloved Garson. The sending of daughters to convents, avoiding the expensive dowry, has a long and less than venerable tradition in this part of the world. Some women adapted, some rebelled and some were torn, like Agata, between the contemplative life and the world beyond the convent walls.

A vignette from *La monaca* sees the family experiencing the effects of a tremor: 'In the silvery moonlight, the central chandelier was swaying; an earthquake. Doors and windows were creaking, servant bells were chiming.' This time, the effects are limited but the city was not always so fortunate. Johann Wolfgang Goethe passed through in May 1787 in the wake of a devastating earthquake, finding the place 'accursed'.

His initial reaction to the port was condemnatory, 'There can be no more dreary site in the world than the so-called Palazzata, a crescent of palazzi which encloses about a mile of the harbour waterfront.' The harsh language is unfortunate as even he notes the gaps in the crumbled buildings which can only have been due to seismic activity. His Teutonic mindset goes on to expound the virtues of local building techniques, or lack thereof. He later regrets these initial impressions but has already committed himself to an early departure.

A more modern take on the experiences of devastation and reconstruction is present in Elio Vittorini's book, *The Women of Messina* (*Le donne di Messina*). The plot centres on the construction of a postwar commune where the local women struggle desperately to create some form of community from the rubble, literal and metaphorical, of the war. Vittorini continued to tinker with the text as he became increasingly disillusioned with Italy's inability to change. The collective women have a degree of anonymity, their actions small but significant in the grand sweep of history. It is an experimental work fitting for this Sicilian literary modernist who, when working for the publishing house Einaudi, rejected Lampedusa's *Leopard*. He saw it as static, in terms of the central character and the situation, which some would say was the whole point.

### Taormina

From Messina, the coastal road down the eastern side of the island leads to the precariously perched town of Taormina, *the* Sicilian resort. Since the days of Goethe, when the German heaped praise on the stunning location of the town's Greek theatre, Taormina has been an essential destination on any tour of the island. Many creative souls have sought extended solace here; backed by Etna and bathed by the pearlescent light dancing on the waves of the Ionian below, it is a sensualist's seventh heaven. From a small village, it grew to accommodate the louche literati of the western world. Its twenty-first-century reincarnation embraces both the day-tripper and those who can afford the luxurious suites of hotels with illustrious roots.

The original draw for visitors was the ancient theatre, probably one of the most spectacularly sited examples still existing. Carved into the coastal mountainside, its serried ranks of stone seating horseshoe the central performance area. The bay is framed by the pillars behind the stage, with the whole scene observed by the pulsating slopes of Mount Etna in the distance. Nature's bounty has endowed this theatre with more drama than man could ever produce. Goethe was sufficiently awed to note: 'If one sits down where the topmost spectators sat, one has to admit that no audience in any other theatre ever beheld such a view.'

The Grecian tradition continued to work its magic, but in other ways. Writers came to be inspired, to share ideas, to be seen and simply to hang out. In the mid-1880s when Guy de Maupassant arrived in town, Taormina was still a village but starting to attract notable names – a phenomenon that would only continue with full force into the twentieth century. Otto Geleng, the Berlin-born artist, was for many the pied

5 *The Greek theatre, Taormina*

piper who would lead the flight of like-minded types to enjoy these southern climes. His faithfully reproduced, finely depicted art was an unintended marketing campaign of which Thomas Cook would have been proud.

Maupassant is, as we have come to expect, fulsome in his language. His Sicilian travelogue is unequivocal in recommending Taormina to the visitor. He goes on to praise the landscape and the incomparable location: 'a landscape where you find everything on earth that seems made to seduce the eyes, the mind and the imagination'. The Victorian-era expansionism, whether English or French, pales into insignificance compared with Maupassant's admiration for the Greek colonisers and their genius-like thirst for theatrical entertainment. He wonders at the lack of a modern nation's ability to create such architectural drama. For the Frenchman, the blood of the ancients ran with 'love and admiration for the Beautiful'.

Douglas Sladen, that proselytiser for all things Sicilian, was a regular visitor to Taormina. His guide, *Sicily, the New Winter Resort*, includes sections on the town, but he is realistic enough to emphasise that it is 'an ideal loafing place'. He is more scathing of the casual visitor in his 1905 novel-cum-thinly disguised brochure, *The Sicilian Lovers*. In the footsteps of his friends – the lovers in question – the narrator joins them at the Hotel Santa Caterina.

> For there is a certain pleasure in going to a popular place where you see more than meets the eye: it makes you feel quite a superior person. Most people who go to Taormina are content to go to the Greek theatre; the Hotel San Domenico; the Badia, because it comes into photographs and, perhaps, the Palazzo San Stefano.

As Sladen was publishing his novel, another author was to die on the island, William Sharp. His death will be covered in the chapter on Etna and Catania, but Sharp was also a regular visitor to Taormina during his extended sojourns. He, or should we say she, was a guest of Alexander Nelson Hood, the Duke of Bronte who penned the book *Sicilian Studies*. Sharp was not a Victorian transvestite, but chose to write secretly under the pseudonym of Fiona Macleod, a literary pretence he kept up for many years. His writing focused on poetry and literary biography. William was part of the Rossetti group and a participant in the Celtic revival movement along with W. B. Yeats. Yeats, antagonistic to Sharp, but initially respectful of his alter ego Macleod, was one of the few writers to have an inkling that they were one and the same.

William's works include a study of Dante Gabriel Rossetti, the pre-Raphaelite artist and poet; accounts of the lives of Shelley and Heinrich Heine, and numerous compilations of Macleod's poetry. After his death, Elizabeth Sharp compiled a *Memoir* from his diaries and correspondence, which included letters to Oscar Wilde, Robert Louis Stevenson, Yeats and Rossetti. In 1901, he writes from Monte Venere, Taormina:

> To-day it was too warm to work contentedly indoors even upon our little terrace with its superb views over Etna and the Ionian Sea – so at 9 a.m. Elizabeth and I, with a young painter-friend, came up here to a divine spot on the slopes of the steep and grand-shouldered Hill of Venus, bringing with us our writing and sketching materials and also fruit and wine and light luncheon.

This scene among the pastoral muses was not confined to the Sharps, but a commonly enjoyed expatriate outing. Sladen's 'loafing' is amply illustrated by the fact that Sharp does not seem to have got much work done; by 3 p.m. they have 'lain here for hours in the glorious warmth and cloudless sunglow'.

William was in correspondence with Oscar Wilde, although none is related to their separate visits to the island. In 1897, Wilde left his lover Bosie (Lord Alfred Douglas) in Naples. Their supposed split was to satisfy their respective families, who threatened to withdraw financial support, but they had every intention of meeting up again. Oscar accepted an invite from an elderly Russian of significant means who suggested they go to Taormina. This was Wilde's first visit to Sicily and he was to meet the Prussian Baron von Gloeden, who had set up residence in the town. Von Gloeden was a photographer who specialised in taking pictures of naked Sicilian youths, posing them in suggestive Greco-Roman style. His clientele were the moneyed and artistic classes of northern Europe. With the long lens of history, von Gloeden has been partially exonerated artistically as a photographic pioneer, but not from a moral perspective given some of the subjects' ages.

Von Gloeden was part of the underground cultural circle who considered 'Sicily', with all its Grecian connotations, as a code word for 'homosexual'. Works with the island in the title are common in this era, including one of Victorian society's most bold homo-erotic poems, which was entitled 'To a Sicilian Boy'. It was written by Theodore Wratislaw and appeared in *The Artist* magazine in 1893. Bosie himself was to write a poem called 'Sicilian Love Song'. The list goes on, including works by Edward Cracroft Lefroy and John Addington Symonds with his 'Syracusan Stone-Quarries'. These educated men were used to using classical allusions to refer to their sexual preferences and Sicily, with its ancient past, landscapes and Grecian traditions, was an obvious choice and destination.

Wilde, even before he had set foot on the island, was inspired by its mythology in his own poetry, which was often a biographical outlet for the emotional battles he waged with his own sexual feelings for young men.

> He was a Grecian lad, who coming home
> With pulpy figs and wine from Sicily
> Stood at his galley's prow, and let the foam
> Blow through his crisp brown curls unconsciously,
> And holding wave and wind in boy's despite
> Peered from his dripping seat across the wet and stormy night.

During Wilde's stay, he received several photographs from the Baron as presents, two of which still survive. Oscar was not slow in finding other companions to fill the void left by Bosie and equally, Bosie was doing his best to find lovers in Paris. Their grand love affair was beginning to wane and settling into friendship before declining into Douglas' bitter repudiation of his former lover after Oscar had died.

André Gide, a friend of Wilde's during his time in Paris, was also attracted to Taormina. His first visit was in 1896 when he travelled down the eastern coast of the island with his wife Madeleine, whom, it seems, he married for convenience rather than passion. His letters to his brother-in-law are full of the classical imagery so beloved of his Irish friend, including a weeping Arethusa gathering flowers between stone tombs.

In Gide's novel *The Immoralist* (*L'Immoraliste*) published in 1902, he tackles head on the themes of morality, desire and sexual orientation. The protagonist, Michel, who has married out of duty, becomes very ill and travels to North Africa for its warmer climes. Here, as he convalesces, his eyes are opened to the physical attractions of an Arab youth. Returning to Europe, he throws off the dusty sheets of historical research and looks to reinvent himself. On the steep Taormina–Mola road, he shouts, 'as if to summon him up within me, "A new self! A new self!"' This sounds very close to Gide's own personal journey undertaken in foreign climes, among which Taormina is a prominent destination.

As the novel progresses, Michel no longer wishes to suppress his inner nature and befriends Ménalque, whom he recognises as a fellow soul in torment – a character, although shunned by society, who remains true to himself, rejecting the boredom of conventional social order. Michel is torn by the affection and guilt he feels towards his wife, Marceline, who by this time has lost a child and has become very ill herself with the tuberculosis that had afflicted her husband. On a trip back to the island, the coach driver at Taormina railway station compliments Marceline but the protagonist's eye is on the flatterer: 'He was a little Sicilian from Catania, as beautiful as a line of Theocritus, resplendent, fragrant and delicious as a piece of fruit.'

Needless to say, the story of a man in pursuit of his own desires and truths has consequences for those around him and it is Marceline who pays with her life. Gide's own story was complex and somewhat parallel. Ménalque is a thinly veiled Oscar Wilde, with Wilde's own personality acting on André in the same manner as Michel experiences in the book. The problems in Gide's life were compounded by marriage, but he remained affectionate to his wife, whilst still pursuing his true sexual nature. He was joined in Sicily by a coterie of like-minded souls, most notably the writer, Jean Cocteau and his lover Jean Marais, the film actor. Truman Capote, whose own Taormina story will be revealed shortly, describes an early encounter with Gide in his essay 'Fontana Vecchia'. Although the veracity of this has subsequently been questioned, the account given by the author of *Breakfast at Tiffany's* is nonetheless evocative. He says he was strolling across the shaded square near the Messina Gate when he spied a curious figure amongst the usual array of locals:

> I was startled to see perched upon this wall an old man wearing velvet trousers and wrapped in a black cape; his hat, an olive fedora, had been dented into a peaked tricorne crown, and the brim threw a shadow over his broad, yellowed, somewhat Mongolian face.

Gide must, indeed, have appeared an odd bird to the villagers, even in a place so accustomed to eccentric foreigners: a plushly velveted aesthete amongst the well-worn cloth of the cap-wearing Taorminese. At this time, he was relatively fresh from the belated international recognition that saw him awarded the 1947 Nobel Prize, which cited his truthful insight into the human condition.

Taormina can boast the visits of at least eleven Nobel laureates, some more fleeting than others, including Rabindranath Tagore, John Steinbeck, Anatole France, W. B. Yeats and Ernest Hemingway. Hemingway's stay in Taormina is interesting in its denial by the author. In November 1918, Captain James Gamble, who was part of the Proctor and Gamble empire, invited Ernest to spend some time in the Mediterranean with him. A war-weary Hemingway saw this as a good opportunity but the nurse with whom he had fallen in love during the conflict, Agnes von Kurowsky, was strongly against the idea, convinced that her fiancé would end up as an aimless drifter throwing himself on the mercy of richer patrons.

Hemingway later told the story of how he had headed for Taormina but never reached his destination. He liked to claim that the hostess in his first hotel had taken his clothing and seduced him into staying.

His letters, however, betray the real story. He did stay with Gamble in a rented villa on the slopes of the town but deeply regretted not staying for longer. In a letter to his friend, he writes nostalgically: 'I think of old Taormina by moonlight and you and me, a little illuminated sometimes, but always just pleasantly so, strolling through that great old place and the moon path on the sea and Aetna fuming away [. . .]' Instead, he passed up the chance of spending a year hopping between Taormina and Majorca for a relationship which turned out to be full of infidelity. The twist in the tale is a short story.

This short piece of Hemingway's, 'The Mercenaries', was written in 1919 just after his visit to the town, but remained unpublished until 1985, when it appeared in a biography written by Peter Griffin. Ernest did originally try to get it into print but shelved the idea after several refusals. It is a story of soldiers for hire meeting at the Café Cambrinus in Chicago, a bar frequented by gangsters. A Frenchman and an American recount their adventures, which include Perry Graves' duel over the love of a Taorminese woman with dark eyes and ruby lips. The narrative develops against a backdrop of Hemingway's obvious bittersweet fondness for Taormina, recalling the lemon orchards and citrus groves on the hillsides, their fruit contrasting with the vivid green of the foliage. He must have been struck by the intensity of life 'under the orange trees, jasmine matted on the walls, and the moon making all the shadows blue-black'. Graves, the main protagonist, feels that everything is 'so pretty that it hurts to look at it'.

Amongst those laureates whose works were significantly affected by extended stays are two of Scandinavia's greatest writers, Selma Lagerlöf and Halldór Laxness. Selma, the first female writer to win a Nobel Prize in 1909, was awarded a Swedish Royal Travelling Scholarship, which enabled her to undertake a long visit to Sicily during the years 1895–6, when she conceived and wrote *The Miracles of the Antichrist* (*Antikrists mirakler*). It is set in and around the foothills of Mount Etna and includes the kind of descriptions of the mountain with which a visitor to Taormina would be so familiar.

Her fellow Scandinavian, the Icelander Laxness, also wrote a work with a religious theme. Instead of Lagerlöf's weaving of socialism and

Christianity, Halldór's *The Great Weaver from Kashmir* (*Vefarinn mikli frá Kasmír*) takes his protagonist, Steinn Elliði, on a journey encompassing the pursuit of pleasure, political ideals, aesthetic views and monastic withdrawal. Elliði has rented the Villa Valverde off Via dei Vespri and his steps along the street are often dogged by a one-legged, flute-playing beggar, Leonardo Peppino, who sleeps rough 'on the open street in the five-finger-thick dust, and sleeps deeply and sweetly. Fortune lives in Taormina in Sicily, and Taormina is called the pearl of Europe. Fortune sleeps in the open on the Via dei Vespri.'

Laxness' complex story, where appearances are deceptive and the soul 'swings on a pendulum oscillating between angel and devil', is amply shown by the fact that Peppino's rustic idyll is far from the sunny Bohemian life of the street which the quote above would purport to illustrate. The beggar's carefree life is due to his attack on the local notary's daughter. The Icelander, unusually a Roman Catholic, knew the sweep of his novel reflected his own search for the soul's peace and his first-hand research shines through. In later life, Laxness' Catholicism waned, but during his Taormina sojourn he was enthralled, yet aloof from the decadent life he observed. His description of his favourite Old India restaurant captures this melange:

> Here all the world's languages blend together in one cacophony: Chinese potentates click glasses with prudish girls from America and wealthy painted Mesdames from Fiume and Marseille extend the backs of their hands to the lips of half-destitute artists from the northern parts of the world.

This was a scene repeated throughout the haunts frequented by foreigners, amongst which were Halldór's Hotel Castello a Mare, the Bristol, or those retreats for the monied and famous, the Hotels Timeo and San Domenico. The San Domenico is, as its name suggests, a former Dominican monastery built in the fifteenth century. Its entrance is through a romantic stone archway which perfectly frames the monastic courtyard. The hotel is a blending of the sacred and profane, with much of its religious past still intact, including frescoes and sculpture. The terraces look over the bays of Naxos and Taormina with Etna in the background. No wonder it was the chosen destination for so many filmstars, such as Ava Gardner, along with authors and artists, from the likes of Wilde and Dumas to Klimt and Dalí.

D. H. Lawrence was another visitor who was happy to recommend the establishment in a 1920 letter to Lady Cynthia Asquith: 'they'll give you pension at San Domenico, the swellest place, for 40 francs a day – which is 10/-.' Times have changed somewhat and the several thousand euros for a suite in the Domenico would have priced many out of the market. The other luxury hotel of choice was, and is, the Timeo. Situated next to the ancient theatre, its colonnaded entrance deceptively masks the Olympian views available to those taking a morning cappuccino on the hillside patios. It is not difficult to see how Friedrich Nietzsche was able to pen a significant proportion of *Thus Spake Zarathustra* in Taormina, its ancient powerful landscape giving impetus to his philosophy of the superman acting as his solution to the death of an Abrahamic god.

The Timeo was also a retreat for Tennessee Williams, the American playwright. His notebooks from 1954 recount one of several stays in Taormina. He was fully involved in a complicated relationship with Frank Merlo, a would-be actor of Sicilian ancestry, and his island muse found a release in *The Rose Tattoo*, the story of an immigrant community on the Gulf Coast of Louisiana. In the play, Assunta, an apothecary, reflects the peasant attitude to overblown ideas of social status – 'in Sicily everybody's a baron that owns a piece of land and a separate house for the goats!' The Timeo, however, had much more than a goat pen, its belle époque luxury a place of comfort Williams was happy to embrace.

On one occasion his drug taking and fragile mental state led to a panic attack on the way back to the hotel. After a late-night visit to his friend's bar, he decided to walk the owner, Franco, home. Williams had several favourite bars, including the Caffè Wunderbar, which still nestles between a church and the clock tower on Corso Umberto. On this occasion, after he had stopped drinking and started on his way home, he was reassured by the music from another club, only to be spooked by the eerie silence as it abruptly stopped. He was overcome by panic as his chest tightened and his breath ran short. He took a barbiturate sedative – his second of the day – but found it difficult to swallow: 'Even after I reached the main square, in sight of Hotel Temio [sic], my sanctuary, the panic persisted.' He stopped, leaned back and 'plucked a leaf of wild geranium and tried to admire the stars which are said to calm fear.'

Once in his hotel suite, he turned to alcohol to calm his shattered nerves. This was also the day of his first sexual affair in Taormina on a nearby islet. His first barbiturate had calmed the panic he felt leading up to this liaison. The drugs, alcohol and infidelities are characteristic of his relationship with Merlo which lasted a turbulent 14 years; the stability and happiness were counter-balanced with dark depression.

Williams became dependent on prescription drugs and died in a bizarre accident in which he choked on the lid of his eye-drop solution. This was to happen in another hotel, in New York, many years later. It was an ignominious end which may have been facilitated by his over-reliance on medication, but at least he escaped the fate of an early drug-induced death – the destiny of a young English poet, Edmund John, who died in the Timeo of an overdose in 1917. John was inspired by the likes of Algernon Swinburne and his symbolistic poetry was not considered fashionable at the time, although rather decadent. He is best known for his works, *The Flute of Sardonyx* and *The Wind in the Temple*. His poetry is bathed in southern light but riven with sad undercurrents. Howard Agg, the music critic and a later resident of Taormina, thought the poem 'Chant du Marais' revealed the angst behind his suicide:

> And strange, mad sins, pale with their own delight,
> And funeral chord, and hope, and drugs and wine,
> The burning sun, the enchantment of the night,
> The flashing of the sea – have all been mine.
>
> Yet all my life has been a hope in vain,
> A seeking for the treasure no man finds;
> And all the answer is a song of pain,
> To my wild cry to earth and seas and winds.

Other authors came and went with less drama and tragedy, taking away the imprint of the town's unique atmosphere and landscape. One such was the novelist and playwright Robert Hichens. He scandalised Victorian England with his satire on the life of Wilde and Alfred Douglas – *The Green Carnation*, openly referencing the characters' homosexuality. It was not long before the publishers had to withdraw it from the market. Happy to tackle socially controversial themes, his Sicilian work, *The Call of the Blood*, deals with the affair between an Englishman and a peasant girl, Maddalena, during the groom's interrupted honeymoon. Murdered by Maddalena's protective father, the errant husband's wife returns from nursing a dying friend only to believe he has drowned. The local influence on this former Timeo resident went as far as a 1948 adaptation of the book for Italian cinema screens.

In the 1920s, D. H. Lawrence was a keen observer of the goings-on at the Timeo. In a letter to Jessica Brett Young he recalls a lunch on the hotel's terrace:

> My hat, the people: the poor ricketty Baroness (American married to a Dane) with buttercup hair: the gaga Duca di Brönte, alias Mr Hood, but always called (by the English, not by natives) The Duca – like The Lord: then the runaway French couple whom the police arrested (what for? is the motto): then Dr Rogers from Cambridge hypnotising Danish damsels with fox-skins over their shoulders and glaucous eyes across the lunch table, over poached eggs, and making the table heave when the oranges are skinned: then the actress from the Opéra, very chic de la chic: then – but why enumerate.

After World War I, Lawrence exiled himself abroad accompanied by his German wife, Frieda Weekley (née von Richthofen), whom he had married in 1914 after the settlement of her divorce. Their war experience was traumatic due to her German nationality and accusations of spying. Controversy also surrounded his works, with *The Rainbow* accused of obscenity.

In February 1920, they arrived in Taormina and decided to go house-hunting. They came across a place known as Fontana Vecchia about 20 minutes' walk from the very centre of town. It was owned by returnee emigrant Francesco Cacopardo, known simply as 'Ciccio'. David Herbert's early letters enthuse about the property's atmosphere: 'Do you imagine the balcony at night? – the Plough pitching headlong into the sea on the left, terribly falling, and Taormina in a rift on the right fuming tremulously between the jaws of the darkness.' Temporarily at least, it seemed that Lawrence had found a place to call home, leaving his troublesome past behind: 'The windows look east over the Ionian sea: somehow I don't care what happens behind me, in the north west. – Lascia mi stare [Let me stay].'

Renting the upper two floors of the villa, in a location he loved, he was now free to begin writing. His correspondence, though, shows a mundane preoccupation we all share with monetary matters and the vagaries of public services. Organising the publication of his works (in March 1920 he writes that *Women in Love* had gone to print in America) was no mean feat. Letters to and from the island would take exasperating weeks, if not months, to arrive and he had trouble persuading the Credito Italiano bank to cash monies from the States. The exchange rate was a further preoccupation, revealing a canny attitude towards financial matters.

Lawrence's problems were added to by a very volatile relationship with his wife. Shouting matches and pot slinging were frequent, including one noteworthy occasion in front of a local dignitary. Frieda was also renowned for taking lovers, including the former mule driver, Peppino D'Allura, who worked for a wine merchant. Peppino eventually emigrated to Pittsburgh but confessed all shortly before his death in the 1990s. It seems that on a visit to Fontana Vecchia, Lawrence's wife appeared naked before him in the doorway and the rest, as they say, is history.

Amongst financial considerations, marital strife and the attractions of the local landscape, Lawrence did find time to devote to writing. During his stay he completed one play, *Touch and Go*, and saw the publication of three novels: *Women in Love*, *The Lost Girl* and *Aaron's Rod*. During this prolific period, he also produced some of his best poetry, a series of short stories and essays, a travelogue and translations of the Sicilian writer, Giovanni Verga. His poetry is imbued with a sense of man's more primitive interaction with nature, a marrying of classical myth and visceral elements, evident in this poem, 'Almond Blossom':

> This is the ancient southern earth whence the vases were
> baked, amphoras, craters, cantharus, œnochœ, and
> open-hearted cylix,
> Bristling now with the iron of almond-trees.

The best place to turn for a description of his beloved Fontana Vecchia, as Lawrence saw it, is in the novella he wrote called 'Sun'. The central character, Juliet, is recommended by her doctor to head for the sun. Leaving behind her lukewarm husband, she sets sail for Sicily with her child, nurse and mother. Her inhibitions are shed as well as her clothing as she leaves behind her former self and allows the heat to penetrate her very being:

> Juliet sat down by the cypress tree, and took off her clothes. The
> contorted cactus made a forest, hideous yet fascinating, about her. She
> sat and offered her bosom to the sun, sighing, even now, with a certain
> hard pain, against the cruelty of having to give herself: but exalting
> that at last it was no human lover.

Juliet, mindful of Ancient Greek references to the unsunned body being unhealthy, bastes herself in olive oil and strolls through the garden's lemon trees, her rosy flesh slowly turning bronze. She is continuously drawn to the cypress tree, an arboreal love shared by the writer himself. The tenant was very protective of his garden's trees and was not above vociferously arguing with Ciccio when he expressed a desire to chop down a particular specimen. The roots of a carob tree were threatening to damage the villa's drainage system, but Lawrence was so incensed by the loss of scenery and shade that he refused to back down and the tree was saved.

David and Frieda lived in Fontana Vecchia from March 1920 until February 1922 with a significant break for the summer of 1921.

6 *Fontana Vecchia, the house rented by D. H. Lawrence, Truman Capote and Howard Agg, Taormina*

Frieda was unable to cope with the searing heat of July and August and hankered to see her relatives in Germany; trips to Baden-Baden and the Black Forest were undertaken, with time also spent in the Austrian lakeside town of Zell-am-See. Lawrence, something of a gypsy, could not remain static in Sicily forever and his restless soul pushed him onwards. In March 1922, he headed for Ceylon, leaving behind perhaps one of the very few places he ever really contemplated spending the rest of his life:

> Ah dark garden, dark garden, with your olives and your wine, your
> medlars and mulberries and many almond trees, your steep terraces
> ledged high up above the sea, I am leaving you, slinking out. Out
> between the rosemary hedges, out of the tall gate on to the cruel steep

stony road. So under the dark, big eucalyptus trees, over the stream, and up towards the village. There, I have got so far.

Today's Fontana Vecchia is not as isolated as this description would suggest. The tourism boom of the twentieth century has led to development all the way along what is now known as Via David Lawrence. A small plaque recognises the location of his stay, but makes no note of the equally famous subsequent resident of the villa, Truman Capote.

In April 1950, Capote and the writer Jack Dunphy, his lover, boarded a Norwegian freighter bound for Palermo. After a three-week voyage and a long train journey, they eventually arrived in Taormina to meet their friend and fellow author, Donald Windham, who had promised to help them house-hunt. Truman was much taken with the word *pace* carved into the doorstep at Fontana Vecchia. The word, meaning 'peace', seemed to sum up an atmosphere he sought and believed he had found. He was so enamoured of the property, he wrote copious letters to his friends describing its charms and an essay in 1951 that carried the name of the house.

He describes the valley, which is still cultivated, laden with almonds and olives as it dips towards the sea and likened its position to 'an airplane, or ship trembling on the peak of a tidal wave'. He was fascinated by the house's position in relation to the mountain tracks that brought the peasant farmers into town:

> Before dawn, when drooping stars drift at the bedroom window fat as owls, a racket begins along the steep, at moments perilous, path that descends from the mountains. It's the farm families on the way to the marketplace in Taormina.

Capote would listen to their laughter and cajoling of their donkeys weighed down with produce to sell, before adhering to his strict morning writing schedule when, despite the socialising, drinking and sometimes late hours, he would scrupulously check each word, sentence and expression until content.

He was also fond of a daily routine involving the early evening stroll into town where he would buy supplies for dinner, take a Martini at the American Bar and exchange a few insults with the cheeky youngsters who liked to badger the tourists. Best of all was the collection of incoming letters from the Post Office. Truman was an avid letter-writer who enjoyed exchanging gossip and inviting his friends to come and visit him in Taormina. Among those who did was Peggy Guggenheim, the art-collecting heiress who descended from her palazzo in Venice. He mentions others visiting the villa, although some of this may be poetic licence. At various times resident in town were André Gide, Cecil Beaton and Christian Dior, all name-dropped by Truman. In one account, he muses on engineering a meeting between Gide and Dior.

A more problematic visitor was his mother, Lillie Mae, who liked to call herself Nina. Their relationship had been difficult from the very outset – Truman being an unwanted baby who was nearly aborted. As a consequence, he was brought up by aunts and distant cousins away from his New Orleans birthplace. Lillie Mae was desperate to improve her social standing and after a rocky marriage to Arch Persons, she divorced and hooked up with Joseph Capote, achieving her long-desired aim of moving to New York, something that Truman would share. He owed his adopted name of Garcia Capote, changed from the unfortunate birth moniker of Streckfus Persons, to his step-father, Joseph.

Despite Lillie Mae fighting for custody of Truman, she continued to push him away, complaining of his effeminate manner. Given this back story, and the fact that she hated his partner Jack, we can imagine the trepidation with which Capote anticipated the arrival of his wayward parent. However, superficially at least, things proceeded better than expected – she avoided alcohol, drinking only coffee, and managed to be civil to Dunphy. This mask of urbanity persisted in hiding the deep divisions between mother and son.

Jack, who would go on to be Truman's long-standing partner, albeit non-exclusively, was also working as he enjoyed the Taormina sun. The portrait of the couple that emerges from Capote's letters is one of temporary domesticity. In his letter to Andrew Lyndon in May 1950, he gives an insight into their more mundane moments, spending endless hours picking ticks from their dog, Kelly, and describing Jack's active hiking to the sea and back, a trip that exhausted the less physically active Truman.

In the same letter he also exposes a tendency to the spiteful comment and character assassination. Gide's stay in Taormina is referred to by the American, whose letters mention the old Frenchman's habit of spending hours in the barber's being lathered with soap by the young boys of the town. In this particular piece of correspondence, he notes the arrival of André's daughter: 'She amazes me by being 1) ugly as a wood-stove, and 2) younger than you can imagine, only twenty-three or four. Do you suppose that old goat is really responsible?' Harsh, but one can imagine the need to speculate.

During his sojourn he worked on many pieces, beginning *The Grass Harp* in June 1950, which he would complete a year later. His correspondence, full of the to-ings and fro-ings between publisher and author, also cites the many books he read during his stay, including William Goyen's *The House of Breath*, Donald Windham's *The Dog Star* and, interestingly, our belle époque favourite, Donald Sladen and his *Sicilian Marriage* – perhaps an unlikely choice as one of Truman's 'favourite' authors given the book's frothy, light treatment of Sicilian mores. Dunphy's furious writing at the Fontana Vecchia also led to the publication of his work, *Friends and Vague Lovers*, in 1952.

Owing to the house's location, trades people would often visit to sell wares, produce or provide services. One such regular caller was the ice boy, not a nickname but a true description of the young man's trade – delivering ice from Etna in order to keep food cool. Capote liked to engage him in conversation about his family and the local characters. Truman and Jack were shocked by the story of the lad's beautiful aunt, beaten badly by her protective brother and of the ice boy's assertion that he would do the same should his sister stray from the straight and narrow.

One of their more surreal exchanges took place on an August night 'when the moons were so preposterous'. Their purveyor of ice started to question the couple on their knowledge of werewolves; the boy even suggested that Capote may be afraid of venturing out after dark. It appears that Taormina was in the grip of a werewolf scare owing to the tale of a youth who had claimed he was attacked by a half-human howling beast on all fours. The author, with his American scepticism of peasant superstition, laughed at the boy's naivety, only to be brought up short for his impertinence when the youth told him that the town used to be infested with lycanthropy, finally reassuring him that just a couple remained.

Fontana Vecchia also hosted a rather more convincing ghostly apparition. The house of the writers, as it became known among the locals, was home to yet another author after Capote and Dunphy left in the early 1950s. Sat in his top-floor Bond Street office, Howard Agg, the music journalist and playwright, was dragged away from a dreary London winter by a colleague's photographs of Taormina. As time passed, this spot of light in the long postwar tunnel continued to play on Agg's mind. He eventually found time to book a hotel and take himself to the town for a holiday.

The holiday, all too short, turned out to be a change in the course of his life. As soon as his BBC commitments allowed, he booked himself a further two weeks in the same *pensione*. Armed with the collected letters of D. H. Lawrence, Howard was determined to visit the Fontana Vecchia and snatch a glimpse of the life the Lawrences had in Sicily. David Herbert was one of Agg's favourite writers, but he only expected to be able to get the usual tourist's restricted access. Prompted by the Dutch owner of his guesthouse, he was put in touch with Signor Cacopardo, who we now know was universally called Ciccio, and, according to Howard, was 'a dapper little man of some age, wearing a bright check shirt, tweed trousers and a panama hat sat at a rakish angle'.

Ciccio was very happy to regale the music critic with stories of the Lawrences' life, showing him where David Herbert used to write and where he liked to receive guests, preferably at breakfast. The writer of *Lady Chatterley's Lover* would like nothing more than to walk out onto the balcony and watch the glorious Sicilian sun rise over the sea towards the land of Homer – a poetic image, although somewhat marred by the fact that he would do so wearing that most middle class of night attire, the pyjama.

On finding out that Agg was, himself, a writer, Ciccio suggested he rent the apartment. He had some bourgeois Romans interested, but was much keener to have a single artist in residence. Howard dismissed the idea as delightful but impossible; however, the seed had been planted. He returned to London, investigated the possibilities of continuing to fulfil his writing contracts whilst abroad, put his affairs in order and upped sticks for Sicily the following February.

The stillness of the villa at night was a complete contrast to his busy London life, but, initially, not unpleasant. During his stay, he began to put down his experiences on paper, which would later become his own Sicilian odyssey, published as *A Cypress in Sicily*. Certain incidents began to mirror those of the illustrious previous residents, including an argument with Signor Cacopardo over the removal of a particularly fine tree in the garden. Agg, like Lawrence before him, won the day. One experience, though, was proving too close for comfort.

The usually deep sleeper was beginning to struggle to get a decent night's sleep. Agg, with finely tuned senses, often found himself awoken for no apparent reason. Sometimes the house was lulled back into its lazy Mediterranean rhythm, but he often experienced 'the eerie sensation that the air was stirring round me, and that I was not alone in the room'. To add to the unease, he once heard footsteps on the stairs from the balcony. The only conclusion Howard could reach was a supernatural one – a spirit from the Fontana's long history had come back to haunt the property.

This conclusion led to initial feelings of panic and the all-too-human reaction of flight. But he had cut the ties to London and there was no immediate way back. He decided to stick things out but the phenomena intensified. Not only were there footsteps, but now a voice and a mysterious light. Agg picks up the story in his own words:

Staring into the darkness I saw to my consternation a light shining on the wall facing my bed. In shape it was square, resembling a tiny window, and it never moved, but fluctuated from one minute to the next – now glowing faintly, now brightly – until finally, after about ten minutes, it faded away until all was dark again. It reappeared on several other nights, always in the same spot, and always behaving in the same mysterious way.

It would be easy to dismiss this as lights from the road, a passing lantern or even fishermen in the bay, but in the next episode, things worsened. The square illumination extended to the height of the wall and shone with brilliance. Howard checked all the possibilities and could find no reasonable explanation for this manifestation. The weirdest thing of all was the lack of the obvious shadow his body should have cast in front of such a powerful beam. He was not the only one to experience these oddities: Saro, his cook, was also uneasy and complained of an unsettling atmosphere.

Agg, wary of being thought foolish, decided to approach Ciccio tactfully by asking if anyone had died in the house and, apparently, the landlord's father had breathed his last there. The sceptical Ciccio joked that if Agg bumped into his dad he'd like a word with him. Finally, Howard spilled the beans and was pointed in the direction of an old sage called Signor Adolfo, who was supposed to have a connection with the spirits. It seems he already knew of the supernatural goings-on at Fontana Vecchia: 'You have a presence in the house. There is no doubt of that. All I can tell you is that it is a man – a man with a beard.'

He refused the protection of a talisman but listened to the advice that he should talk to the presence. By now, Agg was convinced his ghostly apparition was that of D. H. Lawrence himself and delved into his letters to explain a possible link. He found what he was looking for in this particular passage: 'Here the past is so much stronger than the present, that one seems remote like the immortals, looking back at the world from their world.' Reading on, he realised what a wrench it had been for Lawrence to leave.

A friend from London arrived to stay whom Agg felt had an insight into the spirit world. To begin with, he told her nothing of the nightly goings-on but was keen to see her reactions to the villa. She appeared to avoid the *salone*, sitting in the garden instead, even when the nights started to chill. The stairs were another no-go area. Prompted by her reluctance to linger in certain places, Howard told her the full story. Her reaction was to confirm the house's haunted nature. When she returned to England, she sent the author a thank-you letter and informed him that the ghost belonged to a man. Over time, he became accustomed to the presence and assumed it meant him no harm. During the friend's second visit, the living room was no longer off limits and, to Agg's relief, she told him the spirit had gone.

Howard had been inspired to visit the Fontana by his love of Lawrence's writing and could not have imagined that he would experience such a closeness to the man's presence. Had David Herbert really returned to one of the places to which he felt most attached? Whatever the truth of the mystery, it is apparent that the music critic believed he had been visited by the spirit behind *Sons and Lovers*, *The Rainbow* and *Women in Love*.

There is a second dwelling in Taormina that could equally be dubbed the house of the writers – Casa Cuseni. Robert Kitson, an engineer, first went to Taormina in 1900 and decided to build and design his own house. He used local stone, marble, wood and terracotta, stuccoing the walls a golden yellow colour. He commissioned Frank Brangwyn, the celebrated Anglo-Welsh artist and designer, to create the dining room and furniture. The frescoes completed by the artist are a fine example of his work at the height of his artistic achievement. The house in Via Leonardo da Vinci is now a museum and luxurious bed and breakfast under the careful eye of London's Victoria and Albert Museum and the Italian government's listed building status.

One of the first celebrities to take up residence was the then unknown soldier, Alan Whicker of *Whicker's World* television fame. During World War II, Whicker was part of the army's film and photo unit. He was posted to Sicily to cover the invasion by the Eighth Army. His commanding officer, Geoffrey Keating, and the war artist Edward Ardizzone were the first to arrive in Taormina and they climbed the eight hundred feet from the coast to requisition the Casa Cuseni as their base. In his memoir of these years, the television journalist describes the villa: 'Its garden was heady with the exotic scent of orange blossom, its library equally heady with pornography.'

He remembers these headquarters with fondness – one of the few places where he was able to relax during the conflict. The crew of photographers larked about taking pictures of each other in between bouts of more serious planning for the future campaign to come. Their evenings were spent on the 'demon vino' whilst sitting on the terrace admiring the view. For the writing of *Whicker's War*, he returned to the house at the beginning of the twenty-first century to find the property little altered and in need of some attention. He must have been pleased by the subsequent protection offered by museum and national monument status.

After the war, Daphne Phelps, Kitson's niece, reassured her uncle that she would act as his executor in the event of his death, with the promise that she would inherit the house. Complications over the will ensued, resulting in Daphne's aunt being the inheritor, but this comfortably off relative was more than happy for her niece to take on the responsibilities in Sicily. In 1948, Daphne gave up her career as a psychiatric social worker and relocated to Taormina.

Life was initially difficult, the privations of postwar Italy affected everybody and she had a new culture to contend with, including the attentions of bachelor Sicilians seeking the perceived wealth of an English heiress. To her amusement, she quickly realised they were after the 'marriageable house' rather than the marriageable woman. Daphne noted that the inhabitants demonstrated two identities: one strand, she mused, would outwit the invader with intelligence and cunning, and the other would pull together with extreme sang-froid.

Her artistic friends were soon keen to come and visit her, which suggested a possible solution to her financial worries – the house would become a *locanda*, the least taxable or bureaucratically influenced of Italian rented accommodation. Daphne's rules, however, were that her guests would have to be recommended and she made no bones about her preference for 'creative people'. Some were more welcome than others.

One guest she tried to avoid was the heavily drinking widow of Dylan Thomas. Caitlin Thomas was being looked after by a friend of Daphne's, Wyn Henderson. Wyn had written a few times to suggest a stay but on each occasion Daphne had declined – she neglected to reply to the third letter. Wyn was certain that a bit of peace and quiet was all that Caitlin needed to write her book, *Leftover Life to Kill*, and much

7 *Casa Cuseni, the house of Daphne Phelps, Taormina*

to Daphne's dismay, two figures appeared on the hillside pathway one moonlit night: 'I just had time to see that one, an assisted blonde, her hair dazzling in the moonlight, had a large wicker basket out of which was sticking a large, half-empty bottle of wine.'

Daphne was happy with Wyn's company, finding her entertaining and fun. Peggy Guggenheim had described her as 'Wyn Henderson of the hundred lovers', a potential libel that Phelps was less certain of after just one week – 'Her intimate friendships had, it seemed, been mainly with the authors of books on my library shelves.' Caitlin was more problematic. Having formed a relationship in Ischia with an abusive Sicilian director's assistant, Giuseppe Fazio, she was now separated from him thanks to Wyn's machinations. The split did not last long and he turned up on Daphne's doorstep in order to whisk Thomas' widow away with him.

Caitlin did write *Leftover Life to Kill* and the intense pain of losing her poet husband is evident throughout. It spans much of the emotional distress she suffered, being treated for mental health issues in London, Rome and Catania, where she eventually settled. Her later years were spent with Giuseppe, who must have had more attributes than seen by Phelps; they had a son together and she stopped drinking through an Alcoholics Anonymous programme.

Another house guest was the philosopher Bertrand Russell. After the BBC's Reith Lectures were finished in 1949, Russell planned to retreat to North Wales, finish his autobiography and then fulfil some engagements he had in Rome and Marseille. He had been invited to Cuseni by Daphne in an attempt to repay the hospitality the Russells had shown when Phelps was stranded in the United States during the war. As events transpired, this neat plan did not run as smoothly as anticipated, the ever-worsening breach in the Russells' marriage obstructed any of Bertrand's endeavours on his biography and culminated in a monumental argument when the couple eventually met up in Sicily.

Patricia, Russell's wife, bizarrely known as Peter, strongly believed that Bertrand was going to restart his relationship with Colette O'Neil and was in dispute with him over money earned through his work, *The History of Western Philosophy*. Russell, in turn, had threatened to change his will and leave part of his money to the offspring of a previous marriage, John and Kate, rather than bequeath it all to her. The scene was set for a disastrous stay which reached its denouement during a moonlit picnic and fishing expedition with Julian Trevelyan and Mary Fedden. The potent mixed wines and fishing expertise were supplied by their local friend, Rocco. Peter had stayed behind at the Casa, piqued by the discovery of a letter from Colette to Bertrand that still had the potential overtones of an affair.

Late into the night, the somewhat worse-for-wear band arrived back to the house, Bertie being steadied on the arm of Phelps. Peter, aka Patricia, screamed at Daphne for not inviting their son Conrad, who loved fishing, whilst Russell took cover in the lavatory. An indignant Peter left the house the following morning without her son, who took great delight in shouting wine-based insults at his father. On 2 April 1949, Bertrand wrote to Colette from Taormina, 'there has been one immense upheaval, involving at best an amicable separation. It appears that for the present it would be unwise for me to see you.'

Daphne only saw her friend Bertie twice more. On one occasion she met him in London and they arranged to go out for a meal. By this time, Russell had been through four marriages but had the comfort of the children he loved. After the restaurant, he walked her home and, not for the first time, made a pass at her. He was convinced of Phelps' inhibitions; she more of his unsuitability.

A pattern of eccentricity and excess is beginning to emerge amongst Daphne's guests, reaching its zenith with the arrival of the poet and artist Henry Faulkner. Daphne devotes an entire chapter to him in her book, *A House in Sicily*, which she starts with, 'I am still surprised at myself for having done it. I cannot think what made me.' She's referring to her invitation to let him stay rent free in the small flat that usually housed a gardener. Henry started out as a would-be novelist, but turned his hand to painting and poetry, finding himself in Sicily thanks to an art patroness, Alice Delamarr. He had soon spent his allowance collecting antiques along the Corso and was essentially eating and drinking for free at the Casa – doing the occasional decorating job.

Phelps was amazed to discover his qualities as a poet in addition to his more obvious ones as an artist. She quizzed him with regard to their possible publication and if anyone with a serious critical eye had read them. Off-handedly, he dropped the names of Tennessee Williams and Ezra Pound. Daphne was thrown by such illustrious names and wondered, 'Wherever had these three met? Could it have been in a mental hospital? It seemed likely' – which was not far from the truth as Faulkner had spent time with Ezra Pound at St Elizabeth's Hospital in Washington.

Henry's bizarre manner and unabashed showmanship was also beginning to gain him notoriety in town. He made an instant connection with Roberto, the owner of Mecambo's Bar. Roberto – who was himself to become notorious, thanks to Claire Rabe's thinly disguised portrait of him in the erotic novel, *Sicily Enough* – was fond of Faulkner's flower-dancing antics among the bewildered tourists. Roberto also appreciated the artist's ability to communicate with animals. On one occasion, he arrived at the Casa Cuseni with three dogs and six cats which he had saved from the inevitable. Ever forgiving of Henry, Daphne managed to accommodate them. He later adopted a goat, Massimo, that was going to be slaughtered and he would sometimes feature fantastical representations of these animals in his art.

Faulkner's attraction to waifs and strays did not only extend to the animal kingdom. Daphne was shocked to see a blousy woman, 'a sham blonde', entering Henry's flat with a key he had obviously given her. His explanation was as complicated and bizarre as ever: she was a German prostitute who had had her money stolen and was destitute. Faulkner was sure it would not take her long to earn it back again and get enough money together to return to Germany. A horrified Phelps felt this was one step too far but she did not need to ask her to leave as the German disobeyed Henry's instructions to keep the animals separate and was therefore shown the door.

Eventually, Faulkner's increasingly erratic behaviour lost him friends, particularly Roberto, who nearly reported him to the carabinieri, but Daphne remained faithful. To her surprise, Henry wanted to put her in his will along with Alice Delamarr. One of his parting shots was a wish that she should meet his friend, Tennessee Williams, which she later fulfilled. The stilted early conversation only loosened when the pair spoke of their mutual tolerance and forgiveness of Henry's peculiar ways.

Daphne continued at the Cuseni, receiving guests with the occasional famous name, including Roald Dahl when he was negotiating a contract with RAI, the Italian state broadcaster, for putting his *Tales of the Unexpected* on the air. She died six years after the publication of her memoir, leaving the house to the care of her family and, as we now know, it has umbrella support from the Victoria and Albert Museum.

After much literary endeavour within the walls of Taorminese property, the town's literary reputation finally began to wane. The 1960s, 1970s and 1980s continued to see visits from the rich and famous, but these were more likely to be due to the Taormina Film Festival. The rough edges of bohemian life were gradually being polished by the glamour of Hollywood money.

Even in the 1950s, Evelyn Waugh and his travelling companion, Harold Acton, had noted a difference. In his 1930 book, *Labels*, Waugh tells how he had scrupulously avoided Taormina, staying onboard his ship whilst the other passengers scrambled in a mad frenzy of cars to reach the town. The closest he came was a binocular view from the deck as his boat made its way down the Ionian. His subsequent visit to Sicily in 1952 conspired to enforce a stay instead of the planned train journey to Syracuse.

The only hotels available were in Taormina. Recalling the Palermo chapter, we know that Evelyn's temperament was, at best, variable and he complained of the sulphurous smells and a lack of sleep. For once, Acton joined his companion's dismay, describing the roads as overrun with Scandinavians in charabancs. Even the theatre provided no comfort – a contemplative view being obscured by tourists swinging their Kodaks. He lamented the absence of the likes of Wilde and Gide: 'Where were the Grecian lovers and Uranians, those who came hither to cultivate "les Amitiés Particulières".' His is the bewailing tone of any elite who find they no longer have the space or time to indulge their whims. He goes on to explain that in his youth, 'Taormina had been a polite synonym for Sodom: now it was quite as respectable as Bournemouth.'

# CATANIA
# AND MOUNT ETNA

## Under the Shadow of the Volcano

### *Catania*

Catania lies approximately halfway down the eastern coast of the island. It is the second largest city in Sicily, and as such, has a unique rivalry with Palermo. The close proximity to Mount Etna means that the name Catania is inextricably linked to the mountain that Sicilians call Muncibeddu or Mongibello in standard Italian. Made from the very lava rock of its slopes, parts of the city have a rather sombre appearance that contrasts with its reputation for the lively nightlife enjoyed by the university students of the town.

The centre is dominated by the Baroque central piazza bordered by the city's cathedral, which looks upon a fountain dominated by a curious elephant obelisk. Incised into the lava stone are a series of hieroglyphs that refer to the goddess Isis. At turns Roman and Egyptian, the medley is topped by the insignia of St Agatha, the patron saint of the city. A great deal of this square was designed by the architect Vaccarini who was to find his work cut out by the great earthquake of 1693, which followed a monumental lava eruption 24 years previously.

This Piazza del Duomo leads into Via Etnea – a long, sweeping boulevard of elegant shops reminiscent of Paris, appearing to stretch all the way to the mountain itself. Bisecting the square is Via Vittorio Emanuele II, leading in one direction to the sprawling suburbs and, in the other, the few hundred metres to the coast. This takes you past the run-down exterior of a property distinctly recognisable through its balcony architecture. The house is commonly associated with the local poet, Domenico Tempio, whose risqué works fell foul of the censors in the eighteenth century. The balcony depicts male and female characters openly masturbating so it is no surprise that it became synonymous with his poetry. However, he is more likely to have written about these figures than to have actually commissioned them, owing to his limited resources.

Whether strolling from the seafront, past Tempio's balcony, or heading towards Etna, you will encounter the two names most closely associated with Catania: Giovanni Verga and Vincenzo Bellini. Bellini, the opera composer, whose home can be visited in Piazza San Francesco, also has some tranquil gardens named after him to one side of Via Etnea. An interesting reference to the man appears in Henry T. Tuckerman's book, *Isabel, or Sicily: A Pilgrimage*. Published in 1839, it is that unusual hybrid of the time, also favoured by Douglas Sladen – part novel, part travelogue. Tuckerman was a Bostonian critic and novelist who visited the island on extended travels during the early part of his writing career; these are reflected in his prose and poetry.

In the preface to *Isabel*, Henry admits he is trying to avoid the 'egotistical tone' so prevalent in more formal travel journals, hence the amalgam of styles softening the effect of his work; his more strident voice is otherwise apparent in the preface as he complains of the 'want of commodious inns' and 'the long and rigid quarantines'. However, Isabel, his heroine, is travelling with her uncle on a mission to surprise her father, who had exiled himself to Europe after the death of his wife.

In Catania, accompanied by Vittorio, a local aristocrat, the fictional travellers are taken to Bellini's house, not long after the composer had died. Tuckerman, through the conduit of Isabel, is obviously a great admirer of the man whose music 'has created yet another joy in the dim circle of our experience: and woven a fresh and perennial flower into the withered garland of life'. Vittorio, their distinguished guide, leads the couple to the Benedictine monastery of San Nicolò, the very same institution we will shortly discover in Federico De Roberto's masterwork. It seems the young Bellini, at the tender age of eight, was capable of playing the grandiose organ in this prestigious location.

Tuckerman lists the operas in their progressive development until he reaches *Norma*, which he calls 'frequently sublime'. The astute American was aware of the political climate in the declining years of Bourbon rule and his narrator notes the press censorship of the day, it being a harsh rein on the literary output of the island's writers but not so on its musicians: 'musical genius is untrammelled, and human sentiment may, through this medium, find free and glorious development.'

Not far from the composer's house, now the Museo Belliniano, is the home of Catania's other famous son, Giovanni Verga. This writer, famed for his realistic portraits of Sicilian peasantry, lived in Via Sant'Anna, nestling between the two arms of Vittorio Emanuele II and Via Giuseppe Garibaldi, some two hundred metres from the elephant obelisk.

Despite the fact that he moved to Milan in 1872, whilst in his thirties, the author's great works – *The House by the Medlar Tree* (*I malavoglia*) and *Mastro-Don Gesualdo*, in addition to numerous other stories – were written about his native land. Verga grew up and died at 8 Via Sant'Anna and a plaque between the balconies, level with the second floor, commemorates this fact. The blackened façade, its already dark lava stone deepened by pollution and the residues of Etna's intermittent awakenings, is punctuated by long, elegant balconied windows.

The house is a national monument and the second floor a museum to Giovanni. In the hallway is a writing desk that the author took with him to Milan. The study has an inlaid walnut table at its centre overhung with glass lamps; the patterned floor is edged with dark-wood glass cabinets, heavy with books. The overall effect is one of austerity and simplicity but of lasting quality, a material reflection of the man and his works.

Verga was a verist – a style that portrayed the realistic, often gritty, lives of the poorer echelons of society; not for him the decaying aristocracy of *The Leopard*, despite a youthful phase of elegant authorial romanticism. In his day, he had as much European fame as his stylistically different contemporary, the northern Italian, Gabriele D'Annunzio. Giovanni's novels and short stories focus on fishermen, peasants and the hardworking people of small-town Sicily. D. H. Lawrence was so taken with Verga's work that he translated much of it into English, including his *Little Novels of Sicily* (*Novelle rusticane*) – a good introduction to his approach. The book includes the short story 'Malaria', said to be one of the first literary treatments of the disease:

> And truly the malaria gets into you with the bread you eat, or if you open your mouth to speak as you walk, suffocating in the dust and sun of the roads, and you feel your knees give way beneath you, or you sink discouraged on the saddle as your mule ambles along, with its head down.

In Verga's day, villages like Lentini, Francoforte and Paternò, which surround the big city, were malarial and in the process of depopulation. Giovanni's vivid language captures the desperation as the disease grabs the inhabitants and 'nails them in front of the doors of their houses whose plaster is all falling with the sun'. His prose, beautifully translated by Lawrence, depicts the incredible poverty that this corner of Sicily experienced in the latter part of the nineteenth century.

Giovanni dabbled with studying law at the University of Catania but his vocation was always literary, aided by his family's wealthy background. He was uninterested in the kind of fame and popularity that his work had brought him, preferring the privacy of his spartan apartments. As Lawrence points out, some of his work was autobiographical in nature: for example, in the story 'Across the Sea', which switches between Naples, Messina and south-eastern Sicily. Undoubtedly, though, all of his work was closely observational with certain stories springing from experiences witnessed as a youth.

He never married, although he kept mistresses. The rather serious moustachioed figure of an older Verga, with his 'proud dark eyes', was happy to embrace a literary family, acting as something of a mentor to younger writers, notably Maria Messina and Federico De Roberto. Messina, whose works have only recently been rediscovered, was championed by Giovanni. Her stories are a unique female voice, depicting the lives of women often kept at home in conditions of servitude. Interestingly, she writes of the middle class while some of her mentor's poorer female characters are out in the fields, living a more raucous, earthy existence. A collection of her stories appear in the book *Behind Closed Doors*.

De Roberto met Verga in Milan and their friendship remained for life. He was half Sicilian and born in Naples; on the death of his Neapolitan father, he was sent to Catania to be educated with his mother's family, the Asmundos, whose lineage was Spanish. This Hispano-Sicilian connection, so prominent in much of the island's aristocracy, was a definite influence on the writing of his foremost novel, *The Viceroys* (*I vicerè*). The English translator of the book, Archibald Colquhoun, explains in his introduction that the Garibaldian invasion of Sicily to unify Italy in 1860 was the touchstone for so many local writers, and that Verga believed the Catanian *veristi*, the writers of truth, were haunted by the sour post-unification experience – De Roberto is no exception.

Central to the piece is the Uzeda family, a fictionalised noble clan originally hailing from the town of Uceda in Spain. As with *The Leopard*, their feudalistic lifestyle is coming to an end, but unlike Lampedusa, Federico was in the midst of the changes and a keen observer of those trying to cling to power. The backdrop is Catania itself and the locations for many of the scenes still exist today. De Roberto once worked as a librarian in the municipal reading rooms, part of the former monastery of San Nicolò l'Arena.

The monastery was sequestrated in 1862 and is now part of the University of Catania. Its income at the time was derived from a whole series of other estates. Federico uses its opulence as a demonstration of hierarchical gluttony: 'The monastery, vast and sumptuous, ranked with royal palaces, in token of which chains were hung in front of the gates [. . .] The excellent food, good living and almost complete liberty to do what he liked, did not dissipate the monks' soreness at the forcing of his will.' The characters may have been fictional, with the occasional deliberate nod to prominent figures known to Federico, but the novel is interwoven with the politically and geographically accurate.

The former monastery is in Piazza Dante; the Francalanza Palace, home to the Uzedas, is associated with the Palazzo San Giuliano, which dominates the Piazza dell'Università, a servant's stone's throw from the elephant. The servant perspective is very much part of the plurality of the novel, leading Lampedusa to describe it as 'a picture of the Sicilian aristocracy seen from the servants' hall'. No layer of society escapes De Roberto's truthful eye. Corruption, obsession with power and moral decay are all part of *The Viceroys*' 600-plus pages – witness Prince Consalvo Uzeda's view of himself: 'It was to that historic name, to those sonorous titles that he felt he owed his place in the world, the ease with which avenues opened before him.'

In addition to his prolific writing career, Federico also managed the city's museums and it is fitting today that his library of books, over four thousand volumes, is housed on the floor below Verga's rooms in Via Sant'Anna. Like his friend and mentor, De Roberto also remained unmarried, but his biographical background contains none of Giovanni's illicit trips to northern Europe with mistresses in tow. In truth, Federico's work was his life but, in looking at both, it is difficult to avoid the conclusion that something deeper lay beneath the surface. As Colquhoun stresses, his writing represents a certain aspect of the Sicilian character, 'its subdued fervour and sadness, its solitude behind the smiles'.

Nonetheless, De Roberto was a well-recognised figure in Catania. Complete with monocle, magnificently pointed handlebar moustache and starched white collar, he would stroll along Via Etnea during the evening *passeggiata*. This scene still repeats itself to this day, minus the formality of dress, as does that other ritual so beloved of Catanians – the feast of their patron saint Agatha (Sant'Agata). It was the ephemeral witnessed in moments of such collective fervour that Colquhoun feels must have resulted in this poignant note left on the writer's desk at the time of his death: 'Among all human constructions the only ones that avoid the dissolving hands of time are castles in the air.'

The psychological impact of death, in this case violent, makes an appearance in one of De Roberto's other ground-breaking works, *Agony* (*Spasimo*). At the heart of the story is an investigation into the presumed suicide of a Milanese countess. The resultant enquiry points to a possible murder; it is an early example of what the Italians now call a *giallo*, sometimes flippantly described in English as a 'whodunnit', but more appropriately as a psychological thriller. It would be an interesting comparison to see how the genre has developed by setting it alongside *Blood Rain*, an Aurelio Zen mystery set in Catania and written by the English author Michael Dibdin.

Originally from Wolverhampton in the English Midlands, Dibdin took an English degree at a time in the 1960s when literature was experiencing something of a revolution. Drawn to Italy, he moved to the central peninsula town of Perugia and his detective, Aurelio Zen, was then born. Zen is a Venetian with a strong moral centre who, at times, seems lost in the maze of corrupt double-dealing officialdom. Like his Sicilian counterpart, Andrea Camilleri's Montalbano, his cases are not always neatly resolved – loose ends dangle and justice can be more poetic than literal.

The posting Aurelio fears most is a Sicilian one, which is likely to be reflected in the actual forces of law and order in Italy. It is not that Sicilians will be hostile or that he finds the culture disagreeable, but rather it is the simple fact that to understand the Sicilian underworld, it is necessary to have grown up in the very same streets. This is a truth that was pointed out by the real-life judge Giovanni Falcone.

In the novel, seventh in the series of Zen mysteries, Aurelio is seconded to Catania on the trail of events that resulted in the discovery of a decomposed corpse in a railway wagon. He is joined by his adopted daughter, Carla Arduini, who is setting up a secure computer network for the anti-Mafia unit. The first time we encounter them together is in a local bar in Piazza Carlo Alberto, a very macho micro-world troubled by the unaccompanied arrival of this unknown female. Dibdin describes the 'almost oppressive' atmosphere of deferentiality which only relaxes when her father arrives.

Zen is cautious and the picture painted is one of paranoia and distrust, heightened by the unfamiliar Catanese surroundings. The tension leaps from the pages, yet he is simply having a coffee – a morning routine he has established since the beginning of his posting. He is not blind to the city's attractions despite this palpable wariness. The mornings see him rise early and throw the windows open 'in time to watch the astonishing spectacle of sunrise over the bay of Catania; an intense, distant glow, as though the sea itself had caught fire like a pan of oil'.

His routine continues, passing a woman roasting peppers on a brazier as market traders set up their stalls with everything from fresh meat to olives, artichokes, fennel and sundry household wares. He crosses Via Etnea with Etna in the distance, ending up at the *questura*, the local police headquarters – an early morning stroll through the beauties of Catania before the rigours of the day, and rigours they surely are. Things do not end well for Zen or his daughter, the latter dying while the former disappears into a Dibdinian version of Sherlock Holmes' supposed demise at the Reichenbach Falls, courtesy of Mafia-planted Semtex.

If Zen's Sicilian world is one of macho posturing, then he has caught the essence of a particular stereotype that was truly investigated by the native writer, Vitaliano Brancati. Brancati wrote of *gallismo* – best translated by that borrowed Spanish equivalent of machismo, to describe the strutting 'cock-of-the-walk', full of bravado and conquest. But it is a hollow boast, an outer cloak to hide the inner insecurities of some southern males. Vitaliano was born in Pachino, south-eastern Sicily, in 1907, but it is to the city of Catania that he owes these astute observations of a certain Sicilian masculinity. He graduated from the university in 1929 having written a dissertation on Federico De Roberto, a passing of the baton that De Roberto himself received from Verga.

Brancati steeped himself in the works of Ibsen, his fellow Sicilian Pirandello and the likes of Proust, Gide and Joyce. After periods in Rome and the central island town of Caltanissetta, he returned to Catania to teach, contribute to magazines and write. The upshot of this period of creativity was the novel, *Don Giovanni in Sicily* (*Don Giovanni in Sicilia*), actually written in nearby Zafferana Etnea. At the height of Fascist rule, it can be read as a critique of this very male ideology, a credo Brancati had dabbled with and rejected.

His language and themes were daring for the age, dealing as they do with sex and obsession. The eponymous bachelor, Giovanni, is cosseted by his sisters, living his imagined sexual conquests through a group of similarly minded men. Their trips in search of seduction end in the merely platonic and the relationshipless central character resorts to prostitutes. His world is turned upside down when he marries a northern Italian baroness and is somewhat amazed to find an atmosphere of sexual frisson in the Milanese salons frequented by his wife's friends. Rather lackadaisically, the torpid Giovanni engages in some of these invitations to extra-marital sex but finds the realities of his Milanese life leave him on the sidelines.

He is magnetically attracted back to the idle ways of his Catanian lifestyle, reverting to the childlike state of idleness and fantasy we saw at the outset. The name, Giovanni, was carefully chosen by Brancati as a pastiche of Don Juan, the infamous Spanish seducer. But, as we have seen, he's a man of straw, not the only such character in Vitaliano's work. In another of his novels, *Beautiful Antonio* (*Il bell'Antonio*), the protagonist is desired by many women but his impotency brings shame on the family when his marriage is annulled.

Alejandro Luque was sufficiently inspired by the person of Don Giovanni to write of his fading years in 'The Decline of the Don Juan' ('Ocaso del donjuán'), a short story forming part of his compilation, *La defensa siciliana* (*The Sicilian Defence*), which was written in homage to Brancati. Interestingly, the Spanish author has also pointed out that the matriarch often harbours the worst aspects of machismo. The Catanese matriarch, in her most encompassingly protective sense, is Sant'Agata – saint and martyred protector of her people. Predictably, it is the male populace that lead her feast day.

Along with the Palermitan festival celebrated in honour of Santa Rosalia, Sant'Agata's Day is the other great religious procession renowned outside of the island. Theresa Maggio, a second-generation Sicilian American, was drawn home in the 1990s to search for the lesser-known mountain villages in the interior – particularly, many around the base of Mount Etna. In such close proximity to Catania, she could not resist attending the Feast of Sant'Agata. The account of her experiences was published in her travelogue, *The Stone Boudoir*.

Maggio's story is not one of a single trip, but of a lifetime observing the Sicilian experience through the immigrant Sunday gatherings of her grandparents, who had left the town of Santa Margherita Belice to the west of the island in search of a better life in America. They eventually ended up in New Jersey with a garden and enough land to grow grapes. On expressing a desire to see the Sicilian interior, Theresa was dissuaded by her grandmother, who exclaimed, 'there's nothing there'. Sicily was a taboo subject for conversation with her granddaughter, but an experience to share with her peers – a sad nostalgia for a lost earthquake-riven home town.

Theresa first went to Sicily as a very green student in the early 1970s. Taken under the wing of a young man returning to see his fiancée, she was taken on a mad-cap late-night drive in a car full of strangers, all the way to the doorstep of her Margheritese relatives. The positive experience of connecting with family and the kindness of strangers brought her back for subsequent visits, including a trip with her father to the Palermitan beach resort of Mondello to see where he had served in World War II. The Mondello connection proved fateful as she soon became enamoured of a lifeguard-cum-fisherman.

The relationship was not to last, leaving Maggio to return to a journalist's job in the States. Like so many grandchildren of immigrants, the generation that skipped the heartache but was drawn to the culture, she could not resist the lure of those deep veins of familial truth. It was the film *The Star Maker* (*L'uomo delle stelle*), by the director Tornatore, that gave her the final impetus to return to her tour of the hill villages, many of which were portrayed in the film.

Mount Etna is garlanded with a necklace of these little settlements and towns which are caught between the twin pulls of the forbidding volcano and the bright lights of the city. They are in the direct line of fire when the gods awaken inside the crater but, as we have seen, Catania itself is not immune. Their only recourse in the face of such helplessness is to pray to their saint. What Rosalia did for Palermitan plague victims, Agata does her very best to do for Catanians in the face of molten anger.

The hagiographic details date back to the year 252 when Agata refused to marry the Roman proconsul Quintian, having promised herself to God. Her vows and his pagan traditions were wholly incompatible, and as a consequence of her disobedience, Quintian had her breasts mutilated and her body subjected to burning coals. The place of her imprisonment is now known as the Church of Sant'Agata al Carcere. Her relics are housed in the cathedral and on the 4 and 5 February, her effigy, containing these body parts, is paraded on a carriage through the streets.

As Maggio illustrates, it is essentially a male-dominated event with the grudging acceptance of women in the procession after years of them demanding their rightful place. The saint is adorned with a crown laden with jewels donated by that legendary English king, Richard the Lionheart, and her robe has gold stitching with yet more sparkling accoutrements. Spanish viceroys, Savoyard queens and even Bellini himself have contributed to her finery.

Theresa was awed and slightly fearful of the pressing multitude and, at one point, she was told of a boy's lucky escape from the heightened fervour of the populace. A city maintenance man's son became so entangled in the throng he had to go home 'with no hat, no shoes and one ripped sleeve'. His father vowed to wait until the boy could protect himself before returning. The crowds are not the only hazard: the dripping wax from the thousands of candles turns the streets of Catania into one big skating rink.

The real work is done by the men pulling on the ropes of the carriage, orchestrated by one captain keeping all involved in tune. When the chariot, known as a *fercolo*, reaches Via Etnea, the scene mirrors the volcano beyond:

> Boys in white robes shouted, 'Siamo tutti devoti tutti?' and pink and white fireworks lit the ultramarine sky over the cathedral. When the sky turned blue velvet the *fercolo* moved off slowly with a hundred ten-pound candles blazing, as Agata was hauled up the boulevard towards Etna [. . .] The mountain was a geyser of fire but Agata smiled at it.

For some uptight Anglo-Saxons, the health and safety repercussions of such a scene would be staggering: unfettered hordes, molten wax, the massive weight of a hand-drawn effigy careering up steep slopes and sleep-deprived worshippers in a state of ecstasy. The very idea.

Agata does her best to protect her citizens, but sadly, her best is not always good enough and Catania lives under the constant threat of potential annihilation – just as the citizens of Naples fear the wrath of Vesuvius. However, the curse of a volcanic location can also be a blessing as the resulting layers of ash provide all the nutrients for an abundance of produce. The slopes and plain below Etna are the market garden of Sicily. Lemon and orange groves line the asphalt veins conducting the container lorries to all points of Europe. The area's citrus production is famed but another crop is gaining ground among the world's cognoscenti: the vine.

### *Mount Etna and Aci Trezza*

One author who came to Sicily in search of this flourishing viticultural activity is Robert Camuto, an American wine writer based in France. His book, *Palmento*, subtitled *A Sicilian Wine Odyssey*, is just that – a text that takes wine as its protagonist but looks deeper into the ritual and tradition that the fruit of the vine manifests in the island's wider culture. Camuto is convinced that Sicily is living through a key period in its history and there is no better way of introducing his journey than quoting from the introduction:

> I am not a wine critic but a writer who sees in wine metaphors for us all. Wine to me is food (physical and spiritual), an expression of humanity and nature and that zone where the two merge into something larger. In this communion of life forces, I know of no place richer than Sicily – no place at this moment that has more to say.

It is especially Etna and its mixture of eccentric wine-makers that attracts Robert, particularly *il belga pazzo* (the crazy Belgian), Frank Cornelissen. Frank's land is at Solicchiata on the northern slopes of Etna, where everything was left untended for years, until he breathed new life into the grapes. These high vineyards still have a ramshackle appearance: 'The terraces' dry walls – built from stacked lava stone – followed the contours of the mountainside and were often broken and overtaken by brambles. Century-old stubs of vines were planted in irregular rows [. . .]'

Frank is not the only foreigner drawn to the mountain's fecundity and distinctive *terroir*, that wine lovers' unique mixture of geology and geography that produces an individual identity to the wines of the area. There are Americans, passing Dutch and even an English rockstar – the Italianophile of Simply Red fame, Mick Hucknall. Camuto went to visit Hucknall's wine consultant in the hilltown of Sant'Alfio on an estate appropriately named Il Cantante (The Singer), and was witness to the star being interviewed about his new venture. Able to get a word with Mick, Robert was surprised at his knowledge and engagement in the process of quality wine-making:

Over a glass of white wine Hucknall told me – a diamond filling flashing in his front tooth – that while he had numerous offers to buy vineyards, making wine on Etna was an opportunity to do something unique in the wine world with grape varieties that were unheard of outside Sicily.

In many ways, this is the key to the distinctive nature of modern Sicilian wine. Grape varieties like Nerello Mascalese, Nero d'Avola, Grecanico, Inzolia and Frappato are not the usual bottles of Chardonnay, Merlot and Shiraz that line the supermarket shelves of northern Europe and North America.

On one particularly fine October morning, Etna showed its most powerfully beautiful face to Camuto. As Maggio must have wondered before him, Robert tried to imagine the difficulties that led his grandfather to emigrate. Full of these thoughts, he drove to Passopisciaro and was able to take in the full vibrancy of that unique time of the wine-makers' year: 'The changing colors of the vines from green to yellow seemed to vibrate against the backdrop of volcanic stone terraces [. . .] In those moments it all seemed like Eden.'

This paradise, however, was a mythical Hell for the Greco-Sicilian philosopher Empedocles. A citizen of the southern town of Agrigento, he was known for his philosophy of Love and Strife – Strife usually gaining the upper hand thus leading to the conflicting forces seen in our world. He also delved into theories of light and vision, as well as respiration, reincarnation and vegetarianism – a real pre-Renaissance man.

The legend of his death comes down to us from the biographer of Greek philosophers, Diogenes Laërtius, who believed that Empedocles had thrown himself into the jaws of Etna so that the people would believe he had vanished into the realm of immortal gods. His ploy was uncovered by a truculent volcano which spat out a bronze sandal for all to see. Horace, in his *Ars Poetica*, was more forgiving, believing that philosopher-poets of Empedocles' quality had the right to give themselves up to the fire.

This myth endures through the works of authors such as Friedrich Hölderlin and Matthew Arnold, who wrote the dramatic poem *Empedocles on Etna*. There is nothing to suggest that Arnold actually visited the mountain but he was steeped in the classical tradition, also lecturing on the translation of Homer during the 1860s. The poem takes the form of a dialogue with the philosopher as one of the characters. In his final moments gazing into the crater there is a manifest release, a freedom: 'Ah, boil up, ye vapours! Leap and roar, thou sea of fire! My soul glows to meet you.'

Death in the crater is a theme that occurs in another of Alejandro Luque's short stories, 'The Sicilian Defence', part of a collection with the same name. The tale within a tale chronicles the frustrations of an author whose work becomes a publishing phenomenon before his book is ever finished. The reluctant writer's magnum opus concerns the history of Cenerina Maria, who grows up in a convent only to be reunited with her father later in life. Her increasing Electra complex, the female Oedipal equivalent, comes to an inevitable conclusion when she takes her volcano-obsessed father on an excursion to the summit. Like Empedocles before him, he disappears into the flames, aided by the guiding hand of his psychologically damaged daughter. The troubled author Di Giovanni, who has partially penned this tale, finds his deified position in the avant-garde of Italian letters a deception too far. His end is less poetic, shooting himself through the head.

There are those who feel inspired to write about the mountain, and those who feel the need to climb or explore it. Goethe allowed his keen geologist's eye to roam over the lava fields noting the mixed composition of minerals that contributed to the 'alluvial hills'. The scene was one worthy of an artist's palette and his friend, Kniep, took full advantage of the sketching possibilities on offer: 'Here Nature shows her predilection for high colours and amuses herself by arraying the black-blue-grey lava in vivid yellow moss, red sedum, and a variety of purple flowers. Cacti and vines give evidence of meticulous cultivation.'

Patrick Brydone showed the same spirit that would lead his compatriots to throw themselves down the Cresta Run on glorified teatrays or risk life and limb skiing full pelt down impossibly vertical slopes. In the 1770s, he tackled the trek to the summit, more of an endurance than a helter-skelter feat of recklessness. His observations and descriptions were meticulous and became the most celebrated aspect of his published travelogue. Their fame even led some critics to analyse the text in an effort to prove the Scotsman never actually reached the top in the way he claimed.

He left Giardini on the coast and his route took him through the town of Piedimonte Etneo, where he first noticed craters and stones created by the mountain. The streets of Piedimonte are now paved with similarly regurgitated Etnean stones, giving the straight central avenues that sombre air so noticeable in Catania. The little town's construction owes much to Ignazio Sebastiano Gravina Crujillas, and if the name sounds familiar, he was part of the same aristocratic family as that other Prince of Palagonia whose monsters so horrified Goethe in Bagheria. Ignazio's periwigged statue stands proudly surveying the organised layout of the town from his position in the central piazza.

Brydone found the next region above Piedimonte to have been stripped of its wooded vegetation owing to the boiling torrents poured down the mountainside in 1755. Etna is truly a living entity, its molten heart pulsating and contours constantly reshaping. Patrick noticed this phenomenon when he saw the 'little mountains' that had newly bulged from the sides of their angry parent. This volcanic activity is also responsible for the area's prodigious capacity for growth and, even so soon after being stripped of ground cover, he noticed the beginnings of rapid recolonisation which he put down to the 'nitre' in the ash-rich soil.

Giving up the attempt to summit from this direction, the party returned to Acireale, where Brydone was curious to observe the meeting of lava and sea water which, in this particular case, had formed a dark promontory. Considering it to be a recent phenomenon, he was surprised to learn that this flow, halted by the waves, was mentioned by the ancient historian Diodorus. Between Giardini and Acireale is the infamous Fiume Freddo – the Cold River of Acis and Galatea fame. The two lovers were separated by that ubiquitous villain, the Cyclops Polyphemus, who had killed Acis in a fit of jealousy. The dead suitor's blood became the waters of the Fiume Freddo. Brydone was surprised by the rapidity of the flow and its extreme icy coldness, yet 'it never freezes; but, what is remarkable, it is said often to contract a degree of cold greater than that of ice'. Its roar reminded the author of the agonies inspired by Cyclopean pain.

The Scotsman was but one of many to gain inspiration from this myth – not least of whom include Handel, Poussin, Lorrain and Dostoevsky. Many of the towns along this area of coastline also bear its imprint – witness the prefix of the following: Aci Catena, Aci Sant'Antonio, Aci Castello and, most famous of all, Aci Trezza. It was here that Giovanni Verga set his novel, *The House by the Medlar Tree*; as we know, one of his most famous works. It was also turned into a film, *La terra trema* (*The Earth Trembles*), by the director of *Leopard* fame, Luchino Visconti. Just off the main street, there is a small museum commemorating both the film and book. Its partially obscured stone entrance arch leads to a courtyard planted with a medlar tree, another corner being strewn with fishing nets. Movie memorabilia are also augmented by the kind of simple furnishings known to the fisher folk, along with letters written by Verga to his brother Pietro.

The plot of the story centres on the Toscano family who live in a house by said medlar, hence the English title. The widowed paterfamilias, Ntoni, lives with his son, Bastian, his wife and their five children. Their income is derived from a fishing boat named *La Provvidenza* which initially proves a misnomer as Ntoni's son and a rashly bought cargo are lost at sea. This is the beginning of a chain of misfortune leading to debt, house repossession, imprisonment, prostitution and broken betrothals. It is only thanks to the most hardworking of Bastian's sons, Alessi, that the family are able to buy back the beloved house.

Verga's portrait of peasant struggle is full of the very real hardships faced by fishermen in this area during the turn of the nineteenth century. Like fishing communities the world over, they had to deal with the twin vagaries of market price and nature's wrath. As the *Provvidenza* slips out of Aci Trezza harbour, we observe life in the little town continuing, unaware of the boat's drastic fate to come:

The *Provvidenza* went off on Saturday, towards evening, when the Ave Maria should have been ringing; only the bell was silent because Master Cirino, the sacristan, had gone to carry a pair of new boots to Don Silvestro, the town-clerk; at that hour the girls crowded like a flight of sparrows about the fountain, and the evening-star was shining brightly already just over the mast of the *Provvidenza*, like a lamp. Maruzza, with her baby in her arms, stood on the shore, without speaking, while her husband loosened the sail, and the *Provvidenza* danced on the broken waves by the Faraglione like a duck.

At least the boat and its crew did not have to deal with the incident that gave rise to the *faraglioni* mentioned above. They are three pointed rocks rising from the sea and punctuating the Aci Trezzan horizon, also referred to as the Cyclops' Rocks. Legend has it that our old friend Polyphemus hurled these massive boulders at a fleeing Odysseus who had driven a beam into the monster's single eye. Odysseus himself picks up the story, recounting how the Cyclops, in rage and pain, 'tore the top from off a high mountain, and flung it just in front of my ship so that it was within a little of hitting the end of the rudder'. Warned against further provocation, Odysseus continued his taunting. The second rock,

8 *The* faraglioni – *Cyclops' Rocks* – *mythically attributed to Polyphemus,*
*Aci Trezza*

hurled in fury, created a bow wave that drove the ship on to a meeting
with the commander's anxiously waiting comrades.

Brydone punctuates his Cyclopean interval with a quote from the
Sicilian poet Anguillara, who in turn borrowed his inspiration from
Virgil; as Patrick highlights, some even claim Virgil looked towards
Apollonius Rhodius – the author behind Jason and the Argonauts. He
goes on to say there is nothing new under the sun: 'Poets have ever
been the greatest of all thieves; and happy it is that poetical theft is no
felony, otherwise, I am afraid, Parnasus would have been but thinly
peopled.'

Patrick began his second assault on the mountain from the village
of Nicolosi, once known for its figs and spotted with those breaches in
the mountain wall he had previously spied near Piedimonte. The road

was strewn with former lava fields, regularly interspersed with vineyards and orchards. It has ever been a shifting landscape where lava-stone constructions or random fields of rock melt away on contact with newly formed rivers of molten material, when 'in the course of a few hours, churches, palaces, and villages, have been entirely melted down and the whole run off in fusion, without leaving the least mark of their former existence.'

In Nicolosi, Brydone's party was surrounded by distrustful locals who believed them to be treasure hunters. Upon their innocent search for lava stone, the villagers laughed mockingly, bantering in a dialect that even Patrick's Sicilian companions found unintelligible. Striking up a conversation in standard Italian, Brydone explained that curiosity was the simple reason for their visit and that he was 'un inglese'. Setting aside that he was a Scotsman, the locals recognised the appellation and recalled visits from previous Englishmen. They asked him if he believed in Christ but were unconvinced by his affirmitive answer, retelling a local legend that the English had lost a queen to the fires of Etna. They were now certain his mission was in devotional homage to this legendary monarch. Brydone's reply was both sarcastic and deadpan: 'I assured them that the Inglese had but too little respect for their Queens when they were alive, and that they never troubled themselves about them after they were dead.'

Intrigued by the legend, Patrick found out that the queen's name was Anne and she had been condemned to the eternal fires of Etna for turning her husband into a heretic. Suggesting names, Brydone was stopped in his tracks to discover that the mountain harboured none other than Anne Boleyn. He was relieved to find out that her husband had joined her as 'he deserved it much more than she.' Amused but keen to continue, the party rose above Nicolosi through the temperate zone of forests and fragrant ground cover which continues for about nine miles. They spent the evening in a cavern making use of the vegetation as makeshift matresses.

Rising still further, the mountain began to smoke, the hot molten rock within emitting gases through any available vent. The trees gave way to the snow and ice fields, with a distant summit 'vomiting out torrents of smoke'. As is the case today, a good mountain guide was an essential and the unfortunately nicknamed Cyclops proved to be just that for Brydone and his team. Before dawn, they reached an ancient ruin known as the Philosopher's Tower, attributed to either Empedocles' desire to study the mountain or to the worship of Vulcan. A well-deserved swig from the brandy bottle gave them the final impetus to reach their destination. As dawn breaks, Brydone is lost for words but, nonetheless, has a damn good try at capturing the emotions he experienced:

Neither is there on the surface of this globe any one point that unites so many awful and sublime objects. The immense elevation from the surface of the earth, drawn, as it were, to a single point, without any neighbouring mountain for the senses and imagination to rest upon, and recover from their astonishment in their way down to the world. This point, or pinnacle, raised on the brink of a bottomless gulf as old as the world, often discharging rivers of fire, and throwing out burning rocks with a noise that shakes the whole island. Add to this, the unbound extent of the prospect, comprehending the greatest diversity and the most beautiful scenery in nature, with the rising sun advancing in the east, to illuminate the wondrous scene.

The prospect of such an awe-inspiring view from the crater edge can be something of a lottery owing to the shifting cloud formations that often shroud the mountain from within and without. Another intrepid literary explorer drawn to the very top was Guy de Maupassant, fortunate enough to burst through the 'abyss of clouds' and emerge into the immensity of blue, being 'bathed in the heavens'. He found the sulphur fumes problematic and, indeed, their acidic harshness can be overpowering to the unwary. They do contribute to acid rain and have been known to erupt to a height of up to five kilometres (just over three miles).

Both Maupassant and Brydone revered the landscape and drama inherent in nature at its most raw, not least of which was the very discernable temperature alteration felt when ascending the mountain. Both went from burning heat to considerable cold, having previously wondered at the imprecations to pack furs and woollens. As Guy is confronted by a wall of solid lava, he feels the perversely frosty stab of Etna's schizophrenic soul: 'And, little by little, the cold grips us, that penetrating mountain cold, which freezes the blood and paralyses the limbs. It seems hidden, waiting in ambush in the wind; it stings the eyes and eats the skin with its icy bite.'

Like all mountaineering, it is the way up that provides the anticipation, excitement and sense of achievement but descend they must and their accounts are much shortened on the return journey. Washington Irving was not even afforded that luxury – his ascent stalled halfway owing to the amount of snow lying on the ground and the reluctance of the knowledgeable local guides to attempt a summit they knew to be 'hazardous in the extreme, and certainly fruitless'.

D. H. Lawrence, beset as he was with illness, was content to view from afar and calls the mountain 'a pedestal of heaven'. His journey to Sardinia described in the book appropriately titled *Sea and Sardinia* starts from his home in Fontana Vecchia, Taormina. He speaks of crossing the invisible border, both a state of mind and a physical alteration, palpably felt between the coast and those foothills so aptly described by Patrick Brydone. Lawrence's restlessness had yet again proved too strong to deny, yet he questions his own desire to go as he knows it would be so easy to remain at Etna's feet. The magnetism he feels altering his 'active cells' appears a direct comparison to the magma-like revolutions within the body of the volcano.

The peak is both an attraction and a repellent as the writer acknowledges: 'Ah, what a mistress, this Etna! with her strange winds prowling round her like Circe's panthers, some black, some white. With her strange, remote communications and her terrible dynamic exhalations. She makes men mad.' So leave he must – partly to escape the draw of Mongibello and partly pushed by its alarming capacity to devour the soul. Like any anxious holiday-maker, he packs for the journey – flask, sandwiches, fruit and butter – and battens down all the doors and windows, with the exception of one that refused to close having been distorted by temperature fluctuations. Years later, Norman Harrison, the American fiction writer of *The Entity*, who had rented the villa, thus continuing the long list of writers in residence, noted that the very same window would still not fasten.

Eventually, Lawrence made his way to Taormina station and took the train to Messina, skirting the foothills of Etna whilst being spared the sight of its summit which was obscured by cloud – leading David Herbert to suppose it was 'playing some devilry in private'. The worship of a graven image of another sort appears in Selma Lagerlöf's novel, *The Miracles of Antichrist,* principally set in the Etnean town of Diamante. As we know from the Taormina chapter, this Swedish Nobel laureate received a government scholarship to travel. She never married but had a close relationship with the widowed Sophie Elland, who accompanied her on the trip to Sicily.

Whilst exploring the foothills near the coast, she conceived of the plot for the novel and set about writing the finished product. The book is split into short-story-like interludes that begin with the soothsayer, Sibyl, prophesying the birth of Jesus, and Augustus building the Temple of Aracoeli. Cutting to the nineteenth century, an English traveller steals the temple's Christ image and puts a replica in its place. During the dead of night, the true statue returns and a monk discards the false idol, which is first taken to Paris, eventually finding its way back by the hands of travellers to the town of Diamante.

Located on Monte Chiaro, another of those mountainettes identified by Brydone, Diamante could be any small settlement on the ascent to the top. Lagerlöf describes it as 'zigzagging up the mountain' – its ramshackle nature lacking the town planning so evident today in the aristocratic reconstruction of Piedimonte under the watchful eye of the Prince of Palagonia. The author's vocabulary reflects the way in which the mountain itself hurls out the materials that the locals use to construct their settlements: 'When it was far enough up it threw down a town gate and a piece of town wall. Then it ran round the mountain in a spiral and dropped down houses.'

The false Christ image finally resurfaces in Diamante thanks to another English woman, Miss Tottenham, who begins to treat the town as her own fiefdom, albeit with a degree of altruistic intent. She releases the image to a monk, Fra Felice, who places the statue on his altar, but only after a thorough cleaning. Stones and plaster fall on the Christ but it remains intact and the Father is convinced of a miracle – just one of many small interventions attributed to the replica, including the resurrection of the town's theatre.

Revolt and social upheaval bring the ideology of socialism to the settlement. Gaetano, the returning sculptor sent to England by the Signorina, brings his ideals back, having spent time apprenticed to a mastercraftsman with socialist leanings. He is consigned to gaol for his beliefs. Even Gaetano's gaol term is seen as the work of God, potentially a test that could lead him back to faith. The story continues in a series of vignettes which focus on the ordinary people of Diamante and their struggles to survive.

The railway brings progress of sorts to the locale, connecting up the isolated settlements, just as the Ferrovia Circumetnea – the narrow-gauge line encircling the mountain – does to this day. Ease of travel prompted Lagerlöf's character, Father Gondo, to encourage pilgrimages to the town, but all illusions are shattered when he discovers the inscription hidden within the crown – thereby making the connection to the Aracoeli Temple in Rome, '"You have had Antichrist among you, and he has got possession of you. You have forgotten heaven. You have forgotten that you possess a soul. You only think of this world."' Approaching the Pope for advice, Gondo is referred to Signorelli's *Miracles of Antichrist* in Orvieto and advised to embrace the movements of Antichristianity, bringing the likes of socialism to the fold instead of casting them to the flame, '"You cast Antichristianity on the pyre, and soon he in his turn will cast you there."'

Etna, the devourer of souls, has struck again. The very nature of myth and environment combine to create a milieu that breeds this kind of literary contemplation. Lawrence was convinced the Etna Sicilians were 'intelligent, almost inspired, and souless'. Eccentricities are manifest, whether it is Belgian wine-makers or English aristocrats. One such dukedom belonged for many decades to the descendants of Lord Nelson.

## *Bronte*

The town of Bronte lies to the north-west of Catania on the opposite side of Mount Etna. The houses, clinging to the slopes by the Simeto river, are dwarfed by the all-encompassing presence of the mountain. The fertility of the surrounding land is reflected in the pistachio cultivation, which any modern-day Sicilian will immediately associate with the area. The aforementioned Duchy of Bronte was given to Admiral Nelson in 1799 by King Ferdinand III as a reward for his help in putting down the revolution in Naples, which was the seat of the Kingdom of the Two Sicilies. Nelson's help meant that Ferdinand could recover his throne.

The Castello Maniace, some 13 kilometres (eight miles) from the town centre, was the heart of the family fiefdom which passed into the hands of the Bridport family when the Viscount married the Admiral's niece. The castle stands in wooded grounds, fronted on one side with lawns. Its quadrangular pattern gives a hint at its past life as a monastery. Depending on the season, the walls are softened by creeping vegetation that dresses the stone in flashes of green and red. The complex is now a museum administered by the regional authority.

The fact that the ruling aristocracy in this area was English did little to help relieve the conditions of the poor. In fact, the initial reactionary suppression of rebellion in Naples, which handed the duchy to Nelson's family, could be seen as a precedent for the way in which events unfolded in later years. Despite Ferdinand's adoption of some British ideas of constitutional monarchy, Bronte continued along feudal lines, and even Garibaldi's unification movement failed to ease conditions. The peasantry revolted in 1860 but was suppressed, this time by Nino Bixio, Garibaldi's friend and the commander of two battalions of Red Shirts.

Literary connections start with the unexpected link to the similarly named Brontë sisters and their vicar father, whose delusions of associational grandeur led him to change his family name of Brunty to that of the Admiral's estate in Sicily. With no connection beyond this simple change in nomenclature, the famous authoresses put pen to paper, their works eventually seeing the light of day under their Sicilian pseudonym. Time and passing fashion have withered the association, the curious remnant of an accented 'e' being the only faint reminder of Nelson's Sicilian title – a title he liked to use for a place he never visited.

His heirs, however, were far more rooted to their ancestral estate and it did not return to the Sicilian people until 1981. One of the more curious relatives to have inhabited Castello Maniace was Alexander Hood, who sometimes appended Nelson to his name. As we have seen, he spent much time hobnobbing with the literati in Taormina, writing his own book, *Sicilian Studies*, and striking up a great friendship with William Sharp aka Fiona Macleod.

From the years 1901 to his death in 1905, Sharp spent a great deal of time in the company of Alec Hood, both in Taormina and as a guest at the castle. His letters and his wife's explanatory memoir of William's complex literary life are ample testimony to this. The preface to *William*

9 *Castello Maniace, the former ducal seat of the Nelson Hoods and retreat for the Scottish writer William Sharp, Bronte*

*Sharp: A Memoir* sets out the rationale behind the Scotsman's use of a female persona in his poetry, prose and even letter composition. Fiona first appeared on the scene as Sharp's protégé, her work focusing on Celtic imagery and mythology. Yet Macleod's oeuvre went beyond the simple pseudonym which uneducated critics of the day had presumed a joke. It seemed a necessary part of his psyche and, as Professor Patrick Geddes explained in a letter to Elizabeth Sharp, 'Should you not explain that F. M. was not simply W. S., but that W. S. in his deepest moods became F. M., a sort of dual personality in short, not a mere nom-de-guerre?'

Indeed, Elizabeth does go on to explain as comprehensively as possible the duality which she splits into a life of two halves: the first ending with Sharp's publication of *Vistas* and the second starting with Macleod's *Pharais*. During William's Maniace years, he was well ensconced in his double life, as some of his letters written from the castle are signed as Fiona. However, by the 1900s, suspicions among correspondees were no doubt at their height and none other than Yeats worked out the connection.

Elizabeth and William spent the New Year of 1901 in Palermo and were in Taormina when they heard the news of Queen Victoria's death. At the memorial ceremony in the English chapel of Santa Caterina, they first met Alexander Hood, who, at that point, was heavily involved in introducing new farming methods to Bronte. As a result, he inherited the estate from his father in 1904. Only days after this initial meeting, the Sharps were whisked away to Maniace for a tour of the property, an extended visit to be repeated on five other occasions.

In 1902, as himself, William writes to Ernest Rhys from Nelson's castle: 'A few days ago I came on here, to the wild inlands of the Sicilian Highlands, to spend a month with my dear friend here, in this wonderful old Castle-Fortress-Monastery-Mansion – the Castle Maniace itself being over 2,000 feet in the highlands beyond Etna . . .' A further letter in the same month of February to another correspondent, Theodore Watts-Dunton, talks of the appearance of spring on the estate when 'everywhere is a mass of purple iris, narcissus, Asphodel, & thousands of sweet-smelling violets.'

Sharp's wife and his sister, Mary, were very much part of the Fiona deception and he took full advantage of Mary's female handwriting to lend authenticity to the letters penned by Macleod. In October 1902, Sharp's alter ego is writing to Thomas Mosher about her business/publication concerns including copyrighting, and she requests a series of four volumes to be forwarded on to Il Duca Alessandro di Bronte. It seems that Sharp's female counterpart was dogging his footsteps all the way to the castello as 'she' writes again to Mosher in November from the Maniace estate acknowledging the receipt of her book, *By Sundown Shores: Studies in Spiritual History*. She writes of her illness and seems to diverge from the opinions of William when she complains of the altitude: 'On the other hand, at the friend's where I am at present staying the elevation is too great for me (between 3000 & 4000 feet) and the climate too inclement and changeable at this late season of the year.'

Alec Hood was one of the few initiates who understood the true identity of Fiona Macleod. Prior to his visit in the autumn, Sharp wrote to his friend explaining the dilemma he faced living a 'woman's life and nature within', explaining that 'rightly or wrongly I believe that this and the style so strangely born of this inward life, depend upon my aloofness and spiritual isolation as F. M.' Macleod and Sharp continued to coexist, at times happily, within the isolated confines of Hood's realm, but William was always conscious of the need to keep Fiona moving and somewhat aloof. As himself, he wrote an account of the lands, entitled 'Through Nelson's Duchy', which was published in *Pall Mall Magazine* in October 1903. He evokes not only the history but the sensorial experience of staying in the heart of mountainous Sicily:

it is so still in the gardens below that I can hear the continuous indeterminate murmur of the bees in the dense borders of the large and fragrant Sicilian amaryllides, so still that the floating fumes of roses and violets, of heliotrope and the long clustered spires of medlar and lemoncina, rise undrifted by the least eddy of air, an invisible smoke of sweet odours.

He writes of the rushing waters of the Simeto, 'that Symaithos so loved of the poets', the gorges below Maniace, the wind in the mountainous forests of Serraspina and the Bronte vineyards. His ear takes in the folk songs of the peasants along with their praises for the Duke – the latter of which may be the biased opinion of Alec's good friend, or a reflection on the more efficient agricultural practices introduced by Hood. He quotes Matthew Arnold's *Empedocles on Etna* and muses on the Greek remains found in the vicinity. Sharp had found his Eden and a like-minded friend to share his fears and pleasures.

He submitted a similar idea to the American *Atlantic Monthly*, focusing on little-known inland towns and landscapes. He was also working on a projected book about Magna Graecia which would enlarge upon Hellenic Sicily. William's 'Sicilian Highlands' appeared in the *Atlantic* in 1904: 'Is there anything in Europe finer than the beech forests of the Serra del Re when the wind from Etna, blowing at height of six thousand feet, moves across the gold and amber mountain raiment, immense, primeval, solitary [. . .]'

The Maniace years came to an end in 1905, even as William continued to be inspired by his surroundings, working as he was on a drama entitled 'Persephonma, or the Drama of the House of Etna', scenes of which were written at the castello. It was to have been dedicated to the Duke of Bronte. On 8 December, Sharp's diary ends and, as his wife says in her memoir, 'here too ends the written work of a tired hand and brain, but of an eager outlooking spirit.' His last drive took him to a mountain pass and the spectacular sunset over Cesarò. Elizabeth was sure it was fatal to him. Some of his last words were spoken to Alec Hood and he was laid to rest on 14 December 'in a little woodland burial-ground on the hillside within sound of the Simeto'. A Celtic cross was later added to the grave, appropriately carved from the mountain's lava stone; part of the inscription reads: 'Farewell to the known and exhausted, Welcome the unknown and illimitable [. . .]'

Sharp died at the age of 50, his health weakened by a bout of typhoid, a heart condition and other intermittent illnesses. Alexander Hood lived until 1937, long enough to meet D. H. Lawrence during his extended stay in Sicily. By the 1920s, the Duke had become something of a figure of fun, only being called 'Il Duca' by the resident expatriats of Taormina. Lawrence sharpened his sarcastic, satirical pencil when he wrote to Lady Cynthia Asquith about the aristocrat:

> Did you ever hear of a Duca di Bronte – Mr Nelson Hood – descendant of Lord Nelson (Horatio) – whom the Neopolitans made Duca di Bronte because he hanged a few of them? [. . .] We went to see him – rather wonderful place – mais mon Dieu, M'le Duc – Mr Hood I should say. But perhaps you know him.
>
> Tell me where do Dukedoms lie
> Or in the head or in the eye . . .

# ❈ 5 ❈

# SYRACUSE
# AND THE SOUTH-EAST

## The Sybaritic South

### *Syracuse*

The fact that the city of Siracusa bears a name that has long been anglicised to Syracuse is ample linguistic proof of its worldwide significance. Moreover, the English spelling is basically a corruption of the Ancient Greek, Syrakousai, thus giving away the real importance of the city to a world beyond the island. At its classical peak, in around 400 BC, Syracuse was a rival to Athens, showing its power when it defeated an Athenian expeditionary force. Seven thousand men from Athens were imprisoned and kept in appalling conditions in the Latomie stone quarries, which still exist today.

The city has much more to offer than just its stunning Grecian past but it is this legacy that has attracted a fair proportion of incoming writers, from Cicero to the present day. The Greeks knew how to locate a settlement, be it from an aesthetic point of view or from a defensive one. Syracuse was originally founded on the little island jutting out from the mainland, known as Ortygia, a name derived from the Greek for quail. It was a superb defensive location that gave unhindered access to trade routes.

Lawrence Durrell found himself doubly at home when his bus tour reached Ortygia, with both his love of islands, however small, and his Grecian affiliations assuaged. He starts the chapter on Syracuse in his *Sicilian Carousel* with a self-penned poem that includes the lines: 'One day she dies and there with splendour/On all sides of her, for miles and miles,/Stretches reality in all its rich ubiquity,/The whole of science, magic, total time.' The golden stone of the city does seem to capture time; the buildings appear saturated in history, none more so than the cathedral, which has literally consumed the remains of a Greek temple, its columns embedded in the surrounding Christian structure.

Naturally enough, the cathedral is in Piazza Duomo at the heart of Ortygia. Durrell, no lover of Christian doctrine, was simply inspired by the harmony he had feared would be missing from such an edifice: 'I felt like chuckling as I walked about inside this honeycomb – so full of treasures, a real Ark of the human covenant.' The splicing of time and religion does not always produce such seamless results – consider the dark, heavy carved wooden pews parachuted into the middle of the sublime arches of Cordoba's former mosque.

The atmosphere on the streets is something Lawrence could almost smell, setting in place a train of thought that he followed to its logical conclusion – the imaginings of ancient origins. With time to kill, the byways of his daydream encompass Greek garden design, the olive and its rituals, gods, the significance of the rose and Pindaric verse. The latter has some significant Syracusan foundations. Pindar came to Sicily in middle age and he composed odes to the tyrant Hiero here – the first of which was set down in 470 BC. In the sixth 'Olympian Ode', he captures the spirit of Syracuse and gives a fine example of laudatory verse: 'Bid them too be mindful of Syracuse and Ortygia, ruling which with blameless sceptre and perpending honest deeds, Hiero honours the purple-footed Ceres, and the feast of her daughter, drawn by milk-white steeds and the might of Aetnean Jove . . .' In a potential act of atonement, some of his later poetry would attempt to condemn the acts of tyrants.

Durrell was not altogether suited to the strictures of a bus tour. Interruptions in his musings are frequent, and his semi-fictionalised fellow passengers are often a cause of amusement or vexation. Struggling with bags in the lift of his hotel, he does, for once, have the grace to be immensely grateful to a French passenger, whom he calls the Count. Describing himself 'as an "ancient préfet de Paris"', the Count was still travelling like a minor royal. Bag after bag bumps into Durrell's leg, but he receives a gracious apology and the nod of recognition. At this stage in his life, Lawrence had spent a lot of time in France and was something of a literary celebrity, with numerous appearances on television. The exquisitely mannered Frenchman promised not to reveal to the others on board the presence of an illustrious writer in their midst.

Another passenger is the retired Indian army officer, Deeds – a man of meticulous planning who had itemised his own Sicilian itinerary. The entire coach, though, and not just Deeds, sees the Piazza Duomo as its Ortygian highlight. It is not difficult to realise why – the vast expanse of near-white, smoothly paved stone is blissfully car free and arranged in a soft arc that enfolds the stroller and café-goer, particularly during the velvet embrace of a summer night.

Opposite the cathedral is the Soprintendenza per i Beni Culturali ed Ambientali, which houses a detailed coin collection dating from the Greek era. The collection was visited by Ezra Pound and W. B. Yeats. Yeats clearly studied the designs in some depth as the imprint they left was to prove useful when he was given the responsibility of submitting ideas for the coinage of the Irish Free State. The Sicilian-influenced currency, first struck in 1927, contained Syracusan images that would last right until the abolition of the coins upon the adoption of the euro.

The postcards sent home by Pound's wife depict the classical sites of Syracuse, including the Latomie quarries. The party stayed in the Hotel Roma, which is still a hotel and can be found, appropriately enough, in Via Roma. One of her short missives home calls Syracuse 'a queer place', quoting Ezra's opinion that it is 'a trifle of the East' – one of the city's less eloquent sobriquets.

At the far end of Piazza Duomo is the Church of Santa Lucia alla Badia. This church is most famous for housing an original work by Michelangelo Merisi, better known as Caravaggio. The initial frustration when reading the inevitable 'no photograph' sign quickly dissolves into gratitude on the realisation that there is nothing to be done but sear the image onto your retina, detail by detail. The work portrays the burial of Saint Lucy and is fronted by two intense gravediggers. Lucy is stretched out, backed by a contingent of mourners. First impressions also fix on the upper half of the image, which is dark and devoid of detail. It is a masterwork, but clearly done in some haste.

To flesh out the picture and Caravaggio's back story, there are two works that come to mind, both written by Sicilianophiles: *Caravaggio: A Life Sacred and Profane* by Andrew Graham-Dixon and *M: The Caravaggio Enigma* by the writer of *Midnight in Sicily*, Peter Robb. They each approach the subject from a different angle, but either is very worthy of consideration. Robb, whom we know as a surveyor of the murky world that exists between Sicilian politics and organised crime, takes an interesting perspective on the life of the artist. Throughout the text, Caravaggio is simply referred to as M.

Merisi fled to Sicily from Malta after a violent confrontation with a fellow member of the Order of St John. He already had an extremely chequered past, having killed Ranuccio Tomassoni in a botched duel. Robb follows him to Sicily, the place where Caravaggio's friend and fellow painter, Mario Minniti, awaits. The following extract describes how Merisi (M) obtained the Santa Lucia commission and gives a flavour of the book's visceral style. Minniti played a pivotal role in the contract:

> He also used his persuasiveness and *the excellence of his virtue* to win a big commission for M in Syracuse. The Mario who now gave shelter and assistance to his old friend on the run was a rather different person from the wild and beautiful Sicilian boy with a turbulent past who'd shacked up with M in Rome fifteen years earlier.

The whole job took Caravaggio less than two months in total – he was working to a deadline, very conscious of the close proximity of Malta and the inherent risk of pursuers within easy reach. After completion of the 'brilliantly unfocused' work, there were few further opportunities in Syracuse. Robb details the decision which prompted the artist's move to Messina. Despite the supposed manhunt, the Australian writer does highlight one lingering doubt with regard to Caravaggio's believed need to flee the Knights of Malta – there was a priory belonging to the order in that town: 'You'd think a fugitive from the order's maximum security cell on Malta, expelled by his fellow knights as a *foul and rotten limb*, and pursued by the murderous covert vendetta of a very senior knight, might've preferred a more restful destination.'

From the Church of Santa Lucia it is a short walk down Via Picherali to the Fonte Aretusa – Arethusan Fountain. Do not imagine a structure spouting jets of water through the mouths of Grecian nymphs, think more of a spring welling up into a reed-filled basin and you will recognise it immediately. The font has legendary origins, as the name would suggest. Arethusa was a water nymph who enjoyed bathing in the stream of the river god Alpheus. As was the way of things in the ancient world, the god was rather smitten with the young naiad, her nubile limbs gracefully cutting a swathe through his passionate waters.

Not keen to succumb to her insistently aqueous suitor, she ran away and asked Artemis, the protector of women, for help. The solution was to turn Arethusa into a freshwater spring which made its way underground all the way from Olympia to Ortygia, where she surfaced. Undaunted, Alpheus' current changed direction in order to follow the object of his desire and their waters now mingle in the sacred Ortygian fountain that bears her name. This seems like a plot tailor-made for the Romantic poet and some of England's finest wordsmiths were, indeed, compelled to turn the legend into verse.

Percy Bysshe Shelley, whom we will later meet when discovering that other eternal Sicilian legend of Proserpine, wrote a poem entitled 'Arethusa' to accompany the play that his wife, Mary Shelley, had created on the former subject. Intended for a younger audience, the poem covers the entire story, finishing with a Syracusan flourish:

> And at night they sleep
> In the rocking deep
> Beneath the Ortygian shore;
>
> Like spirits that lie
> In the azure sky,
> When they love but live no more.

10 *The Arethusa Fountain at the edge of the island of Ortygia, Syracuse*

Shelley's contemporary and fellow Romantic, Samuel Taylor Coleridge, also dipped his toes in Alpheus' stream. In one of the most famous opening verses in the English language, Coleridge references the mythic waters: 'In Xanadu did Kubla Khan/A stately pleasure-dome decree/Where Alph, the sacred river, ran/Through caverns measureless to man . . .' Unlike Percy Bysshe, Samuel Taylor had first-hand knowledge of Syracuse. In 1804, his opium addiction was deepening and his relationship with his wife, Sara, was going from bad to worse. So it was a mentally agitated Coleridge who stepped ashore in Valletta, Malta, in May of that year. As we know from the Caravaggio story, the route between Malta and Syracuse was a busy shipping lane.

Very soon after arriving in Malta, Coleridge was appointed as private secretary to Sir Andrew Bell, part of the governing English garrison on the island. The required task of report writing was something he could almost achieve in his sleep, allowing the reawakening of his long dormant desire to visit Sicily. There was one poem he had already written with more than just a passing reference to the place. In 1800 he penned 'The Mad Monk', based on 'Anselmo' by Mary Robinson. He had also been reviewing the works of Ann Radcliffe, including the supernatural tale entitled *A Sicilian Romance*. Her Gothic Mediterranean stories could easily have had their own influence here. Coleridge's monk is a somewhat reluctant recluse who is looking for an end to his sadness.

> I heard a voice from Etna's side;
>> Where, o'er a cavern's mouth,
>> That fronted to the south,
> A chestnut spread its umbrage wide:
> A hermit, or a monk, the man might be;
> But him I could not see;
> And thus the music flow'd along,
> In melody most like to old Sicilian song:
>
> 'There was a time when earth, and sea, and skies,
>> The bright green vale, and forest's dark recess,
> With all things, lay before mine eyes
>> In steady loveliness:
> But now I feel, on earth's uneasy scene,
>> Such sorrows as will never cease; –
>> I only ask for peace [. . .]

The poem may also reflect Coleridge's own uneasy state of mind at the time. Peace from the sorrows of opium craving was his quest. For the time being though, happy to escape the landscape of the Valletta hinterland, Samuel boarded a ship to Syracuse in August 1804 for an extended stay on the much larger island, where he remained until November. He based himself in Syracuse with the British consul, Leckie.

He wrote to his wife detailing two trips to the peak of Etna but his real passion was for the opera. In his notebooks, the poet writes fervently about the music: 'Of the Quintetta in the Syracuse opera and the pleasure of the voices – one and not one, they leave, seek, pursue, oppose, fight with, strengthen, annihilate each other, awake, enliven, soothe, flatter, and embrace each other again, till at length they die away in one tone.' Since Coleridge's day, the opera house has been somewhat altered; the present building can be found in Ortygia, halfway down Via Roma. The Teatro Massimo, as it is known, is currently silent, its tones of operatic embrace muted owing to lengthy restoration.

It was not just the music, though, that attracted the attentions of Samuel Taylor. A certain soprano by the name of Cecilia Bertozzoli had taken a shine to him. The trips to the opera became increasingly frequent but his strolls to the performances were tortured. He regularly passed a stand of poplar trees which reminded him of the similar scent he had experienced five years before in more idyllic times with his wife. The association permeated the guilt he felt in making regular post-performance dates with the lead singer – 'the aromatic smell of the poplars came upon me! What recollections, if I were worthy of indulging them.'

Coleridge calls his Sicilian soprano 'P.D.' in his notebooks, short for prima donna. Unlike Byron or Shelley, who gave themselves up to passion, he stopped short of abandoning himself to the inevitable sexual conclusion of their blossoming relationship. In her biography of Coleridge during these years, Molly Lefebre tells us that La Bertozzoli got the poet to her bedside only to see him disappear into the night with his conscience intact; though Lefebre is fairly certain that this incident took place on Samuel Taylor's second visit to Syracuse in 1805, owing to the extended nature of their relationship.

If the opera had become something of an addiction, it paled in comparison to his fight with opium. After initial attempts to break his habit, Sicily was proving too much of an emotional rollercoaster with too ready a supply of opiates to forswear the demon that had taken such a hold. Originally prescribed laudanum to ease rheumatic pain, he had long since been fighting the obsession. Prone to depression, he often lamented his dulled senses and lack of impetus – something which struck home with particular vehemence whilst in Syracuse for his thirty-second birthday.

Sicily grew the opium poppy for the harvesting of the drug, and Coleridge took more than a passing interest in its cultivation and production. However, he was genuinely taken with the raw nature he found on the island, whether it be the olive trees, vines, choking brambles, scampering lizards or the climate. This quote, appearing in *Anima Poetae*, comes from his notebooks and is dated September 1805 – it has the ring of drug-induced fancy but does capture his fascination with eternal Sicily, a land blasted by the sun: 'the dawning and setting sun, at the same time the zodiac – while each, in its own hour, boasts and beholds the exclusive Presence, a peculiar Orb each the great Traveller's inn, yet still the unmoving Sun-Great genial Agent in all finite souls.'

Samuel Taylor's role as an administrator on Malta gave him ample opportunity to observe government at close quarters. His Mediterranean years coincided with the height of the Napoleonic wars and Britain's consequent involvement in the politics of Sicily. With a degree of hindsight, Coleridge wrote in 1834 of his strong opinions on the governance he had witnessed on the island:

> Really you may learn the fundamental principles of political economy in a very compendious way, by taking a short tour through Sicily, and simply reversing in your own mind every law, custom, and ordinance you meet with. I never was in a country in which everything proceeding from man was so exactly wrong.

It has to be said that he must have approached these laws and ordinances with the mindset of an Englishman used to playing by the rules, rather than with the unspoken understanding of a native who realises how the nuisance of government, usually imposed by an outsider, is to be either ignored or manoeuvred around.

Coleridge was scathing of the 1812 attempts by the British to give Sicily a constitution and assembly, noting that it 'passed two bills before it was knocked on the head'. Despite these lofty opinions of a northern

European, he was fair-minded enough to recognise that 'to tax the people in countries like Sicily and Corsica, where there is no internal communication, is mere robbery and confiscation.'

If Coleridge looked back on his Sicilian months with a more political than personal eye, his notebooks written at the time convey a different story. He was not the only poet to have found his time in Syracuse one of personal tumult, although some might say this is the natural state of a Romantic. The war poet, Siegfried Sassoon, however, had more reason than most to understand life's turmoil. Born in Kent of Sephardic Jewish ancestry, he is best known for prose and poetry tackling World War I – some of which was written from the trenches and some with the emotional distance of hindsight.

Sassoon's earlier life was characterised by his indifference to the opposite sex and a strong homosexual attraction which he fought for many years. In 1927, he met Stephen Tennant – a painter, aristocrat and androgynous beauty. Siegfried was smitten, leading the writer, Edith Sitwell, to imagine them as an elder noble and his indulged protégé. Two years later, the pair took a trip to the continent with the ultimate destination of Sicily in order to ease Stephen's lung condition.

On the way, they stopped at Rapallo near Genoa, staying at the residence of Max Beerbohm. This was one of those idyllic periods when conversation, company and wine seemed to make everything shine. Sassoon's biographer, Jean Moorcroft Wilson, reports that whilst in Rapallo they also paid a visit to Yeats – Siegfried's only comment on the meeting being that he considered Yeats something of a poseur. Via Naples, the pair eventually landed in Palermo on 20 December.

Sassoon was caught in the trap of either paying attention to his writing or giving in to the clamorous requests of his insistent partner. Conflict was inevitably on its way. For the time being, the couple travelled Sicily's back roads on a classical itinerary that took in the usual sites, including Agrigento. The final stop saw them take up residence at the Hotel Villa Politi on the Syracusan mainland close to both the coastline and the archaeological zone of Neapolis. The hotel, in ornate belle époque style flushed with rich wooden panels, formerly belonged to the aristocratic artist Salvatore Politi and was later used by Winston

Churchill during the Allied invasion of Italy – the hotel bar now bears his name. Other famous guests have included two of Italy's prominent writers: Edmondo De Amicis and Gabriele D'Annunzio.

Stephen Tennant needed Siegfried's full attention and the sunny Syracusan climate. What the war poet really wanted to do was spend his days writing the work he was currently intent on finishing, *Memoirs of an Infantry Officer*. As the title suggests, it is a true account of his war years, albeit fictionalised on a personal level. It takes the reader from his initial acceptance to a questioning of the mindless slaughter. The pair eventually worked out a compromise whereby Siegfried had the morning to write whilst Stephen sunbathed or sketched. The afternoons were spent sightseeing or beachcombing. Within two and a half months the book was completed.

Another partially autobiographical work to come from his time on the island was the poem entitled 'In Sicily'. When published in the Ariel Poems series, it was accompanied by one of Tennant's drawings of a Sicilian lemon:

> Because we two can never again come back
> On life's one forward track, –
> Never again first-happily explore
> This valley of rocks and vines and orange-trees,
> Half Biblical and half Hesperides,
> With dark blue seas calling from a shell-strewn shore:
> > By the strange power of Spring's resistless green,
> > Let us be true to what we have shared and seen,
> > And as our amulet our idyll save.
> > And since the unreturning day must die,
> > Let it for ever be lit by an evening sky
> > And the wild myrtle grow upon its grave.

The forward track Sassoon references would eventually continue without Stephen. This poem appears to presage the demise of their relationship whilst retaining the power of the memories they shared writing, drawing and exploring Syracuse. Their relationship ended in the early 1930s when Tennant drifted away from his older lover. Implausibly, Siegfried married – once again attempting to conform – and had a son called George. The marriage was not to last, ending in 1944 – he eventually turned to the Catholic Church.

For a more light-hearted approach to time spent in Syracuse, we look to Frances Minto Elliot, the archetypical Victorian female traveller and writer, whose story belies another complicated private life. Her book, *The Diary of an Idle Woman in Sicily*, contains nothing of the divorce, separation and literary friendships with the great and good that form part of her biography. She divorced John Geils of Glasgow and separated from her second husband, the Reverend Gilbert Elliot, all of which took place at a time when any marital disharmony was quietly brushed under the carpet.

Frances spent a significant portion of her life in Italy, and Ortygia was one of those destinations that had magical qualities for her: 'I was dying to see Syracuse. My vision by day, my dream by night.'

She had hooked up with a Scottish doctor she calls 'The Physic' in her diary. Upon arriving in Syracuse, she is literally grabbed by a well-dressed young man who hauls her towards an awaiting carriage, informing the surprised Frances that she is an English princess and that the prefect of the town has insisted she be escorted to the hotel. The high camp of this scene is only added to by the indignant Scotsman, no doubt ranting at the top of his voice, as Minto Elliot tries to explain that he should not be left behind. Elliot translates for the doctor, who is convinced that the young man is going to take off with his baggage.

As with most Georgian and Victorian travellers, the antiquities were the biggest draw. Frances does her best to inform her readers of the fact that from the classical period Syracuse was not simply one area or one district: 'A city consisting of four or five cities or suburbs, each with its own name, history, and monuments, further divided into two parts, Outer Syracuse on the mainland, and Inner Syracuse on the island.' She lists Inner Syracuse as being the new town, a misleading statement to the modern visitor as the outer ruins at Neapolis have been surrounded by development from the 1960s and 1970s. Only one bridge used to connect the island of Ortygia to the mainland but today there are three – a true sign of the incursion of modernity.

For Minto Elliot and Sassoon, Syracuse was the destination; for Washington Irving it was the starting point and his first impressions were not favourable when compared to his expectations – 'But, heavens! What a change! Streets gloomy and ill-built, and poverty, filth, and misery on every side.' That is not to say he was without entertainment; he was quick to take up an invitation to a masquerade, very similar to the one he was to experience in Termini Imerese. Irving's visit in 1804/5 only just failed to coincide with that of Samuel Taylor Coleridge. It is an interesting prospect to imagine the writer of *Sleepy Hollow* conversing with the poet who created the *Ancient Mariner* during a ball being held at Coleridge's favourite theatre.

Irving dressed himself up as a physician ('which was the only dress I could procure') and spent the evening speaking in a mixture of English, Tuscan Italian and French – a pidgin blend that persuaded his guests he was a Sicilian. Happy to blow his own social trumpet, it seems he was the centre of attention: 'As I knew many anecdotes of almost all of them, I teased them the whole evening, till at length one of them discovered me by my voice which I happened not to disguise at the moment.'

Syracuse's reputation always precedes it. Patrick Brydone, another happy acceptor of Sicilian aristocratic hospitality, wrote aboard his boat heading for the city that he was setting sail for 'the mighty Syracuse'. His initial impressions were much less scathing than Irving's, although he found it so reduced in size he could not secure bed and board for any period of time. Apart from the Greek heritage, he was most attracted to the fortifications on Ortygia, namely Castello Maniace, enhanced by the Spanish king and still located at the farthest point, guarding access to both harbours: 'Here he has raised a noble fortification, which appears to be almost impregnable. There are four strong gates, one within the other, with each a glacis, covered way, scarp and counterscarp.' His admiration for the construction stops short of its equipment and manpower, there being no artillery on display and only one battery of cannons designed for salute. This may well have reflected the perilous state of the Bourbon monarchy, fast approaching the nineteenth century.

Both Brydone and Minto Elliot make reference to Cicero, the great Roman orator, lawyer and writer. Cicero's full story will be told when we reach Trapani and Marsala – he was the former regional administrator for that district of the Roman Empire. Nevertheless, it would be a shame to miss his literary and legal input with regard to Syracuse. As we will later discover in more detail, Cicero was given the task of prosecuting Caius Verres, one of the earlier examples in Sicily's long history of foreign-dominated, often corrupt, governors. Caius stood accused of systematically robbing Sicily of its wealth.

Cicero came to Syracuse to gather evidence, but it was also a chance to indulge his Grecophilia, for he clearly acknowledged the debt Roman culture owed to its Greek counterpart. In the written *Pleadings against Caius Verres*, the orator's leanings are clear: 'I will now, my Lords, commemorate and expatiate upon the plunder of Syracuse, the most beautiful and splendid of cities.' The essence of the prosecutor's oratory is worthy of investigation, but the most approachable aspect of his writing concerns the description he gives us of how the city looked in Roman times:

> the part of the city which is called the island, separated by a narrow channel, is joined to the main land by a bridge. So vast is Syracuse, that it may be said to consist of four large cities. One of these, as I before stated is, the island, which surrounded by the two havens, is projected to the entrance of either [. . .] Here there are many temples, but there are two superior to all the others; one is consecrated to Diana, the other, highly embellished before the arrival of Verres, to Minerva.

This description finds echoes in the output of Frances Minto Elliot. Roman Syracuse had a population that considerably outweighed the much reduced settlement when Brydone visited centuries later. It is only the advent of rapid development in the twentieth century that has seen census figures soar past the levels of antiquity. To confuse things further, it would be fruitless to try and look for the temple dedicated to Diana (Artemis) as the authorities have labelled it as the Tempio di Apollo. If churches can change name then it is reasonable to expect something similar with Greek and Roman religious buildings.

Cicero labels the fourth district Neapolis, or New Town – as we know it is a name that still applies today, although most visitors will find it marked on maps as the Parco Archeologico. This 'new' area was the last to be built by the Greeks. The zone, at the top of Corso Gelone, can be visited and still includes much described by the Roman writer. He mentions 'a large theatre' where the plays of Aeschylus were often staged. It is now more common to find Andrea Bocelli performing here, but there is also an annual Greek theatre festival.

Aeschylus' drama has a philosophical core, which Cicero himself attributed to the playwright's Pythagorean thinking. The works performed at the theatre show a belief in the future existence of the soul, the importance of oaths, names, numbers and the need for a moral compass in life. The *Oresteia* trilogy, written whilst he was living in Sicily, has at its heart man's relationship with divinity and all its capricious commands and punishments.

This excerpt from *The Eumenides*, the last part of the trilogy, encapsulates divine whim. Orestes, already overwhelmed by the Furies for having killed Clytemnestra and Aegisthus, now turns up to a summons at the Temple of Minerva:

> Hither, divine Minerva, by command
> Of Phoebius, am I come. Propitious power
> Receive me, by the Furies' tort'ring rage
> Pursued, no vile unhallow'd wretch, nor stain'd
> With guilty blood, but worn with toil, and spent
>
> With many a painful step to other shrines,
> And in the paths of men. By land, by sea
> Wearied alike, obedient to the voice,
> The oracle of Phoebius, I approach
> Thy shrine, thy statue, Goddess; here to fix
> My stand, till judgment shall decide my cause.

If Ancient Greek drama can seem daunting, an easier way into the realm of Grecian Syracuse is through modern-day historical fiction, one of whose leading exponents is the Italian author Valerio Massimo Manfredi. Manfredi has reconstructed in novel form the story of Dionysius. *The Tyrant* (*Il tiranno*) tells the story of Dionysius' rise to power from the ranks of combatant. Witness to the sack of Selinunte by the Carthaginians and tired of democratic practices, Dionysius would raise Syracuse to the heights.

A professor of classical archaeology in Milan, Manfredi is more qualified than most to given a portrait of the city's most infamous ruler. On the plus side, Dionysius was a statesman and man of letters, who invested in his city and its defences. In the sweep of just two paragraphs Manfredi is able to illustrate both this inclination to consolidate battles won and the paranoid side of a dictator who cannot abide to be found wanting – 'As soon as he had returned to Syracuse, Dionysius commenced a couple of ambitious construction projects: a fortified residence connected to the dockyards in the heart of the old city, and a wall that blocked off the isthmus of Ortygia'. It was not the building endeavour that riled his enemies, but the construction of battleships that proved a step too far. His reaction to their anger was swift: 'He unleashed his mercenaries, who conducted massive house-to-house searches, arrested all his opponents and brought them to the fortress in Ortygia.'

The fortress was not the only place the tyrant supposedly kept his prisoners. In the archaeological park there is the so-called 'Ear of Dionysius': the cave is part of the aforementioned Latomie quarries that were used to construct many of the city's ancient edifices. The Ear has a peculiar acoustic property allowing sound to travel to the top like a funnel and to reverberate in a series of echoes back to the floor. Given the shape of the entrance and the amplification of sound, it was a visiting Caravaggio who christened the grotto the Ear of Dionysius.

The space, full of chisel marks from slave workers, would have been an excellent place to corral an ill-used workforce. It is said that the tyrant's guard placed himself at the small outlet near the top of the ear, thereby sitting in a position where he could freely hear all talk from below. This may be a case of artistic licence creating mythical reality, but it is certainly true that the Latomie quarries as a whole were used by some rulers as a gaol.

Frances Minto Elliot was accompanied to the Ear by her erstwhile guide, Giuliano. As Brydone says, the cave and quarry complex was almost inaccessible in the late 1700s, just as it continued to be in the early 1800s; therefore a trip into its heart was something of an adventure – not to mention undertaking the trip alone with a foreign woman. Frances was all too aware of this and seemed more amused than worried; it was her guide who found the excursion a new experience, as 'from crimson his cheeks have passed to purple'.

She longed to quiz Giuliano about the origins of the Ear but her text clearly shows he had clammed up with the anxiety of it all. Relying on her own impressions, she compares the cave entrance to Arab design: 'Dionysius' Ear is the strangest-shaped arch I ever beheld. Long and narrow, and ending in a sharp point, perfectly Saracenic.' This is a beautiful description of what appears to be a Moorish inspiration, although this has no basis in fact. Prior to Minto Elliot, Washington Irving visited and was rather scathing of previous writers' accounts, calling them 'careless'. He is more prosaic and less artistic in his descriptions:

> The Ear is a vast serpentine cavern, something in the form of the letter g reversed; its greatest width is at the bottom, from whence it narrows with an inflection to the top, something like the external shape of an ass's ear. Its height is about eighty or ninety feet, and its length about one hundred and twenty. It is the same height and dimensions from the entrance to the extremity where it ends abruptly.

Such precise analysis is worthy of Goethe but it does give a realistic picture. Why such fuss over a hole in the rock? The approach through lush vegetation and fallen Doric masonry is Brydone's 'subterraneous garden' and we can do no better than agree with his further impression, that it is 'one of the most beautiful and romantic spots I ever beheld'; although, in order to do this, you have to empty your mind of any thoughts relating to its use as a prison. The thousands of Athenian troops held captive in the rocky basin were barely given sufficient food or water to survive. Many withered away to an agonising death.

Like countless places of high romance, the quarry has an infinitely darker side.

One writer and doctor who would become the father of psychoanalysis was well-qualified to investigate the darker side. Sigmund Freud, whom we first met in Palermo, found Syracuse a significant point of reference. The city was a final important stop in his search for Magna Graecia. Freud was much taken with Wilhelm Jensen's story, *Gradiva*, analysing its Oedipal nature, which he concluded was still alive in the normal adult male. Rosalba Galvagno explains that he extended the theory to the actual cities of Rome and Syracuse, the former being the manifestation of the father and the latter, a maternal representation. A visit to Syracuse fed both his love of archaeological investigation and his metaphorical analysis of the city.

Freud, once again accompanied by Sándor Ferenczi, stayed in the Hotel des Ètrangers facing the Arethusa Fountain. The hotel, a grandiose affair, still offers luxurious accommodation. Its modern spa, complete with lion-headed water jets, carries on the long Arethusan tradition of taking the waters. Sigmund was happy with the hotel despite Syracuse being plagued with the foreboding signs of a forthcoming sirocco wind. Perhaps expecting the Ortygia of his analytical dreams, he was less disposed to praise the little island, complaining of the smell and the huddled conditions. His destination of choice was obviously going to be Neapolis.

Freud also found great interest in the archaeological museum and its Hellenistic collections. Galvagno, in 'Freud and Greater Greece', tells us how the depictions of the feminine made the psychoanalyst reflect on Sicily as the island of childhood memories. A month after his visit, the statuary would still be making incursions into his dreams. In addition, Sicily and Syracuse make an appearance in his communications and letters, including those to other theorists like Karl Abraham and Wilhelm Fliess. As Diane Chauvelot indicates, Syracuse 1910 was a watershed in his thoughts.

The city affords any visitor the chance to cherry-pick their historical époque and influence. Greece may dominate the thoughts of the majority but Spain is also very evident. The Spanish imperial domination gave

Charles V the opportunity to raise the city walls and build bridges on the remains of Hiero's palace. As with everywhere in Sicily, history is interlaced. Minto Elliot remarks on this literal mingling of construction in the city's buildings: 'One can see the huge, uncemented Greek blocks worked into the Spanish masonry, a strange link between the Classic Tyrants who trod out political liberty in Sicily, and the mediaeval Tyrant, who failed to tread it out in Flanders.'

If the structures of Sicilian cities are complicated, so are the reputations of great men who have influenced this land. Ask differing nationalities about Charles V and you will receive as many different replies as countries. A similar thing could be said of Lord Nelson, the archetypical English hero in the face of Napoleonic threat. To those fighting against the Bourbons in Naples, he was an oppressor and, to the Maniace peasants, some of his relatives were the worst of 'feudal' rulers.

Despite the ambiguity felt by Sicilians to the years of Spanish domination, there is little doubt they share a common historical bond, evidenced by the thoughts of Leonardo Sciascia. The Andalucian, Alejandro Luque, compares Syracuse to his home town of Cadiz, a similarly situated finger of land jutting into the sea. One of his favourite poets is Adam Zagajewski – a Polish émigré to Paris who returned to Krakow in 2002. In the course of visits to Sicily, Zagajewski penned verses inspired by past glories, including one about the temple at Segesta, but it is his hymn to Syracuse that captures the Greco-Hispanic coupling: 'City with the loveliest name, Siracusa;/don't let me forget the dim/antiquity of your side streets, the pouting balconies/that once caged Spanish ladies.'

That other literary maestro of Luque's, Jorge Luis Borges, referenced Simonides of Ceos in his tale 'Funes, the Memorious'. Simonides, a friend and confidant of the ruler Hiero, spent his last days here. He is said to have created the memory technique of mnemonics. As Alejandro relunctantly prepares to leave the city, he calls up the spirit of Simonides: 'I'd like to be a mnemonic virtuoso in order to retain the names of all the doors, windows, limestone façades shining in the sunset, and so many of the other details too, but it would be all in vain, as this city seems simply unforgettable.'

Unforgettable, yes, but also leaveable. The Sicilian writer and native Syracusan Elio Vittorini was forced to leave to further his career. Few Sicilian writers have escaped the pull of the mainland at some point in their lives, in the same way that Paris and London have sucked in cultural talent from their provinces. Vittorini was born in Via Veneto on the island of Ortygia. His *casa natale* at number 138 is marked with a plaque commemorating the fact. The house, however, is otherwise unremarkable and slipping into gentle decay. The city has a literary centre (*parco letterario*) dedicated to the promulgation of Vittorini's work in Via Polibio on the Syracusan mainland. It forms part of the Pegaso Cultural Association.

Walks are available that take in the sites fundamental to Vittorini's life and work, including those in *The Red Carnation* (*Il garofano rosso*) and *Conversations in Sicily* (*Conversazione in Sicilia*). Not only was his childhood peripatetic, owing to his father's job on the railways, but in adulthood he also moved around, first to Florence then to Milan, where he was arrested for anti-Fascist activity during World War II. After the conflict, he concentrated on his work as an editor and writer. *Conversations in Sicily*, first drafted in autumn 1937 at the height of the Spanish Civil War, tells the story of a man's return to his native island and his quest for meaning in life.

The tracks of his return are literal. Vittorini sends him home on the very railways his father would have worked on. Ernest Hemingway was a fan of the novel and an afterword written by the American appears in the English translation. He compares Vittorini to rain – a metaphor which he extends to critics who only feed on the dried earth of dispute. For Hemingway, Vittorini is 'the smell of sweet-grass and fresh smoked leather and Sicily'. The protagonist's ticket to ride has the penultimate destination of Syracuse's main station, followed by branch lines to his mother's house in Grammichele.

The central character, narrating the text, converses with his fellow passengers, partaking of their packed lunches and discovering a little of their lives. As the train pulls into Syracuse station, he finds himself in conversation with a land registry worker whilst sharing his omelette. The narrator was born in the city but seems indifferent to his arrival.

His internal dialogue recounts the trip he has taken and the rationale for coming – reiterating all his encounters along the way:

> But I had come to know the man with the oranges, With Whiskers and Without Whiskers, the Big Lombard, the man from Catania, the little old man with the voice of a dry piece of straw, the young malaria victim wrapped in his shawl, and it seemed to me that maybe it did make some difference whether I was in Siracusa or somewhere else.

The second half of the book focuses on discussions with the mother he has not seen for 15 years in addition to various other inhabitants of the town. Through the conversations we see a snapshot of Sicily during this period. The book is political but obscured by the linguistic wrapping that Hemingway assures us Vittorini had to use in order to avoid the Fascist censors. It means that we can still appreciate the lives of individuals and understand their interactions without obviously political interventions.

Vittorini's language has a lyrical content; he delights in wordplay as we can see from the use of the nicknames of With Whiskers and Without Whiskers in the above quote. This playfulness was taken to extremes by another foreign visitor to the city, Edward Lear. Lear, of *The Owl and the Pussycat* fame, also found an outlet for his humour through art. His tour of Sicily is commemorated in a letter but, more significantly perhaps, via his annotated cartoons.

In 1847, Edward travelled with John Proby, later Lord Proby. The pair's journey is celebrated in the work *Lear in Sicily*, a text spearheaded by 20 of Lear's sketches. To give a flavour of his limerick style, the frontispiece contains a limerick to Etna: 'There was a young person of Gretna/Who jumped down the crater of Etna,/When they asked "Is it hot?"/He replied "It is not!"/That mendacious young person of Gretna.'

The letter appearing within the main body of the text, sent to Chichester Fortescue, lamented the lack of his company in a city Edward enjoyed so much: 'Siracuse only wanted your presence to make our stay more pleasant: I waited for and expected you every day. We abode in a quarry *per lo più*, & left the place sorryly.' To what extent Lear actually stayed in the Latomie can be taken with a pinch of salt. From Syracuse, Proby and Lear went to another cave complex in the nearby town of Ispica. His letter and drawings refer to his visit.

Lear christened the cave-dwellers troglodytes, trogs and even froglodytes. There is no doubt his intentions were humorous but with the benefit of distance, his drawings could be seen as rather condescending to the proud inhabitants of these grottoes. The caves, built by the Greeks, continued in use until the end of the nineteenth century. Dwellers were thin on the ground when Lear visited and he claimed to have seen the last remaining family. In one of his cartoons, he shows himself and his companion, Proby, dressed in full Victorian regalia complete with spectacles and hat, confronting a hirsute patriarch with rotund belly and pointed ears. The mother, similarly portrayed, is holding a baby which, in another sketch, Lear nurses as if afraid of its impending evacuations.

Edward fleshed out his sketches of the troglodytes in his letter to Fortescue. His patronising tone is, nonetheless, touched with some affection: 'they are very good creatures, mostly sitting on their hams, & feeding on lettuces and honey. I proposed bringing away an infant Frog, but Proby objected.' These excursions were lengthy, through terrain that was not always easy to pass, but their *giro* should have been at a pace suitable to Proby's recovery from 'Roman fever'. It seems that the two were only distant acquaintances before their Sicilian adventure, having met in Rome. Edward found John a companion of 'a perfectly good temper', perhaps a fellow traveller who was too happy to accommodate Lear's whims and speed, given the ill-health that ultimately led to his death only 11 years later.

Lear never married, having two proposals to the same woman refused. His male friendships often reflected the strength of his homosexual feelings. Adopting Italy, he finally settled in the north, in Sanremo, the site of his burial. He was to make subsequent trips back to the eastern side of Sicily, receiving news of Proby's death whilst in Messina. Lear admitted he was never as kind to John as their travels together ought to have dictated. Syracuse was one of the highlights.

Edward Lear was very English in his eccentricities, sometimes introducing himself with extravagant pseudonyms, including the following: Abebika kratoponoko Prizzikalo – just the beginning of a whimsical name that continues with a stream of equally unintelligible syllables. When the Sicilians wanted to label the poet Lucio Piccolo, they placed his work firmly in the fold of Baroque influence, but were happy to categorise his peculiar aristocratic demeanour as English. The Irish, however, are seen in a different light. The website www.medcelt.org, home to *Feile-Festa* (the literary arts journal of the Mediterranean Celtic Cultural Association) contains a wonderful list of comparisons between the two islands.

One writer from the Emerald Isle who went in search of the different and ended up with the recognisable, is Sean O'Faolain. He ends his book *South to Sicily* with the following: 'When I look now at the mountains of Cork or Kerry, silent across a silent bay, I see Calabria and the South. The strange has become more familiar; a life that I have always known has deepened and become more strange.' Born in 1900, he was a story writer, biographer, travel diarist and former director of the Arts Council of Ireland. His trip to the far south-east of Sicily has a flavour of Vittorini's railway return.

In Syracuse, O'Faolain eschewed the luxuries of the Politi Hotel, staying close to the harbour in Viale Giuseppe Mazzini. Victorian travellers commonly complained about the state of accommodation in the town, Minto Elliot being one of them. This lament could be said to date even further back to Brydone and his difficulties in finding somewhere suitable to stay. Just 52 years after the demise of the Victorian era, Sean was more than happy with his arrangements; in fact, Syracuse positively shines – 'We have everything we could desire in Siracusa: scenery, climate, the most affecting antiquities outside Rome, good hotels, a natural town-life, the constant flicker of a pleasant port.'

Guided around the town, he was bombarded with classical facts. Archimedes is one name that leaps from his pages, being born and having died in Syracuse. Most known for his 'claw' used to defend the city from naval attack and his 'screw' to extract bilge water from large ships, this proto-scientist's place in the general public consciousness is forever linked to one word: 'Eureka!' – shouted as his body displaced the water in his bath, thus proferring a solution to the problem of measuring the volume of an object. Archimedes has become a folk legend, a status O'Faolain attributes to Dionysius of Ear fame. His guide was keen to show him the site of the tyrant's battle with the Carthaginians – a location that also saw the landing of Allied troops in 1943.

The city of Syracuse has been gracious enough to donate a stretch of land on its outskirts in memory of those Allied forces who fell in the Sicilian landings of World War II. A plaque on either side of the cemetery entrance states the following in Italian and English: 'The land on which this cemetery stands is the gift of the Italian people for the perpetual resting place of the sailors soldiers & airmen who are honoured here.' Behind the marbled columns lie the serried ranks of pristine white gravestones.

## *Pachino*

Alan Whicker, the iconic British broadcaster famous for *Whicker's World*, served in Sicily as part of the British Army's film and photo unit. If you follow the coastline down from Syracuse, you will come to Pachino, almost as far south as it is practical to go without visiting Sicily's outer-lying islands. The beaches and moderate landscape here provided the perfect point for British troops, particularly the Eighth Army, to come ashore. On the stormy night of 9 July 1943, Alan Whicker was part of that invasion.

In his book, *Whicker's War*, he recounts the story of the landing the following morning. After contemplating the forthcoming horrors with an Australian lieutenant, he waded out into the Mediterranean with his camera held above the waves. They had all been briefed to expect heavy resistance from the Wehrmacht but, with Whicker's usual sang-froid, he tells us what he actually experienced:

> In fact, all we faced were a few peasants and goats, and the usual hit-and-run Luftwaffe dive-bombers. It was quite a relaxed way to start an invasion. So far we had on our side most of the military strength and

all the surprise, and as the troops came ashore some of our hesitant Italian enemies – local farm workers – waved and smiled. It's always comforting to have the audience on your side.

During the evening, he could even afford what he calls his 'first European brew-up'. He sat around with comrades drinking billy-can tea, eating bacon and Sicilian tomatoes. It was a benign start to what would prove a very trying 22 months as his photo unit followed the battles all the way to Venice.

Sixty years after those initial first footsteps, Whicker returned to Pachino for his book and accompanying film. Years of experience in travel had taught him to expect a skewed version of nostalgia – time moves on and vistas are prone to the riggers of development. He was amazed to find that 'this time my old battlefront sanctuaries of 60 years ago were . . . *unchanged*.' It is a bittersweet experience as he alternates between joy and sadness, mourning the fact that not one of his old colleagues or, indeed, enemies are around to hear his news. But it was the same sand, 'soft and sympathetic and still ready to embrace and sustain a flinching body diving for cover'. Today, the yielding sand offers the same comfort to sunbathers and novice windsurfers.

In memory of the fallen we turn to *Poems from Italy*, a slim volume of 72 poems compiled from a competition held amongst troops during the first nine months of the Italian campaign. Private A. Dove wrote 'Impresario, South of Syracuse' in July 1943 – his words speak for themselves:

> On, on, laden with kit,
> Our nostrils twitch with the scent
> Of wild mint and thyme.
> Past olive groves, with trees in rows
> Looking serenely on,
> Tossing their heads, as a faint wind
> Sets them chattering
> On the follies of man.

## *Noto*

From Pachino, *Whicker's War* moved to Noto. Fortunately, for the good of our universal artistic inheritance, Noto was spared any significant damage, at least on that occasion. In 1693 an earthquake obliterated the town and gave a free hand to those intent on rebuilding it. The architect, historian and television presenter Francesco da Mosto describes this new city as 'a masterpiece of Baroque town planning, unique for its size and homogeneity, achieving a marvellous visual balance between the solid structures of the palaces and churches and the open spaces of the squares and streets, and perfect harmony between materials and styles'.

Noto, together with the rest of the region, is designated a UNESCO World Heritage area known as the Val di Noto. The buildings shine with the aura of golden honeycomb – a fitting colour for Vincent Cronin's quest. He was also struck by the town's uniformity of style and attributes the desire to create something special to a blitz-like spirit and the significant patronage of rich citizens.

In common with Zagajewski in Syracuse, Cronin spotlights the balconies, something which the town council literally do when the light begins to fade into night. Vincent says that the 'balconies are highly elegant features of the buildings, with a complex form: in many balustrades the metalwork curves outwards to give a pompous, inflated appearance in harmony with the eighteenth-century building'.

One palazzo in particular which draws most visitors' attention is the Villadorata in Via Nicolaci. Mermaids, lions and rampant horses support the voluptuous, bulging wrought-iron balconies. These sculptures do not have the shock effect of Prince Gravina's grotesques in Bagheria; rather they are playful sentinels designed to entice and attract instead of repel. Cronin compares their forms to those on Gothic cathedrals, but with the lightness of a southern Baroque touch. He also notes the chiaroscuro effect, particularly prevalent when the Sicilian sun catches them at certain times of day. The intricate carving, pushed to depths of scale, is defined by the deep shadows cast by a brilliant sun. The overall tonal contrast is something that would surely have appealed to Caravaggio.

*11 The Baroque cathedral of Noto*

The source of these buildings' beauty is also the source of their potential demise. The limestone with which they are constructed is immensely prone to the processes of elemental weathering. Close investigation of the structures reveals pitting and pock marks on every edifice. It is not long since the cathedral had to be partially reconstructed owing to the crumbling of its central cupola. This fragile beauty is realised in another of Adam Zagajewski's Sicilian poems, 'Noto':

> Noto, a town that would be flawless
> if only our faith were greater.
>
> Noto, a baroque town where even
> the stables and arbors are ornate.
>
> The cathedral's cupola has collapsed, alas,
> and heavy cranes surround it

like doctors in a hospital
tending the dangerously ill.

Afternoons town teenagers
gather on the main street

and bored stiff, whistle
like captive thrushes.

The town is too perfect
for its inhabitants.

Zagajewski is credited with a clear economy of style and a dry sense
of humour. This can be glimpsed in the above verses, where the town's
youthful population are unaware of the iconic architectural jewel they
inhabit – not a phenomenon peculiar to Sicily – we all need to grow
into our surroundings. If the town is too perfect for its inhabitants, the
1970s town planners tried to make it a little less so. The outskirts now
show the all too familiar signs of characterless concrete. Fortunately, the
centre is still living in its Baroque time-warp.

The colourful wordsmith Duncan Fallowell found his perfect view of
Noto obscured by an angular modern hospital he likened to 'a chunk of
Brasilia'. Fallowell had Noto as his ultimate destination, where he was
intent on finding that last flowering of European magnificence before
other cultures pursued their own differing ideas of perfection. In his
book, quirkily titled *To Noto, Or London to Sicily in a Ford*, he details
every experience on the way to his architectural nirvana. When we say
every experience, it is no lie.

Born in 1948 and Oxford educated in history, he started his career
as a critic in the genres of rock music and film, before moving on to
fiction. His first book was a biography entitled *April Ashley's Odyssey*,
the account of a young boy's struggle with his sexual identity resulting
in a sex change that would lead to a successful career as a fashion
model. Subsequent novels written in the 1980s include *Satyrday* and

*The Underbelly*. Much of the decade was spent roaming the byways of Europe in search of the interesting, obscure, the louche and cerebral.

Fallowell's prose veers from the heights of historical insight and academic description to the depths of a seeming obsession with his own bodily functions, faeces in particular. Using a strategically placed tree to obscure his Brasilia hospital, Duncan even indulges his coprophilia to describe the perfect scene he has been searching out – 'by moving not an inch forwards or backwards or to left or right, I find myself gazing at last upon the shitless city of my dreams.'

The journey to Noto was originally triggered by a conversation with Sacheverell Sitwell and is peppered with literary encounters, including Harold Acton in Florence, Gore Vidal in Ravello and Leonardo Sciascia in Palermo. In his book Duncan recounts how he and his friend Von were guided around Noto by an English teacher who was keen to ditch his English as soon as possible, finding the linguistic and physical effort in the height of summer a little tiresome. He tells Fallowell he is a member of Pro Noto, an organisation designed to help fight for restoration. It is an association that still exists to this day, placing an emphasis on the development of responsible tourism in the region – a fact that Fallowell lamented, believing that one of Noto's beauties lies in its role as a 'real town'.

Von, his travelling companion, describes the town as a 'smaller, quieter, fruitier, *hotter* Bath'. The architectural styles are not a perfect match for this south-western English city, but there is a remarkable resemblance in the luminosity of the stone and the creation of a town with coherent historical planning. She goes on to compare the commercial activity of the two, highlighting Bath's prevalence of antique shops and second-hand bookshops. Her suggestion that Noto lacked these, due to a missing middle class, is something that is definitely now changing although it is debatable whether this new business activity is catering to the demands of the local populace or the increasing footfall of tourist traffic.

Continuing their tour, the heat prompted the little party to stop for an ice-cream even though the English teacher opted for water. It is not inappropriate to suggest that the Sicilian ice-cream makers' art has a

Baroque component in keeping with the surroundings of settlements like Noto. Each compartment in the fridge resembles the intricately decorated façade of a building – feast your eyes on the ripples of red swirled through a *spagnolo*, the glistening jewels in a *frutti di bosco* or those balcony-like grilles of dark cacao on domes of *cioccolata*. Fallowell chose a strawberry gelato complete with alpine berries and an intense syrup embellishing the surface.

It was the second to last pleasure before Von had to leave and a slight depression descended. Duncan's last hurrah involved a trip back to Noto Antica – the remains of what existed before the 1693 earthquake prompted the Baroque explosion. Walking through the tumble of cornices and walls, he felt an elemental balance which prompted a bit of nude sunbathing and some musings on the nature of travel. If travel leads to magic and then to exultation, what is the point of it all? 'And the purpose of exultation? . . . To find oneself . . . Which is to say, to lose oneself . . . And the purpose of losing oneself is happiness.' The old town is still worth a visit, if only to feel the peace of nature reclaiming the past. Nude sunbathing may be inadvisable as tourists are more prevalent than in the 1980s of Fallowell's visit.

Sean O'Faolain also visited Noto with a knowledgeable guide who was keen to show Sicily's brightest face to a foreign visitor. He called it a 'flawless day', but was most intent on highlighting the little niggles that any traveller will encounter: no eggs in the restaurant of choice, flies everywhere, two traffic disputes with policemen, one in neighbouring Canicattini. Most of all he felt sympathy for his guide and friend, an intelligent man whose pride had obviously been hurt in the act of doing his best to show the island's worth.

### *Modica*

Having a guide can often prove the key to unlocking understanding. Our own vain attempts at locating the birthplace of Salvatore Quasimodo found us seeking directions from a passing pensioner. With great delight, he took our arms and proceeded to show us not only the house in question, but the nooks and crannies that only a local would know. Quasimodo moved from Modica in his childhood, but the town is happy to claim him as its own. His *casa natale*, in Via Posterla, has the usual wooden shutters and stone supported balconies – it is not a house of Baroque elegance, but a solid presence befitting for a working family. The plaque on the outside quotes in Italian 'And Suddenly it's Evening' ('Ed è subito sera'): 'Everyone is alone on the heart of the earth/pierced by a ray of sun:/and suddenly it's evening.' It also commemorates the date of his birth in 1901 and his Nobel Prize in 1959.

12 *The birthplace and early childhood home of Salvatore Quasimodo, Modica*

In his essay on the origins of his own poetic thought, Quasimodo acknowledges that the borders to his poetry are framed by Sicily: its ancient civilisations in pieces on the grass, its sulphur stone, salt mines, quarries and women crying throughout the centuries for their assassinated sons. His is the Sicily of the Anapo, Ciane, Megara Iblea and the Lentini of Giorgias. Lentini, formerly known as Leontini, is situated to the north of Modica, approximately halfway between Syracuse and Catania. It was home to the pre-Socratic philosopher Giorgias, but also to another important writer referenced by Quasimodo, namely Jacopo da Lentini. In 'A Copper Amphora' ('Un'anfora di rame'), he calls Jacopo the notary of love.

Da Lentini, the thirteenth-century poet sometimes known as Giacomo or Giàcumu, was a notary as well as a versifier who worked for Frederick II. He was considered the cream of the influential Sicilian School of poetry by none other than Dante Alighieri. We know he is best remembered as the presumed inventor of the sonnet form with much of his work concerning the vagaries of love: 'My newborn song, go and sing something new; rise up in the morning and go before the loveliest, the flower of all loving women, more finely fair than gold: "give your love that is dear to the Notary who was born at Lentino."'

If the classical world and Sicily's literary forebears haunt Quasimodo's works, so do the landscapes of his youth, those of Modica and the Val di Noto. Modica is located in a valley, coating the slopes in yet more harmoniously coloured stone. In reality there are two Modicas – the Alta and the Bassa, each with its own impressive mother church. The higher, Alta, is a complete maze of one-way streets looping through tilting buildings which were not designed to look upon the rigours of motorised traffic.

In the former Jewish quarter, further down the hill, there is a hotel called De Mohàc in Via Campailla – a street named after the seventeenth-century philosopher and scientist, Tommaso Campailla, whose birthplace is almost opposite that of Quasimodo's. The hotel was an aristocratic palazzo and its name pays homage to Gualtiero De Mohàc, one of Roger II's Norman admirals. The building is notable on two counts: through the dining room there is an entrance to a cave dwelling complete with stone-carved bed, torch niches and ancient graffiti. Secondly, each of the ten bedrooms bears the name of a writer. You can stay with Sciascia in room 3 or the poet he translated, Pedro Salinas, in room 8, Quasimodo in 7, Emily Dickinson in 9 or Gesualdo Bufalino in 10. Proud to display Modica's connections with Bufalino, the hotel displays a quote of his taken from *Blind Argus* (*Argo il cieco*); placed in the foyer it reads:

> One summer I was young and happy, in 'Fifty-One. Neither before nor after; just that summer. It may have been by grace and favour of the place I live in, a town like a pomegranate split in two, close to the sea yet pastoral, the one half clinging to a cliff-face, the other bespattered at its foot [. . .]

Bufalino was actually born in Comiso, 33 kilometres (21 miles) to the north-west, but he set *Blind Argus* in Modica. It is the tale of a school teacher who has fallen for one of his 18-year-old pupils. She is the local beauty and pursued by many of the town's available young men. Instead, he finds solace with Cecilia, who is staying with Don Nitto, the local 'godfather'. The entire narrative, riven with bittersweet nostalgia, is recounted by the now aged, long-retired teacher. It reflects the lies that we tell ourselves and others in the blind pursuit of love. Modica is essentially another character in the text to whom our teacher must bid a sad farewell:

> So then, to Modica, a long farewell! and to the corner of an Ionian isle in which she lies; to her elegance, her country ways. To the portals of her churches with their surging tides of steps. To the gentle warmth of her courtyards, her benevolent carob trees. To her stone walls shining as words of God. To the easygoing speech of her people. To her festivals and to her funerals. To the wheat of her fields and the honey of her bees.

The association with bees dates back to ancient times, as does the epithet Iblea, formerly Hybla, appended to towns in the area and the

Hyblaean Mountains. In fact, honey is still produced in the area. Honey from Hybla has become a metaphor with which one can sing the praises of a concept or object. With this in mind, James Henry Leigh Hunt produced an amusing and immensely readable little volume entitled *A Jar of Honey from Mount Hybla*.

Designed as a Christmas read to entertain friends around the crackle of a British fireplace, this English Romantic poet included all manner of Sicilian mythology, with quotes from the likes of Edmund Spenser's *Faerie Queen*. He also delves into the Greek–Carthaginian struggles and the pastoral poetry of Theocritus, referring to its influence on English and Italian pastoralists. Looking for the sweet literary honey to fill his blue jar, he quotes the English poet Lodge, from his work 'Glaucus and Scylla' – the comparison with a nymph's beautiful yellow locks is inevitable and sums up Leigh Hunt's feeling for this area of Sicily: '"Her hair, not truss'd, but scatter'd on her brow, surpassing Hybla's honey."'

## *Ragusa*

The Val di Noto continues on to include Ragusa and Scicli – two destinations, along with Modica, that have been used to film television episodes of Andrea Camilleri's Inspector Montalbano mysteries. The Agrigento chapter contains much more detail on the literary locations of Camilleri's books, but rather than use these on film, Palomar and RAI (the Italian state broadcaster) opted for the more photogenic settings of Baroque Sicily to form the backdrop to Salvo's investigations.

The television programmes have become a phenomenon in Italy and are now spreading around the world. Ragusa's central piazza, curtseying at the steps of its cathedral, appears in many episodes and Scicli plays host to the *commissariato* or Vigàta police headquarters. The Montalbano location par excellence is on the coast at Punta Secca, where the Inspector's distinctive two-tiered seaside villa is found. The bottom terrace gives directly onto the beach and the overhanging balcony above is where Montalbano likes to take his morning coffee or sip an evening whisky. Outside of the filming schedules, it is available for bed and breakfast.

The Montalbano trail is an industry in itself, with tours to the key locations and the production of guide books for fans of the programme. Those who read Italian can do no better than turn to the excellent *I luoghi di Montalbano* (*Montalbano's Places*) by Maurizio Clausi et al., which also includes the literary settings. One of the most iconic panoramas, often used for a rendezvous with a witness or a meeting with Salvo's diligent right-hand man, Fazio, is the belvedere atop the staircase next to Santa Maria delle Scale. The whole of Ragusa Ibla, the old town, undulates before the onlooker, sweeping up to the heights of San Giorgio Cathedral.

Vincent Cronin calls this drop a chasm. From these heights it appears that San Giorgio would be easily reachable, but the reality is far more labyrinthine, as Cronin obviously had the bitter experience of finding out:

the journey from Ragusa Superiore to the cathedral takes half an hour, the way being entirely by flights of steps: not an orderly, continuous stairway, but irregular, erratic goat-paths which wind like tangled skeins of wool in and around the houses and sweep under bridges; long, flat steps and narrow, steep grace-notes, tumbling down like a cascade, following the line of least resistance to the gorge below.

A similar route then awaits the traveller prepared to climb the opposite hill. If you have a day with no plans, there is no better way to appreciate the town. Wandering in Ragusa Ibla, the visitor is certain to come across plaques indicating the scenes where Montalbano and other films have been shot. The same central piazza also makes an appearance in the Marcello Mastroianni classic, *Divorce Italian Style* (*Divorzio all'italiana*).

Taken individually, each town in the Val di Noto is a little masterpiece. As a whole the district is a breathtaking gallery with the countryside in-between taking on a character of its own. Gentle pastures or groves and vineyards are separated by dry-stone walls, puzzled together by hand. It does not have the enormous vistas or savage rock faces of central Sicily but a landscape that the pastoralist Theocritus could have lauded with ease. From Avola in the east to Vittoria in the west, it is an important area for wine growers, who have increasingly upped the quality of their produce, now exported across the world.

### Vittoria and the Wine District

Our literary wine companion has to be Robert Camuto, whom we last met on Etna with Mick Hucknall. Camuto started his wine odyssey in the Vittoria wine-producing region, famed for its Cerasuolo di Vittoria appellation. After a hair-raising drive south from Catania airport, Camuto chose the COS winery just outside Vittoria as his first destination. He called his book *Palmento* in honour of the old wine-producing traditions of the region. COS's palmento has been converted into a dining room and reception area, but that is not to say the wine-makers of this establishment have forgotten the old methods. Some of their output is fermented in terracotta amphorae in a return to the Pithean methods that Robert is sure Dionysus would have recognised.

Vittoria has a mixture of land, soil and climate that lends a distinctive nature to the wines produced there. It owes its productivity to a fortuitous combination that Camuto can see in the red soil, dampened by rain on his visit. It 'seemed as light as cake and was carpeted with weeds, clover and wild flowers'. Add to this the southward aspect and a 'relentless afternoon summer sun tempered by cool evenings' and you have the perfect ingredients for vine-growing.

Wine, of course, is a great accompaniment to the region's cuisine and his COS host insisted on driving down to the seaside town of Scoglitti for dinner. The Cerasuolo he drank at the table was a mixture of Nero d'Avola and Frappato grapes. The description of his meal is worthy of Camilleri's Montalbano: 'More than *bene*, the seafood was so finely delicate as to hardly need chewing. Each morsel softened my heart as it slid, dripping its marinade, down my throat.'

The unwary could be caught like Camuto in the pasta trap. Following the exquisite entrée, he was happy to finish the equally delicious pasta dish. However, pasta usually appears as a second plate on Sicilian menus and it is a good idea to specify to the waiter that it will be your main course, otherwise you are likely to mop your lips with a satisfied grin only to be presented with the main dish, as was Robert's fate. This is a phenomenon especially likely to occur in little local restaurants that put on daily meals with no written menu. Luckily, he was able to sip the last of his Cerasuolo.

# 6

# AGRIGENTO
# AND THE SOUTH COAST

## Sulphur Spirits and Greek Temples

### *Agrigento*

Agrigento, centrally located along the southern coastal belt, began life as Akragas in 581 BC when it was established by Greek colonists from the neighbouring town of Gela. The shifting currents of history have led to four further name changes: Agrigentum, Kirkent, Girgenti and its present reincarnation. Urban sprawl from the 1960s onwards hides a medieval heart and a classical soul. Today the ruins of the once-wealthy Greek colony are found on a ridge to the east of the modern town. Despite its lofty position, the site is known as the Valley of the Temples and, from their elevated location, the Grecian columns confront their concrete counterparts on the hill opposite.

The temple complex has been attracting writers since the classical era. One of the first was Pindar, born in Thebes, Greece. As we know from Syracuse, his initial artistic overlord was the tyrant Hiero, but the poet did not restrict his Sicilian life to that city. Struck by the luxury and aspect of Akragas, he was moved to describe the settlement as 'the most beautiful of those inhabited by mortals'. Pindar is best known for his aforementioned 'Olympian Odes', the second of which he wisely dedicated to Theron, the victor of a chariot race but, more importantly, the local tyrant. Aware of Theron's struggles, he praises his noble ancestors, 'who after enduring many woes in mind, held the sacred mansion of the stream and were the eye of Sicilia'.

Empedocles, aside from his infamous Etnean demise, was an esteemed citizen of Akragas. Unfortunately, his pre-Socratic philosophy, which gave birth to the four classical elements, only survives in fragments but his name lives on in neighbouring Porto Empedocle. True to human nature, the legends that have survived the passing of time tend to be of the most gruesome kind. Prior to Theron, Akragas was ruled by a tyrant named Phalaris who commissioned a bronze bull from the Athenian sculptor Perillos – the purpose of which was to roast his enemies alive inside, with the added bonus that the acoustics produced a roar from the screaming victims similar to that of a real bull.

The Greek city's wealth and prosperity were only to last until 406 BC, when it was sacked by the Carthaginians. Subsequently captured by the Romans in 261 BC, control of the city ping-ponged between Carthage and Rome before settling under Roman rule, taking the Latin moniker Agrigentum. After the Saracen invasion in the ninth century AD, it became the Arabic Kirkent, which was Sicilianised to Girgenti after the demise of Moorish domination. Mussolini, in an attempt to stamp his authority, Italianised the modern town to Agrigento in 1927. This game of linguistic pass-the-parcel is ample testiment to a diverse history whose classical epoch, epitomised by Agrigentum, drew the more intrepid Grand Tourist.

Patrick Brydone's Grand Tour inevitably took in the ruins; he wrote to William Beckford that 'the whole strikes the eye at once, and pleases very much.' This observation, that the combined effect of the Valley of the Temples is greater than the sum of its parts, was recognised by other travellers. Johann Wolfgang Goethe, however, was more detailed in his analysis. Comparing the most intact Temple of Concord with Paestum near Naples, he notes how it 'conforms more nearly to our standard of beauty and harmony than the style which preceded it – compared to Paestum, it is like the image of a god as opposed to the image of a giant'.

The Temple of Concord is the archetypical image of classical Agrigento. Its near-complete façade, outlined against the azure blue of a southern Sicilian morning, humbles the individual in the face of such ancient achievement. Henry Swinburne, in Volume IV of his meticulous

*13 The Temple of Concord, Agrigento*

*Travels in the Two Sicilies*, attributes the temple's preservation to its consecration as a Christian church by Saint Gregory, former Bishop of Girgenti. Swinburne is equally awed by the site that greets him:

> This majestic edifice stands in the most striking point of view imaginable, on the brink of a precipice, which formed the defence of the city along the whole southern exposure; from every part of the country the temple of Concord appears the most conspicuous figure of a beautiful picture.

The other temples along the ridge include dedications to Jupiter (Zeus), Hercules, Demeter, Asclepius, Vulcan and Lacinian Juno. Goethe describes the Temple of Jupiter as being, 'scattered far and wide like the disjointed bones of a gigantic skeleton', although they may be a little less disjointed since the restorations instigated by Alexander Hardcastle, British gentleman archaeologist, in the 1920s.

These and subsequent works were considered by some as overzealous – the Temple of Hercules being reconstructed from sundry fragments scattered in the vicinity.

As we have seen previously, Guy de Maupassant's descriptions tend toward the poetically elegiac. His impressions of the entire valley evoke ghosts from the distant past:

> Seated on the side of the road that runs to the foot of that surprising hill, you pause to dream before these admirable mementos of the greatest of all artistic peoples. It seems that all Olympus is before us, the Olympus of Homer, of Ovid, of Virgil, the Olympus of gods delightful, sensual, passionate like us, fashioned like us, who poetically personify all the tenderness of our hearts, all the dreams of our souls and all the instincts of our senses.

Nobel laureate Salvatore Quasimodo, never one to eschew the inspirations of his native soil, in the poem 'Street in Agrigentum' ('Strada di Agrigentum'), paints a more weary image of the weather-beaten plateau, whipped by 'a wind that stains and gnaws the sandstone and the heart of the doleful telamons lying felled on the grass'.

Fresh from Syracuse and the more comfortable surroundings of Taormina, the American poet Ezra Pound tore himself away from the south-east in a bid to see more of the classical sites of Sicily. He could not decide whether Girgenti was an inferno or the land of milk and honey, although he was sufficiently moved to include a reference to Akragas in Canto CVII of the *Pisan Cantos*. His wife, Dorothy Shakespear, the trusty recorder of this trip with the Yeatses, wrote more postcards home to her family. The Hamilton College Library, which holds the Pound card archive, has a significant proportion of these cards, giving us a lasting insight into Dorothy's immediate and personal response to her surroundings.

On 31 January 1925, Dorothy writes to her mother: 'Have been down to Girgenti for two days. There's a row of temples along a ridge with olive, almond, and the sea a couple of miles away – very romantic and lovely.' The beauty of the surrounding vegetation, Dorothy's almonds and olives, is at its height in early spring when the groves are carpeted with Mediterranean flowers, or in February when the almond trees are in bloom. When Vincent Cronin reached Agrigento, the biographer and Renaissance scholar was captivated by this very sight:

> All along the valley in February stretch almond trees in blossom, an indefinable shade between white and rose, like snow at sunrise or sunset, acting as a link between the dark brown fruitful earth, with its cactus and olive trees of similar tone, and the pale blue spring sky.

Cronin is joined in his praise of the sweeping landscape that provides the temples' backdrop by Lawrence Durrell, so used to living in the lands of the olive.

Most writers, however, have been far less impressed with modern and medieval Agrigento. Approaching the town today, you are greeted by a conglomeration of ring roads and nondescript urban development. These suburbs mask a tortuously twisting network of narrow streets. Even after the small gap of 25 years, Robert D. Kaplan, the American journalist and writer, returned in the 1980s/1990s to find Agrigento drastically changed: 'It was over-built, teeming with poor neighbourhoods and luxury boutiques, with Arab and African immigrants selling handicrafts on the streets and hustling near the railway station.'

The original Arab quarter, known as the Rabato, has stirred two very prominent local writers: Andrea Camilleri and Luigi Pirandello. Both authors grew up nearer to the coast, as we shall see shortly, but spent a significant part of their childhood in Agrigento, and they both write evocatively of the district in their novels. In the first of Camilleri's Inspector Montalbano mysteries, *The Shape of Water* (*La forma dell'acqua*), published in 1994, the detective visits the Rabato as part of his investigations, an area described as 'consisting mostly of ruins refurbished and damaged higgledy-piggledy ramshackle hovels'.

In Camilleri's novels, Agrigento is rebaptised as Montelusa – a name he owes to Pirandello, a relative on his mother's side of the family. Although Pirandello refers directly to Girgenti (Agrigento) in novels such as *The Turn* (*Il turno*) published in 1902 and *The Old and* the Young (*I vecchi e i giovani*), 1913, he is just as likely to disguise it with a pseudonym; the aforementioned Montelusa or Richieri. Fellow Sicilian writer Leonardo Sciascia from nearby Racalmuto has pointed out that Pirandello found it difficult to escape the pull of his home town. *The Late Mattia Pascal* (*Il fu Mattia Pascal*) was supposedly set in a Liguarian town near Genoa; however, Miragno is Girgenti and the library where the protagonist works is La biblioteca Lucchesiana in Via Duomo – a library Pirandello knew well thanks to his research in the Lucchesi-Palli archives.

When Lawrence Durrell's *Sicilian Carousel* finally turned into downtown Agrigento, he was less scathing of the disordered nature of the town than he was of his fellow tourists. By now, the coach companion he had christened Beddoes – a failed prep-school master – was really beginning to antagonise him. As a self-confessed older gentleman of 65, Durrell's tolerance of others' idiosyncrasies was on the wane. Rather than stay and have a drink at the bar with Beddoes, or take a dip in the swimming pool, he sloped off to his comfortable hotel room for a whisky on the balcony. He was greeted by this beautiful juxtaposition of the ancient and modern:

> From my balcony I could sit in the warmth of the scented night and see the distant moth-soft dazzle of the temples crowning the lower slopes of Agrigento; immediately underneath me, in loops of artificial light swam the fish-white bodies of northern bathers who as yet had not become nut-brown with Sicilian sunlight.

Agrigento Cathedral has excited the opinions of many writers. Located in the unsurprisingly named Via Duomo, the cathedral was built in the year 1000 and is dedicated to the Norman Saint Gerland. It has been greatly altered over the years, giving it a somewhat time-worn, conflicting appearance. It features in Pirandello's epic story of post-Garibaldian politics, *The Old and the Young*. Set in Agrigento and Rome, the novel highlights the generation gap between Prince Laurentano, iconic of the old Bourbon regime, and his son, a supporter of the socialist

Fasci movement. The Prince tries to persuade the cathedral's Monsignore to invest a proportion of his considerable funds in the restoration of the building, which Laurentano considers 'a splendid example of Norman art, ruined in the 18th century by horrible incrustations of stucco and the most vulgar gilding'.

Swinburne is even more scathing of the building's architectural hodgepodge: 'a clumsy building patched up by barbarous architects'. Ezra Pound's wife Dorothy was more enthusiastic. In a further postcard from Girgenti, she praises the cathedral's Grecian sarcophagus picturing Ippolito and Nutrice and its wonderfully dramatic location. Apparently, the Pounds and Yeatses had been experiencing surprisingly reasonable travelling conditions. Dorothy notes that, 'travelling in Sicily has been quite as easy as anywhere else in Italy.'

Taking the Via Atenea through the heart of Agrigento, a road Pirandello describes as, 'the only level road in the place', you come to Piazzale Aldo Moro, named after the assassinated former Italian prime minister. On a lighter note, Camilleri's fictional hero Montalbano always dreads a summons from his boss, Bonetti-Alderighi, who presides over the police headquarters located in this square. Characterised by a small garden, it is the first piazza on the outskirts of the old town.

Leaving this area behind, the extended sprawl hides an ugly problem. Tobias Jones, the English journalist and writer of *The Dark Heart of Italy*, published in 2003, took a millennial look at Italy's political predicament. He headed for Agrigento to investigate the issue of *abusivismo*, the development of anything from houses to hotels without the necessary planning permission. In his words, 'The most important front of the war against *abusivismo* is the country's beauty spot par excellence: Agrigento.' The economics work against the sweeping lands of olive, grain and grape; as Tobias highlights, a hotel or new apartment block is far more lucrative. From the temples, looking back over the town, he writes how: 'Huge *palazzi* hem in the area, and there are nearby cranes heaving new (illegal) breeze blocks into place. Agrigento itself, about a mile away on the hilltop inland, is a wall of white concrete.'

### Caos and Porto Empedocle

To the south of Agrigento, the ring road bestrides the valley and, turning towards Porto Empedocle, you arrive at the seemingly unremarkable suburbs of Villaseta and Càvusu – seemingly, that is, until you realise that Càvusu, or Caos in standard Italian, was the home of Luigi Pirandello. He once famously remarked, 'I am a son of Chaos.'

A gravel-strewn drive leads to Pirandello's birthplace. His ancestors, on his mother's side of the family, moved to the property in 1817 after a cholera outbreak in Girgenti. Declared a national monument in 1949, it was then taken over by the Sicilian government, who have turned it into a museum and archive dedicated to the author. A small wooden café sits at the entrance to the literary park; the house itself is nearer to the cliff edge, surrounded by a well-maintained garden.

As the author is best known to the English-speaking world as a playwright, it is fitting that the property contains a collection of opening-night posters from some of his most famous plays, including *Six Characters in Search of an Author* (*Sei personaggi in cerca d'autore*). This radical creation of a play within a play, prompted jeers of 'Manicomio! Manicomio!' on its opening night, implying that the author should be carted off to an asylum. Further performances saw the text established as a modernist classic, paving the way for the likes of Sartre, Beckett and Pinter.

Luigi's father was the manager of a sulphur mine, an industry providing jobs for many and wealth for a few in the local province. Initially, this brought prosperity to the family, not to mention a fount of future literary inspiration for the young Pirandello. After his university education in Rome and Bonn, Luigi married a shy girl from Girgenti, Maria Antonietta Portulano, the daughter of one of his father's business contacts – the *fin de siècle* equivalent of a dynastic marriage and a decision he would later come to question.

Pirandello's works centre on the unpredictable nature of reality and self. The exterior masks we wear hide the interior self – a psychological battle with which he would become all too familiar when his wife suffered a mental breakdown precipitated by the literal collapse of the family sulphur mine. Luigi's father had sunk all of his wealth into this particular mine, along with his daughter-in-law's dowry.

The son of Chaos was now truly born. Suicidal and facing financial ruin, he was forced to rely on his teaching and writing, a career that reached international success with the serial publication and subsequent translation of the book *The Late Mattia Pascal*. Pascal also marries a local woman and is stuck in a life he can no longer endure, prompting his disappearance. After the discovery of a corpse, the locals believe him to be dead – a situation he turns to his advantage by changing his name and taking on a new existence: a desperate idea that had probably lurked in the shadows of Pirandello's subconscious. Forced back into his old life by the hopelessness of his rootless reality, he is finally confronted by his own gravestone, "'It's me! I'm me! Mattia Pascal! I'm not dead! Look at me!'"

Politically disillusioned by the failure of the socialist Fasci revolt, Pirandello found an outlet for his disappointment by writing *The Old and the Young*. His private life continued its tortuous path; Maria Antonietta, now becoming increasingly delusional and physically violent, accused him of having affairs. Still affectionate towards his wife, Luigi did his best to hold the family together, but, with agreement from his children, she was finally admitted to an asylum.

Seeking to find order in a chaotic world, Pirandello continued to write prolifically whilst dabbling with early Fascism, an ideal he would later reject by ripping up his membership card, declaring himself 'apolitical. I'm only a man in the world.' The playwright died alone in Rome on 10 December 1936. With the minimum of fuss, he wanted his ashes walled up in the rough country stone of his birthplace. From the family home, a path winds through the olive groves along the cliff edge, overlooking Luigi's 'African Sea'. The urn is interred in a clearing, above which there once stood a solitary pine – a source of tranquillity and inspiration during his turbulent life. The fallen trunk now rests on the impacted soil.

Leaving the literary park, you are scrutinised by the deep gaze of Pirandello's sculpted bust. His appearance, somewhere between magus and stage magician, has all the intensity of his troubled existence –

a man, despite his best efforts, apparently incapable of masking his inner turmoil.

Not far from Chaos is paradise. The lush garden of Colimbetra forms the lower part of the temple complex of Akragas and is the point at which three valleys meet. The ancients established a fishpond here made from a great basin of water which also irrigated the surrounding land. In *The Old and the Young*, one of the main characters, Don Ippolito, calls his nearby property Colimbetra because he too had created a basin to catch the winter torrent running below Bonamorone: an oft-repeated focal point in Pirandello's works.

In another of his books, *The Turn*, the impoverished Don Marcantonio Ravì wants to marry his daughter to the elderly but wealthy Diego Alcozèr. Marcantonio is impatiently waiting for the feckless younger suitor, Pepè Alletto, to return from a duel, whilst looking over the valley:

> leaning on the iron rail of the avenue at the exit from the town, with his eyes on a familiar point of the wide, green, undulating landscape that lay at the foot of the hill on which, apparently, Girgenti was built. From time to time he would snort with impatience and take a few steps, or else shake the rail hard, his eyes fixed on the dark stain of the cypresses in the cemetery, down there in Bonamorone.

The road downhill from Colimbetra leads to nearby Porto Empedocle. Once known as the Marina di Girgenti, it was named after the Agrigentine philosopher, Empedocles, in the 1860s. One of Pirandello's characters describes how the two long breakwaters of the new harbour 'make me think of a pair of arms stretched out to all the ships of all the civilised nations of the earth'. Part of the refurbished dock was built from stone scavenged from the temple remains and served to worship the exploitative exports of nineteenth-century sulphur mining rather than the ancient Grecian gods. It is along these now modern industrial jetties that Andrea Camilleri's Inspector Salvo Montalbano likes to walk off a heavy lunch and ponder his cases.

Andrea Camilleri is a native of Porto Empedocle, a town reincarnated in his novels as Vigàta. A theatre director, his literary career did not spark into life until he was late into his sixties. In 1992, his first successful novel, *The Hunting Season* (*La stagione della caccia*) was published. This bloody tale of a pharmacist who kills for love has a dream-like quality with touches of black humour – a thread which will continue to run through much of his later work.

His historical novels often draw on real events in Sicily's period of upheaval from the abortive 1848 revolution to the years of disillusioned unification. Works such as *Taddei's Great Circus* (*Gran circo Taddei*) and *The Disappearance of Patò* (*La scomparsa di Patò*) weave fiction and reality into Vigàta's decades of expansion, a time fraught with hardship and possibility.

These books have yet to find their way into English translation, a fate that has certainly not befallen his series of detective novels featuring Inspector Montalbano. Despite worldwide success, Camilleri has made no concession to his international readership, remaining faithful to his idiosyncratic use of language and very personal view of Sicily. The Montalbano novels are suffused with Sicilian slang and local dialect, often with comic effect – a nightmare for translators, as Camilleri well appreciates. Outside the confines of common European reference points, he wonders what on earth the Japanese make of his characters' innate Sicilianess.

His childhood home still exists, although in a perilous state of repair. Via dello Sport heads north from the Porto Empedocle bypass and peters out next to the ruin of a once-stylish country house. The broken shutters hang limply from the walls above a porticoed entrance gradually being devoured by the encroaching vegetation. Recycling his early years for authenticity, the property makes an unexpected appearance in the case of *The Patience of the Spider* (*La pazienza del ragno*). The glassless windows still gaze over the distant Monte Crasto where Montalbano finds a hidden terracotta dog, in the book of the same name:

> The Crasto mountain, which for its part would never have dreamed of calling itself a mountain, was a rather bald little hill that rose up west of Vigàta barely 500 yards from the sea. It had been carefully

pierced by a tunnel, now boarded up, that was supposed to have been an integral part of a road that started nowhere and led nowhere, a very useful bypass route for diverting funds into bottomless pockets.

It once struck Camilleri like a thunderbolt that his famous detective displayed many of his father's traits and qualities. In Montalbano, we see a thoroughly Mediterranean man. His mood swings are dictated by the vagaries of the weather; living by the sea in the suburb of Marinella, one of his instinctive morning rituals is to throw open the balcony doors with an espresso in hand and survey the state of the sky. In *The Terracotta Dog* (*Il cane di terracotta*) Montalbano experiences:

> one of those days when someone who is sensitive to abrupt shifts in weather and suffers them in his blood and brain is likely to change opinion and direction continuously, like those sheets of tin, cut in the shape of banners and roosters, that spin every which way on rooftops with each new puff of wind.

This meteorological irascibility extends to his relationships at work. There are three triggers guaranteed to try his patience: the bungling Sicilian-speaking desk sergeant, Catarella, mangling Italian; his deputy, Mimì, chasing skirt rather than criminals; and the pedantic Fazio insisting on conveying every last detail about a possible suspect.

The inspector's innate sensibilities reflect the core Sicilian values relating to the world of food. From the first book in the series, *The Shape of Water*, Camilleri makes it clear how importantly the detective treats his palate. His favourite restaurant, the Trattoria San Calogero, wraps his tastebuds in the comforting cuisine of southern Sicily – a rustic experience relying on local ingredients and a million miles from Michelin stars. Via Roma, the heart of Porto Empedocle, was home to the real San Calogero, the last ghost of which disappeared a few years ago when the forlorn sign of the defunct restaurant was removed from the corner of Via Granet. This tree-lined central thoroughfare also houses the Caffè Albanese, now christened Bar Vigata in honour of the town's favourite son. In *The Scent of the Night* (*L'odore della notte*), Salvo picks up some home-made fresh cannoli from the Albanese; these pastries, ubiquitous throughout Sicily, are filled with sweet ricotta, candied fruit or chocolate nibs.

Further along Via Roma is the recently commissioned statue of Camilleri's most well-known character. Montalbano leans against a lamp post staring towards the centre of the boulevard. The portrayal is a literary one – a full head of hair and moustache have little to do with Luca Zingaretti's appearance in the phenomenally successful, eponymously titled, RAI television series. The statue has a benign, congenial air with the quality of a paterfamilias, one who casts a steady eye over his beloved Vigàta. Almost opposite, Luigi Pirandello stands in contrast, high on his plinth. Although looking dapper with one hand in his pocket, it is his

*14 Bronze statue of Andrea Camilleri's detective, Inspector Montalbano, Porto Empedocle*

face that gives him away. Gaunt, pensive, the muscles taut, as if secretly grinding his teeth, he clenches his jaw against the world.

Although Montalbano is a man of instinctive action, Camilleri has been careful not to neglect his intellectual side. The books are interspersed with literary references. From Leonardo Sciascia's *Candido*, to Pirandello's *Mountain of Giants*, the inspector's reading reflects the author's literary tastes and the greats of Sicilian literature. His horizons even extend across the Atlantic to William Faulkner and to the Catalan shores of the Mediterranean, particularly the Barcelona of Manuel Vázquez Montalbán. The name is no coincidence. Camilleri paid the Spanish mystery writer the compliment of using an Italian version of the name for his own fictional detective.

From Porto Empedocle harbour, looking back up to the town, it is possible to see how the cliffs blocked expansion, squeezing development along the beachfront, as alluded to by Pirandello in *The Old and the Young*. Modern construction has endeavoured to carve links to the upper districts with rivers of asphalt climbing up the hillside, but the two areas maintain a separate identity. At the top of the hill, the Osteria al Timone restaurant greets the unwary. The bizarre sight of a stranded ship whose bridge points downhill, replete with life-belts and helm, is the actual incarnation of Da Enzo's, as Clausi and his fellow authors point out in *I luoghi di Montalbano: una guida* (*Montalbano's Places*). The restaurant is recommended to Inspector Montalbano by his deputy, Mimì, when the San Calogero is forced to close. With trepidation, he samples the food for the first time:

> The antipasto of salted octopus tasted as though it were made of condensed sea and melted the moment it entered his mouth. The pasta in squid ink could have held its own against Calogero's. And the mixed grill of mullet, sea bass, and gilthead had that heavenly taste the inspector feared he had lost forever.

The aged Camilleri returns from his home in Rome to Porto Empedocle at least once a year where he can retune his ear to the local dialect and reinvigorate his palate with the local cuisine. Clearly, his formative years and early career have left an indelible stamp on his works. The aforementioned familial link to Pirandello has resulted in the occasional knowing glance in the direction of his relation and sometime neighbour. It is thanks to Luigi's symbolic Saracen olive, a synthesis of 'memory and imagination', that Montalbano sits under such a tree to contemplate life.

A series of crime novels set in Sicily should automatically bring to mind the subject of the Mafia. However, the Cosa Nostra is demoted to fleeting mentions or a subsidiary role, largely in the form of Don Balduccio Sinagra, the decrepit yet stereotypical Mafia don. The threat is evident but shadowy. Andrea Camilleri made a conscious decision not to give this criminal organisation the oxygen of his substantial publicity. The crimes that do make appearances in the novels are a catalogue of Sicily's current-day woes, including people smuggling, kidnap and murder; however, many of the books focus on familial betrayal, feuds, affairs and crimes committed by the psychologically unstable – a deliberate spotlight on the more intimate aspects of societal breakdown. Even Salvo's old school friend, Gegè, operates on the other side of the law, running a prostitution ring near to the abandoned chemical works. Livia, Montalbano's northern Italian girlfriend, is amazed at their continued friendship, a loyalty born of the fraternal geographic link that supersedes notions of class and status.

## Racalmuto and the Sulphur Zone

One of the first Sicilian authors to tackle honestly the thorny subject of the Mafia was Leonardo Sciascia, born in Racalmuto, 18 miles to the north-east of Empedocle. As soon as you pass Agrigento, the countryside opens out into an unforgiving, but starkly beautiful, agricultural landscape – a sight not lost on Johann Wolfgang Goethe. Travelling from Girgenti inland to Caltanissetta, he writes:

At last we can say we have seen with our own eyes the reason why Sicily earned the title of 'The Granary of Italy'. Soon after Girgenti, the fertility began. There are no great level areas, but the gently rolling uplands were completely covered with wheat and barley in one great unbroken mass.

Goethe would have passed Racalmuto as part of this journey. The origin of its name is not one to entice the visitor – the Arabic *rahal-maut* literally means 'dead town'. Fortunately, the name has been Sicilianised over the centuries and has lost its original connotation, although it does have the sleepy air of so many Sicilian towns dotted throughout the interior.

Leonardo Sciascia, best known for his novel *The Day of the Owl* (*Il giorno della civetta*), spent his formative years here, before moving with his family to Caltanissetta in 1935. Returning to teach at the local elementary school, he used his experiences to write the semi-autobiograhical *Le parrocchie di Regalpetra*, changed in translation to *Salt in the Wound*. The fictional Regalpetra is, in Sciascia's own imagination, a place which borders on Racalmuto but could easily be its twin. The author did not always cloak his home town in anonymity. In his book of short stories with a title borrowed from Homer – *The Wine Dark Sea* (*Il mare colore del vino*) – the tale entitled 'The Ransom' recounts the history of playful antagonism between his place of birth and neighbouring Grotte. In contrast to Grotte's 'bad roads, mean houses and dreary festivals', Racalmuto 'staged a festival that lasted a whole week and was splendidly colourful and extravagant'. In the same breath, he also admits to the town's tranquillity throughout the rest of the year.

In recognition of such praise, the good citizens of Racalmuto have created two monuments to their very own internationally recognised author. Sicilians seem to have a penchant for recreating their literary heroes as statues, destined to stroll forever through the heart of town. While Montalbano leans on his lamp post, Sciascia, hand in pocket, strides down Via Garibaldi towards the central piazza and the sandy façade of the twin-towered *duomo* – usually etched into the clamorous blue of a Mediterranean sky. The second tribute to the author is a literary foundation and museum established after his death in 1989.

Arriving in the higher part of town, the preponderance of poetic street names, Via Neruda for one, is a clue to the proximity of the Fondazione Leonardo Sciascia in Viale della Vittoria. The building has an exhibition of photographs from the writer's life on the ground floor and a small museum located above. The rows of Sciascia's works translated into many languages reflect his worldwide impact. More fascinating still are a collection of pen portraits accumulated over the years by the writer himself. They are a gallery of literary influences and a hymn to world literature; Byron sits next to Borges and Maupassant stares over at Voltaire. Nods to these greats are liberally sprinkled throughout Leonardo's work – no less so than in his reworking of Voltaire's *Candide* which he called *Candido, ovvero un sogno fatto in Sicilia* (*Candido, or a Dream Dreamed in Sicily*).

The most intimate part of the museum is the collection of his old school registers and reports from his time as a school teacher. His small, neat handwriting lists the local children who would go on to toil in the fields and mines, emigrate in search of work or find less legal means of gaining a living – a well-spring of inspiration for novels like the aforementioned *Salt in the Wound*, *The Day of the Owl* and a host of short stories. Sciascia is clearly a writer with a social conscience. At a time when *omertà* (the Mafia code of silence) was at its height, Sciascia wrote *The Day of the Owl*, a detective's attempt to discover the murderous chain of events behind the assassination of a local businessman. Doors close in his face, witnesses have seen nothing, leading him to bend the law in order to trap the guilty. Ultimately, the case falls apart.

*Salt in the Wound* gains its English title from the miners who toil in the salt and sulphur mines of the area. Sulphur, in particular, was a major industry in the Agrigento region, especially near the town of Comitini. The last remaining mines closed in the 1970s. As Sciascia illustrates:

> The sulphur and the salt are mentioned in the royal privileges from the fourteenth century on, but the golden age of the sulphur mines was in the nineteenth century, when new people who suddenly perceived the

yellow veins of wealth gleaming beneath their tired farmlands began to burrow in the arid plateau.

Other writers have been equally drawn by the horrific allure of the sulphur industry. Guy de Maupassant, leaving behind the romantic sites of antiquity, visited a mine and was sickened by the child labour: 'They pant and gasp, these wretched urchins, weighed down under their loads. They are ten, twelve years old, and they repeat, fifteen times in a single day, the abominable voyage.' One American writer and campaigner, Booker T. Washington, who was all too familiar with the burdens of slavery, took a long hard look at the conditions in the sulphur mines. Booker T. began his life as a slave on a plantation in Hale's Ford, Virginia and later experienced salt mining first hand. His remarkable story took a fortunate turn when a kindly employer gave him the opportunity to study. In 1871, he attended the Hampton Institute and just ten years later was able to found the Tuskegee Institute in Alabama – a college promoting the education of African Americans; it was his life's work.

In addition to teaching, he was a dedicated writer and his last book, *The Man Farthest Down*, was an attempt to analyse the exploitative working conditions that prompted Europeans to emigrate to America. Naturally, given the large number of Sicilians flooding into Ellis Island, he included the sulphur mines in his research. His shock is palpable as he describes his first sight of a miner:

On the vast slope of the mountain and at a distance they looked like ants running in and out of little holes in the earth. It was at the mouth at one of these entrances to the mines that I got my first definite notion of what sulphur miners looked like – those unfortunate creatures who wear out their lives amid the poisonous fumes and the furnace heat of these underground hells. There was a rumble of a car, and presently a man, almost stark naked, stepped out of the dark passageway. He was worn, haggard, and gray, and his skin had a peculiar grayish-white tinge.

In the 1950s, Lawrence Durrell was fascinated by a glimpse of some miners in downtown Agrigento. His guide, Roberto, explained who they were:

> 'They are Zolfataioi,' said Roberto with a smile. 'We have been shielding you from the uglier side of Sicily, but we have our own black country here like you have; only it's not black, it's yellow. The sulphur-workers live a sort of grim separate life except for their occasional excursions like this.'

Their troglodytic existence also moved Pirandello to write 'Ciaula Discovers the Moon' ('Ciaula scopre la luna'). The story focuses on Ciaula, a miner's helper, who is so brutalised by his life underground that he has become accustomed to man-made darkness and has a fear of the real night. The metaphorical sign of hope comes in the shape of a brilliant Mediterranean full moon, bathing his troubled subsistence in tears of joy.

It was precisely this reputation that deterred D. H. Lawrence from choosing Girgenti as an alternative to Taormina. Prompted to relocate from the lush surroundings of his garden at Fontana Vecchia by his fiery imaginings of Mount Etna, he looked for an alternative: 'Where does one go? There is Girgenti by the south. There is Tunis at hand. Girgenti, and the sulphur spirit and the Greek guarding temples, to make one madder? Never.' Lawrence, who always tended towards a sardonically elemental view of Sicilians, would have been completely contradicted by Booker T. Washington who, despite the miners' reputation, found that 'every Sicilian with whom I came in contact in the sulphur mine treated me in the most kindly manner, and I came away from their country having the highest respect for them.' Despite the appalling conditions he discovered in Sicily or, for that matter, throughout the rest of Europe, it is with a sinking heart we learn that Washington concludes, 'the man farthest down in Europe is woman.' Excluding the present day, this accounts for the fact that Sicily had so few renowned female writers, apart from the occasional honourable exception, notably Maria Messina.

These days, one of the few traces of the gaseous activity which created the sulphur deposits can be found near Aragona. The Vulcanelli di Macalube is a protected area where gases force liquid mud to the surface in miniature volcanoes. Tourists wait patiently for the next bubble to emerge, the thin tremulous crust betraying the imminent upsurge. Guy de Maupassant found this natural phenomenon rather monstrous, 'filthy, shameful little volcanos, spurious, leprous burst abcesses'. A rather extreme reaction.

The wounds of man's sulphurous intervention have now largely healed. The landscape around Racalmuto, so fertile in Goethe's day, was brought to life by Leonardo Sciascia in *Sicilian Uncles* (*Gli zii di Sicilia*):

> We used a goat track which took us to a stone quarry, and then out to the open countryside. There was fruit there: almonds, green and bitter on the outside, white as milk inside – curd-almonds, we call them – and May plums, just as sour and green, which make the mouth dry.

The description is based on his house and garden in Noce on the outskirts of town – a retreat he would return to every summer to write. It calls to mind the landscapes of Andalucía in southern Spain – a comparison Sciascia would have celebrated, being familiar with the notion that Spain is a way of being: a way of being he considered closer to that of Sicily than most would imagine.

### Palma di Montechiaro

To the south-east of Agrigento and Racalmuto is the ducal town of Palma di Montechiaro. It sits on a rocky outcrop some four miles from the sea with its focal point being the Chiesa Matrice, a church that crowns a flight of imposing steps lined by sloping terraces of more humble buildings. Mentioned by Camilleri in his Montalbano novels, the town's real claim to literary fame is its connection with Giuseppe Tomasi di Lampedusa and *The Leopard*, that wistful tale of a declining

Sicilian aristocracy. As mentioned in the chapter on Palermo, the novel has many scenes in the capital, but it was to Palma that Lampedusa turned when he needed a model for the Convent of the Holy Ghost. Palma itself was founded by Giuseppe's ancestor, Carlo Tomasi, in 1637 and the convent, home to a closed order of nuns, was host to some of Lampedusa's more eccentric ancestors, particularly one who spent the last years of his life there sleeping in a coffin. In life as in art, the Prince was granted the right to enter this closed convent, something the fictional Prince of Salina particularly enjoyed:

> This faculty of canonical intrusion was the chief, but not the only reason, for his liking The Convent of the Holy Ghost. Everything about the place pleased him, beginning with the humble simplicity of the parlour, with its raftered ceiling centred on the Leopard, its double gratings for interviews, a little wooden wheel for passing messages in and out, and a heavy door whose threshold he and the King were the only men in the world allowed to cross.

Henry Swinburne, who actually slept in the 'manor house', was more concerned with the town's reputation for having a native in every gaol in Sicily. This beggarly image in such an aristocratic environment is highlighted by Peter Robb in his book *Midnight in Sicily*. As the title suggests, Robb is not one to avoid the more murky aspects of Sicilian history. In 1959, just a year after *The Leopard* was published, a parasitologist from Bologna spent time in Palma studying the conditions there. Robb quotes his startling findings:

> He found a town where over half the people were illiterate and child mortality ran at fifty percent. Farm animals [. . .] lived with their owners in their houses. Only a third of the houses had running water, in any case polluted, and twenty council cleaners, who hadn't been paid for seven months, carried off the night soil in open mule carts.

Palma has wasted no time in lifting itself from these medieval depths. The only animals you are likely to see on the streets now are the odd stray cat and beautifully groomed horses pulling carriages for the tourists or carrying a bride to her wedding at the imposingly Baroque Mother Church.

## Gela

Following the coast eastwards to Licata, the road is lined with olive groves, gently sloping to white sandy beaches backed with prickly pears. Farmhouses interspersed with holiday lets sporadically break up the landscape. It is precisely on these beaches, from Licata to the town of Gela, that the Americans and Canadians landed in World War II. Operation Husky, as it was known, saw the Allies move swiftly inland and was followed by the then war reporter, John Steinbeck. Steinbeck already had renowned works under his belt, including *Of Mice and Men*, *Tortilla Flat* and *The Grapes of Wrath*. He turned to war reporting in 1943 and we know he trailed the invasion all the way to Palermo. His focus on the ordinary individuals involved in the campaign provides a sobering insight into the horrors of war. His experiences were only collated into the book format of *Once There Was a War* in 1958. One soldier was an individual nicknamed Bugs:

> Bugs, when the battle for Gela in Sicily had abated, was poking about among the ruins, when he came upon a mirror – but such a mirror as to amaze him. It had survived bombing and shell fire in some miraculous manner, a matter which created wonder in Bugs [. . .] The whole thing must have weighed about seventy-five pounds, and it was so beautiful that it broke Bugs' heart. He just couldn't leave it behind.
>
> Bugs probably fought the toughest war in all Sicily, for he carried the mirror on his back the whole way. When the shell fire was bad, he turned his mirror face down and covered it with dirt. On advances he left it and always came back in the night and got it again, although it entailed marching twice as far as the rest of his outfit.

The heartbreaking end to this story is that, having successfully carried the mirror to Palermo, Buggs was billeted in a tall house with balconies. Hauling the mirror up, he hung it on a nail, only for the plaster to give way and the mirror to come crashing down onto the floor in a thousand pieces. The phlegmatic Bugs simply shrugged his shoulders, deciding that it probably would not have looked right in his flat anyway.

Fortunately for the Allies, the broken mirror did not cast its bad luck over the progress of the Sicilian campaign. Some attribute the swiftness of the American advance to the enlistment of certain notorious Mafiosi, including the Sicilian American Lucky Luciano. Alan Whicker, furthering his mission for the British Army's film and photo unit, saw the campaign unfold. He emphasises how this decision was to reverse the Mafia's suppression by Mussolini: 'Now in their rush to pacify an island already peaceful, the Americans resuscitated another convicted Mafiosi, Don Calò Vizzini, and put him in control of the island's civil Administration with military vehicles and supplies at his disposal. The Mafia was born again, fully grown.'

Whicker also highlights the pacific nature of the Sicilians' attitude towards the Allies, with ripples of applause greeting the army's entry into town, a restrained but approving welcome. Just as Whicker was to return in later years, so did Steinbeck, both finding the comforts of Taormina more conducive than the privations of the war.

Gela, like Agrigento, has a long and proud history. It was the Gelans, as we have seen, who established the city of Akragas and it was to Gela that the Ancient Greek playwright Aeschylus retired. An apocryphal story has it that he was killed by a tortoise shell dropped onto his balding head from the claws of a passing eagle. Whatever the veracity of this tale, he certainly wrote his famous trilogy of plays, the *Oresteia,* whilst living out his peaceful retirement in the town. Aeschylus' fame would lead to his grave becoming a pilgrimage site for other authors of the period, a fact not lost on the journalist Robert D. Kaplan, who vowed to reread the trilogy that he had found so tedious when a student at college.

Unlike Agrigento, most of Gela's past is confined to the archaeological museum in Corso Vittorio Emanuele. The modern town is punctuated by industrial development and commercial warehousing which reminded Kaplan of Marseille – a complete contrast if you have come from the interior of the island; yet, like Washington, he was struck by the warmth of the people: 'Gela was dominated by oil rigs, auto and tyre shops, and bleak, unfinished apartment blocks. Hordes of men gathered at night around bars as tacky as those in the hilltop towns were elegant. Yet Gela was the warmest and friendliest place we found in Sicily.'

The high incidence of unemployment has led many from this area to emigrate. One of Sciascia's stories from *The Wine Dark Sea*, 'The Long Crossing' ('Il lungo viaggio'), tells how a group of would-be immigrants gather on the beaches between Gela and Licata, believing they are taking a boat trip to America. They are in fact the subjects of a scam and end up being deposited back on Sicilian soil believing it to be the USA. Coming ashore, they are confused to find Americans speaking Italian, driving similar cars and living in similar circumstances – a con trick played on the vulnerable in search of a better life. As Aeschylus would have empathised, 'These toils oppress me, as with breathless haste/I urge the keen pursuit: o'er the long tract/Of continent, and o'er th' extended ocean.'

## *West to Sciacca*

Returning to Agrigento and taking the coastal road in a westerly direction, the first landmark of any significance is the Turkish Steps – a stunning natural cliff formation. The brilliant white marl has been sculpted by erosion into a gently declining stairway to the sea. Sun-worshippers offer their bodies to the ray-reflecting stone that will turn their skins to mahogany. The best view, one that appears on a thousand postcards, is from the road above, where the panorama of sea, sky and land can be appreciated to the full. This stretch of coastline was chosen by Andrea Camilleri as a clandestine meeting place for Inspector Montalbano and his childhood friend, the shady Gegè. Under the cover of darkness, the two meet to pass inside information and trade friendly insults about the old days.

The road continues to hug the coast all the way to Sciacca, passing the mythical beach and ruins of Eraclea Minoa. The settlement, originally called Minoa, was so-named after the legendary Minos, King of Crete. He is said to have chased Daedalus to Sicily and the discovery of a Minoan-style tomb in the vicinity would seem to give some substance to the tales. Daedalus, the Cretan master craftsman of labyrinthine fame, was forced from hiding when he solved a riddle set by the king. Plotting with locals, Daedalus saw to it that Minos was boiled in his own bath.

Sciacca, some 19 miles from Minoa, is one of the prettier towns along the southern coast and claims the father of Sicilian history, Tommaso Fazello – a Dominican friar who wrote the first printed history of the island. Ceramic artisans, whose works adorn the steps down to the port, live cheek by jowl with the local fishermen. Visitors also come for the more benign aspects of volcanicity found in the thermal waters captured by the local baths and spas, the most elegant of which was established at the Grand Hotel Delle Terme built on a cliff near the public gardens. In Goethe's day, the natural phenomenon was a little less tamed: 'Shortly after Sciacca we halted to look at the thermal baths. A hot spring, with a pungent odour of sulphur, gushes out of a rock. The water tastes salty but not foul.' Goethe, who had an eye for geological phenomena, wondered if the fumes only began to smell when in contact with the open air.

Henry Swinburne recounts the very Shakespearean tale of bloody revenge and murder between the houses of Perollo and Luna that saw the streets of Sciacca run red. The original quarrel over marriage to an heiress in 1410 was finally brought to an end over a century later by Charles V of Spain, the then ruler of Sicily. Much bad blood had flowed under the bridge: a poisoning, the public flaying of a dead body and wholesale slaughter.

Buildings bearing these two infamous names are still to be found in the town, including the cylindrical tower and remains of the Castello Luna, although Swinburne would have viewed it before its sad decline in the nineteenth century: 'Sciacca is defended by ancient walls and the castle of Luna. It stands upon very steep rock, hanging over the sea, and excavated in every direction into prodigious magazines, where the corn of the neighbouring territory is deposited for exportation.'

Sciacca's other literary connection is equally sad. In January 1947, Accursio Miraglia, a communist and trade unionist from the town, was shot dead by the Mafia. It provided the template for Leonardo Sciascia's *Day of the Owl*, which, as we know, was one of the first novels to have organised crime in its sights. Miraglia's motto, 'Better to die on your feet than live on your knees', succinctly sums up his philosophy.

## Santa Margherita di Belice

The road inland heads towards Santa Margherita di Belice, the summer residence of Giuseppe Tomasi di Lampedusa. In the account of his childhood, *The Places of my Infancy*, he describes the journey through the mountains as an immense desert landscape – a feudal vision without a breath of wind, oppressed by a leaden sun. Modern-day Santa Margherita is very different from that experienced by Lampedusa. On 15 January 1968, this part of Sicily was struck by a devastating earthquake which virtually demolished the entire town. To truly understand the effects on the populace, you need to turn to someone with inside knowledge.

As Theresa Maggio was roaming inland Sicily in search of lost stories hidden in the hill villages and towns, she could not fail to visit Belice, the ancestral home of relatives and one of the motivators behind her book, *The Stone Boudoir*. Returning to her family's roots, she was given the full picture of that fateful day in January: '"Then we heard it, the end of the world." A booming rumble, a deep, hollow sound like thunder, like an avalanche, it lasted fifteen seconds. The town rolled on waves of earth. The ground split and swallowed buildings. All ten churches in town crashed to the ground.'

It left Lampedusa's palazzo in ruins, with only the façade standing; the source of the town's pride was now an empty shell, as Theresa illustrates, 'The old Santa Margherita had been abandoned and the palace that had been its soul lay in pieces on the ground.'

The building was the model for Donnafugata, the Leopard's summer residence, and in homage to Lampedusa's only novel, the grounds and edifice have been rebuilt using some of the original plans, keeping the façade intact. The book's two young lovers, Tancredi and Angelica, wander its seemingly limitless number of 'guest rooms, state rooms, kitchens, chapels, theatres, picture galleries, odorous saddling rooms, stables, stuffy conservatories, passages, stairs, terraces and porticos'.

In reality, officially known as the Palazzo Cutò-Filangeri, the building cuts a lonely figure in a town largely reinvented – quite fitting for a palace Lampedusa described as 'self-sufficient [. . .] a kind of Vatican'. It resembles a dowager duchess at a debutante's ball. After years of misappropriated funds, the new town has grown alongside the ghostly remains of Baroque Belice: now a sad reminder of the awesome power of nature.

# 7

# ENNA AND THE INTERIOR

Sicily's Bread Basket

*Enna*

The soil of central Sicily is full of life and colour: the meadows surrounding Lake Pergusa are dressed in vivid whirls of wild flowers buzzing with insect life. The balmy climate allows a gentle zephyr to sway the delicate grasses as a beautiful young maiden walks barefoot through nature's abundant floral carpet. Dark flint eyes watch this idyllic scene with jealous intent – every paradise has to have its serpent and this lakeside Eden, near to the central town of Enna, is no exception.

The young woman in question is Persephone and the evil onlooker is the shadowy figure of Hades. This god of the underworld, intent on carrying out his plan of abduction, was to appear through a crack in the earth's crust in his chariot, dragging the young maiden down to his lair in the Stygian gloom. Despite brave attempts by Cyane, Persephone's friendly nymph, all was lost and not a trace remained of her presence.

Her mother, Demeter, the goddess of fertility, was frantic in the search for her daughter and put aside her responsibility for sharing with man the secrets of grain production. As a result, everything fell into decay and infertility; fruit no longer hung in abundance and the spectre of starvation stalked the land. Such are the essential ingredients for this timeless Greco-Roman myth. However, the Pergusan waters are considerably muddied by the varying names given to the participants. For the Romans, the Greek Persephone, also known as Corê, became Proserpina, and Demeter is often referred to as Ceres or Cerere in standard Italian. Hades (Pluton) makes an appearance as Dis or even Aidoneus.

Versions of the myth vary further with regard to Demeter's eventual discovery of her daughter's whereabouts. Some say it was the sun god Helios who shone his all-seeing light into the underworld for Demeter to see the fate of Persephone. Others believe it was the Syracusan, Arethusa, who, having been turned into a stream, directed her waters to show the frantic mother her daughter's location. At this point, Zeus usually makes an appearance as a somewhat harsh arbitrator owing to Demeter's refusal to return to Olympus. He decides to send a messenger to the depths of Hell, asking for Persephone's return.

The situation is complicated by a pomegranate – the mythical fruit of love. Unfortunately, the young maiden had consumed the seeds which she should have refrained from eating. This enabled the devious Hades to drive a bargain – Persephone would spend part of the year with him in the barren gloom of the underworld and the other part in the sunlit uplands with her mother, thus giving birth to nature's seasons with periods of growth and times of dormancy. This myth has an endurance and resonance that has long outlived others, and reading Vincent Cronin we discover a good explanation of its lasting quality; it illustrates 'the multiple pattern of human life, of the rhythm between sorrow and joy [. . .] It is at once a particular, quite simple story and a universal truth susceptible of countless interpretations.'

It is this universality that has attracted the attentions of poets, writers and artists, both to the myth and the locations. Lake Pergusa is approximately 11 kilometres (seven miles) to the south of the central city of Enna and is Sicily's only remaining natural lake. It bears little resemblance to the paradisiacal descriptions above, although part of the area has been designated a nature reserve. Its banks still abound with wild flowers in the spring, but the view has been all but obliterated by a motor-racing circuit that outlines the entire lake.

Mary Taylor Simeti, the American who married a Sicilian and entitled her book, *On Persephone's Island*, could do no less than visit the site of the maiden's disappearance. Like most visitors, she was shocked by this man-made scarring of the countryside, 'Lake Pergusa proves to be a bitter disappointment, a brilliant example of the Sicilians' best efforts to ruin their landscape.' She goes on to explain how much of the wooded and meadowed interior has been eroded by grain production. It seems Demeter taught her mortals too well and the fertility of Sicily's bread basket may be in danger of sliding back into the darkness.

The main road that runs through the town of Pergusa slips past neat but architecturally unremarkable villas, built by those attracted to the pastoral associations of this area of Sicily. A sharp curve takes you from this main road onto the lane that competes with the motor-racing circuit for views of the lake. The closed-off track wins the race and those visitors meandering around the waters will find themselves peering over fences and gantries to try and gain a glimpse of the legendary location.

There is a nearby archaeological zone known as the Cozzo Matrice, which has a collection of ruins from the Grecian period, including a temple dedicated to Demeter. It is at this site that some versions of the myth have Persephone's abductor ascending and descending through a cleft in the rock. Diodorus Siculus was a Greco-Sicilian historian from Agira who wrote between 60 and 30 BC. Among classicists, he is known for his monumental *Library of History* which originally consisted of 40 books, only 14 of which still exist. Fortunately for us, Book V survives and has been translated into English – it being the volume that contains descriptions of the Pergusan legend.

Diodorus clearly locates the story here: 'And the Rape of Corê, the myth relates, took place in the meadows in the territory of Enna. The spot lies near the city, a place of striking beauty for its violets and every other kind of flower and worthy of the goddess.' He is a bit more cagey about the exact appearance of Pluton – he reserves the term Hades for his dwelling place rather than his name – but does mention a large grotto containing a chasm 'which leads down into the earth and opens to the north, and through it, the myth relates, Pluton, coming out with his chariot, affected the Rape of Corê.' The Cozzo and the chasm may be one and the same place.

Unsurprisingly, the story is a gift for poets. It would be far too long winded to reference or quote them all but it is worth noting that some of the English language's most renowned versifiers have produced works that touch on the subject. As part of Book IV of *Paradise Lost*, John Milton makes reference to Proserpine in her Roman guise:

> Not that fair field
> Of Enna where Proserpine gathering flowers,
> Herself a fairer flow'r, by gloomy Dis
> Was gather'd, which cost Ceres all that pain
> To seek her through the world;
> [. . .] might with this Paradise
> Of Eden strive.

In an interesting collaboration between the Shelleys, Mary wrote a play entitled *Proserpine* which was principally aimed at a younger audience, and her husband, Percy Bysshe, contributed 'Arethusa' (see the Syracuse chapter) and 'The Song of Proserpine' which begins:

> Sacred Goddess, Mother Earth
> Thou from whose immortal bosom
> Gods, and men, and beasts have birth,
> Leaf, and blade, and bud, and blossom,
> Breathe thine influence most divine
> On thine own child Proserpine.

The Shelleys were great Italianophiles but their life in Italy was chiefly confined to the north, especially Venice, Florence, Pisa and Livorno, off the coast of which Percy Bysshe drowned.

In his description of *Lord Byron and Some of his Contemporaries*, the author and poet Leigh Hunt puts paid to that apocryphal story of Byron and Shelley's boat trip to the island. It was said that in the face of bad weather, Percy had behaved less than bravely, but this was so out of character that the whole story was clearly a fabrication from start to end. As Hunt says, 'Lord Byron and he never were in Sicily, nor ever sailed together, except on the Lake of Geneva. Mr Shelley's bravery was remarkable and was the ultimate ruin of him.'

Shelley was much admired by a later generation of poets, including the pre-Raphaelite Dante Gabriel Rossetti, who was perhaps more well known for his painting. In both genres, he contributed to the further expansion of Enna's place in mythical folklore:

Afar the flowers of Enna from this drear
Dire fruit, which, tasted once,
must thrall me here.

Dante Gabriel, or Gabriel Charles Dante Rossetti as he was christened, was the son of an Italian émigré and poet, Gabriele Rossetti. His mother, Frances Polidori, was the sister of John Polidori, Byron's physician. Given Dante's background, the subject must have been appealing and his iconic painting of Proserpine shows a dark-haired young woman with a rent pomegranate clutched to her breast, the damage having been done; her silk robe ripples seductively from her shoulder.

Like the Arethusian river pointing its way to the lost maiden, poets followed the current of each other's work. Algernon Charles Swinburne, a one-time housemate of Rossetti, also wrote on the myth. Demeter's list of poetic offspring is a long one, from Virgil, Ovid and Thomas Moore, all the way to the folkloric narratives of writers like Gioia Timpanelli, the Italian-American storyteller whose hermit-like character, Costanza, conjures up 'the wild woodlands of the ancient days'. Closed in her green Palermitan palace, the strains of ancient poetry are an escape, giving flights of fantasy to her imagination.

The main road from Pergusa soon leads to the fortress-like rock upon which the city of Enna rests. Its pinnacle is crowned by two proud structures: one, the Castello di Lombardia, is impossible to miss – its crenellations and imposing walls closely guarding the city's peak; the second is a rocky outcrop lying beyond the castle which still bears the faint marks of man's alterations – this is the Rocca di Cerere or Ceres' Rock. Once a temple to Demeter, it is a porous rock weathered by all that the central Sicilian climate can throw at it, not to mention the many tourists and locals who clamber up its sides for the views. The relatively flat upper level gives a spectacular outlook over much of the Sicilian landscape and it is easy to see why ancient writers, Diodorus Siculus and Callimachus included, have referred to the area as the navel of the island.

In the late Victorian days of Douglas Sladen, Enna was known as Castrogiovanni, from the Arabic 'Kasr Yannas', which itself references

*15 Demeter's Rock, known locally as the Rocca di Cerere, once a temple to the goddess, Enna*

classical Enna. Although the interior backroads were supposedly plagued with brigands, he made the journey and was pleasantly surprised. His guides took him to the Rocca and he ably describes the scene before him:

> We had on our left Calascibetta hanging round its mountain-top and the snowy outline of the Madonian Hills, and on our right the fields of Enna and the sacred waters of Pergusa, while in front of us was the huge square mass of snow-white rock, climbed by an ancient stairway, once crowned by the temple of the earth-goddess.

As we have discovered, to the locals our earth goddess is always known as Cerere, but varying traditions have taken her to their hearts whilst applying their own nomenclature. As Sladen believes, she is 'A many-headed daffodil' who 'still flourishes on the slopes of her mountain'.

Sladen was happy to stay in Enna but could not resist a side-swipe at the flea-ridden bedrooms. In so doing, he inevitably referred to Goethe, whose brief stay was blighted by poor accommodation – so widespread in the 1700s. Johann Wolfgang's room had a 'plastered stone floor and shutters but no windows, so that either we had to sit in the dark or put up with the drizzling rain'. The town's height and central position puts it at constant risk of scudding cloud, mist and potential rain; it is always a few degrees cooler than the hotter coastal resorts.

Douglas, however, made the most of his lodgings and paints a simple portrait of a provincial inn where a pecking order existed according to status: 'the principal inn of a minor Sicilian city is always a kind of club at which the commandant of the garrison or the captain of the local carabinieri is the principal personage.' He was convinced he was staying in the same apartment once frequented by Goethe, albeit with a few simple extra modernisations, windows being one.

Enna may not have been lauded for its inns, but it was, and still is, known for its many churches. One little example found in Piazza Mazzini encapsulates much of the city's history within its walls. The Church of San Michele was once an Arab mosque instituted by the invading Saracen, al-Abbas. Its current façade presents a Spanish colonial face to the world. Sladen was much taken with the building and mentions it in his travelogue, *In Sicily*, and his novel, *Sicilian Lovers* – as we now know, a favourite book of Truman Capote.

In the *Sicilian Lovers*, the early action takes place in Enna or, as Sladen calls it, Castrogiovanni. Tommy Cust, accompanied by his friend, the narrator, first meets the Sicilian woman of his dreams in the centre of town. This Montese goddess strikes Cust with love at first sight:

> She had the finely chiselled face, the delicate nostrils typical of well-bred Sicilian beauty and the great dark Sicilian eyes which have no brown in them, but are of a deep grey that sometimes looks black and

sometimes blue. But the feature of the face was the mouth, the exquisite Italian mouth, whose red lips set off the clear dusky skin.

It is fair to say that the narrator is somewhat smitten too. The two men, watching from a café, pay their bill and career up the main street towards the churches of Santa Chiara and San Michele in distant pursuit of their quarry. They pretend innocently to admire the ecclesiastical architecture. Tommy persuades his friend to return to San Michele on the following day in order to catch sight of his beloved amongst the congregation. In so doing, Sladen gives us a detailed description of the church, which he compares inside to the shape of a lemon. For the sake of his companion, the narrator engages the priest in a small tour of the interior – 'and there in the midst of the fine old Spanish arabesque tiles he pulled away a dirty piece of matting, and showed me a picture made up of ever so many tiles, of San Michele himself threatening the devil with a baton.'

Sladen's reverence for the building in its entirety was not matched when he saw this mosaic picture, whether through the eyes of his narrator or in person, as he goes on to describe it as 'comical'. He is much more respectful of the visit paid to Enna by the then Anglican priest who would go on to become a Catholic cardinal – John Henry Newman. He describes Newman's sojourn in the city as the 'turning point in his life'.

During his life, Cardinal Newman embraced the full gamut of British religious thought. Starting out as an evangelical Calvinist, he was ordained as an Anglican priest during his Oxford years, after which he turned towards High Church Anglo-Catholicism. His Mediterranean trip, starting in 1832, did indeed prove to be the turning point that Sladen mentions. At the beginning, he was accompanied by Hurrell Froude, an Oxford friend, who contributed ideas to the poetry that Newman wrote as they travelled around Malta, the Ionian Islands, Rome, Naples and the key destination of Sicily. The works would eventually appear as the *Lyra Apostolica*.

With the trip nearly at its conclusion, Newman made the almost fatal decision to return to Sicily alone, or at least without his English companions. He employed the services of a Neapolitan servant, Gennaro, and planned an itinerary that was intended to take in Messina, Taormina, Catania, Syracuse, Agrigento and Palermo. In his letters, Newman was convinced that the trip from Catania to Syracuse had been the straw that broke the camel's back of his health, added to the damage from 'any bad state of the atmosphere, by the sleepless nights and famished days'.

After returning to Catania, he struggled across the island until he reached Leonforte, a short distance to the north-east of Enna. Gennaro, clearly noticing the signs, told the priest he was coming down with a fever, to which Newman replied that it was only a stomach ache. After a night prostrate on a less than comfortable bed at an inn in the town, it was clear his servant's diagnosis had been correct. With an eye for a potential opportunity, the Neapolitan hinted heavily that, as Newman might die, it would be a nice idea to make a will bequeathing all the luggage to his servant. His wily ways, however, balked at further deception and he proved loyal to the seriously ill Anglican.

After the ministering of herbal drinks, and with the help of a passing medic, Newman was able to gain a small amount of strength, allowing Gennaro to sit him on a mule and guide him up the hill to Enna where they could seek greater comfort and informed medical assistance. Apparently the fever was rife in the city and, in order to find passable lodging, they had to conceal the depths of his condition. Although close to death, the priest was convinced he would live because he believed that 'God had work for me'.

According to time-honoured tradition, he was bled by a medic with whom Newman conversed in a Latin considerably better than the doctor's, despite his high fever. At times, he must have been muffled and powerless as Douglas Sladen recounts an amusing story heard, first hand, from the Cardinal himself. Newman knew he had to sleep and rest but it was the seemingly endless ringing of Enna's many church bells that prevented him from doing so. His only course of action was to bury his head under the bedclothes notwithstanding the burning heat. Thanks to this behaviour, the rumour spread that the Protestant vicar was possessed by a devil.

This story, owing to Sladen's writing, made it all the way to the inner chambers of the Vatican where the Pope found it hysterically funny that a future prince of the Church should have been gossiped about in this way and he 'laughed till his sides ached like an ordinary man'. John Henry may not have seen the funny side at the time as it took a long while for him to recover fully. Only after eight days was he able to walk with support, yet the then Protestant was still keen to debate with a visiting Catholic priest.

Gennaro continued to minister, simply but ably, to his sick employer and when things really began to pick up, he cooked the obligatory chicken soup and little cakes which the future Cardinal really craved. Once recovered, Newman wrote from Palermo in June 1833 about his illness and his words show the gravity of the situation: 'I have surprised everyone by my improvement (though I cannot run yet; the weather is very relaxing). When I came here I could not read nor write, nor talk nor think. I had no memory, and very little of the reasoning faculty.'

Despite this near-death experience, the priest's letters reflect a profound delight in Sicily and to the self-directed question concerning the failure of his expedition, he retorts, 'By no means'. To him, Sicily was like 'the Garden of Eden, and though it ran in the line of my anticipations (as I say), it far exceeded them'. By 1845, he had converted to Catholicism and continued to write prodigiously throughout his Catholic years. His most well-known work amongst the general public is *The Dream of Gerontius* – a poem about a dying man whose prayers are answered by an angel and a demon; it was set to music by Edward Elgar in 1900. In the same decade as he wrote *Gerontius*, he set down his religious autobiography, *Apologia pro Vita Sua*, in response to criticism from the Anglican Charles Kingsley. Biographers have noted the metaphorical threads of his Sicilian experience running through the text of the *Apologia*. Perhaps it needed this distance in time and geography for a spiritual rationale to emerge from the physical wreckage of such an ordeal.

As we have seen, his writing during the actual trip concentrated on the verses of the *Lyra*. His letters to his mother make this clear but also show the long period in which the illness obliterated almost every attempt to put his thoughts down in writing: 'I was very idle in verse-making till June, when I made a start, and have done one every day since June began, having done only three in April and May.'

Verse was the perfect form for a religious man like John Henry to express his spiritual beliefs through allegorical visions. He admired the likes of Walter Scott and Robert Southey but believed poetry should have a higher purpose. In his verse 'The Good Samaritan', he implicitly gives thanks to the care he received from the Montese medic and his Catholic bretheren:

> There on a foreign shore,
> The home-sick solitary finds a friend.
> Thoughts, prison'd long for lack of speech, out-pour
> Their tears; and doubts in resignation end.
> I almost fainted from the long delay
> That tangles me within this languid bay,
> When comes a foe, my wounds with oil and wine to tend.

The subsequent poems written during his Palermitan recuperation period further show his concern about reforms in the Church of England, possibly hinting at the steps he would take towards Rome. Eventually becoming a cardinal in 1879, Newman lived a long life, dying at the age of 89. He was beatified during Pope Benedict's visit to the United Kingdom in 2010.

If Goethe had to put up with Enna's fogs, and Newman its constant clanging, then Vincent Cronin was happy to embrace both, calling it 'a city of mist and bells'. He compares it to 'a Spanish mountain city such as Toledo' and the comparison is apt both architecturally and spiritually for Enna is home to one of Sicily's most extravagant and Spanish-inspired Easter celebrations. The hooded figures in their white and wine-coloured robes recall the Semana Santa (Holy Week) processions that can be seen the length and breadth of Spain, but particularly in Andalucian cities such as Seville.

The figures of Christ and his mother are painfully and sombrely paraded through the streets, accompanied by the hooded worshippers who belong to various confraternities – laymen who contribute time and effort to their specific church of choice, an affiliation that is usually based on family, trade or district. On Good Friday, the procession is accompanied by the plaintive brass sounds of that distinctive brand of funereal music heard in Sicily. Some of the confraternities wear a pointed hood, which to the uninitiated bears a startlingly unsettling resemblance to that sported by the Ku Klux Klan.

On Easter Sunday, the statue of Christ changes to reflect his resurrection and the whole celebration climaxes when the much happier Madonna finally gets to meet her risen child in the main square by the cathedral. Enna is steeped in this religiosity, whether pagan, Christian or, indeed, both at the same time – observe the town's patron saint, Saint Mary of the Visitation, whom some theorise is an extension of the cult of Demeter.

One church, the Montesalvo, built to supplant the Temple of Ceres, has the claim to fame that it stands at the very geographical centre of Sicily and there is an obelisk next to the *chiesa* which testifies to the fact. In short, the city is the island's mythical heartland, the home of its medieval spirituality and a layercake of historical influence. Vincent Cronin's quest, so eloquently related in *The Golden Honeycomb*, was to search for a legend, a place at once imaginary and very real. Daedalus and his flight to the island from Crete is Cronin's mythological touchstone but the everyday presence of the legendary, buried and adjusted by a complex history, is the real honeycomb at the centre of his work. Enna is arguably the best example of this entangled web of influences which Vincent knows is so difficult to unpick:

Logically Enna is representative of the island's medieval life, of the disturbed period between the extinction of Norman rule and the age when Sicily became a Spanish dependency, but to isolate one particular layer of history from those before and after is virtually impossible in the case not only of Enna but of all Sicilian towns. In each the strands of multiple civilisations are interwoven, just as among the people can be glimpsed here a profile from a Hellenistic vase, there a coarse and swarthy African face, and in their speech now a Lombard, now an Arab word. Sicily is an island lying outside time.

## *Caltanissetta*

Caltanissetta is Sicily's other central city worthy of literary mention. Some 35 kilometres (22 miles) to the south-west of Enna, this former sulphur-mining capital spreads over more rolling terrain cut by valleys. It was bombed by the Allies prior to land invasion during World War II and, as a consequence, some of its streets bear the hallmarks of hasty redevelopment, though it is still well endowed with the kind of architecture that Cronin found so difficult to separate into well-defined epochs.

One of the city's best-known literary connections involves Vitaliano Brancati and Leonardo Sciascia. In 1935, Sciascia's family moved from his birthplace of Racalmulto to Caltanissetta and he was enrolled in school at the Istituto Magistrale 'IX Maggio' where Brancati was teaching. The young Leonardo, then 14, was an avid reader and went on to read *Omnibus*, a magazine with content contributed by Vitaliano. Brancati's years as a writer for this weekly were abruptly shortened when it was closed by the Fascist censors in 1939.

The older teacher would act as a mentor-like figure for Sciascia and it was thanks to him that Leonardo became acquainted with the greats of French literature. He achieved his school diploma in 1941 and, luckily for the world of letters, he escaped the fate of so many of his classmates who were to die in the freezing trenches of Mussolini's flawed campaign in Russia.

To briefly reiterate Chapter 6, Sciascia went on to emulate Brancati in two ways: he became a teacher, albeit at an elementary school, and an author, becoming one of Sicily's best-know writers on the international stage. Brancati's work, so rooted in the satirical exposure of a macho society, has had less international success. His works make it very difficult to capture in any translation the subtlety and, sometimes, overt place-driven sardonic content. His books have been called burlesque, theatrical and, in the more nuanced sense of the word, grotesque depictions of reality. Seemingly Sciascia's complex, ethically driven cries for justice in a world that lacks a moral compass are more recognisable to a wider audience.

The Istituto Magistrale still exists, now rechristened the Istituto Magistrale 'A. Manzoni' after the famous writer of *I promessi sposi* (*The Betrothed*). It is located in Viale Trieste, one of the city's nondescript thoroughfares lined with concrete apartments and unprepossessing banks, hairdressers and shops selling anything from household wares to jewellery. It is an unusual location to have spawned or furthered the careers of two great writers, but they both derived material from their surroundings and produced works that showed a profound love for their island whilst recognising its deep-rooted difficulties.

Perhaps it is no surprise that Sciascia's formative years in Caltanissetta had an impact. Its central location and 'island within an island' mentality have left distinctive traces in Sciascian thought. Rumour has it that Leonardo never bathed in the sea – an apparently harmless little biographical detail, but it is indicative of many a Sicilian's attitude to the water surrounding their island. Despite the bounty it brings, notably the tuna and swordfish that find their way onto restaurant plates from Trapani to Syracuse, the sea has also been a source of trouble; after all, invaders cross the waves.

Sciascia has been famously quoted as saying that Sicilians turn their back on the sea and pretend it does not exist. This may appear a nonsense when strolling the promenade in Cefalù or looking down on the beaches of Taormina, but it makes a lot more sense when you visit the likes of Enna and Caltanissetta, where islanders could pull up the metaphorical and literal drawbridge. These embattled fortress towns and cities of central Sicily were the last bastions of resistance to the next invader. Eventually overrun, they would bear the heavily embossed footprint of the conqueror's culture but retain a great deal of their Sicilian soul – a soul almost as old as the island itself.

### Piazza Armerina

As the crow flies, the town of Piazza Armerina is almost equidistant from Caltanissetta and Enna but if you are approaching from the north-west it is likely you will have come from the Enna direction via the Palermo–Catania motorway. The town of Armerina is attractive enough, draped over a trio of rolling hills and presided over by a castle and Bároque cathedral. The closer you edge to the south-east corner, the more extravagant the Baroque and the lusher and more opulent the market gardening. Yet, despite the town's Palio – a celebration in honour of the island's long-dead first Norman ruler – it is for the nearby Villa Casale that most visitors or, for that matter, writers come to this area.

In 1997, the villa was designated a UNESCO World Heritage Site. To see why it is so important, one can do no better than to quote the organisation's own rationale for conferring this status: 'Villa del Casale at Piazza Armerina is the supreme example of a luxury Roman villa, which graphically illustrates the predominant social and economic structure of its age. The mosaics that decorate it are exceptional for their artistic quality and invention as well as their extent.'

The title 'villa' conjures up images of a whitewashed box, a nouveau-riche pile or a somewhat tasteless architectural hodgepodge. Casale is none of these and would be better described as a palace, although some have argued for its nouveau-riche status in Roman times. Its most famous feature is the mosaic pavement found in the long Corridor of the Great Hunting Scene, depicting the capture of wild animals in Africa. The corridor joins the fourth area of terracing to the other parts of the villa. In this zone, there is a reception hall, basilica and a series of private apartments which also display mosaic floors of more gentle, everyday scenes, including the iconic bikini-clad Roman girls cavorting in sporting activity – forerunners of today's beach volleyball players.

Two writers with different perspectives were drawn to Casale: Bernard Berenson, the academic and art historian, and Robert D. Kaplan, the travel writer and foreign correspondent. Berenson was born Bernhard Valvrojenski in Lithuania but his parents emigrated to the United States in 1875, hence the name change. His love of classical imagery and the Italian Renaissance led his professional career to be inextricably linked with Italy and he set up home in the Villa Tatti in Settignano near Florence, now the Harvard Center for Italian Renaissance Studies. Owing to its classical past, it is not surprising that Berenson was attracted to Sicily and his diaries written between 1947 and 1956, published as *The Passionate Sightseer*, reflect this.

Bernard was grateful for the existence of accommodation at Piazza Armerina so he could manage two extensive excursions to Casale. The modern-day approach will usually be clogged with coaches dropping off parties of tourists, but for Berenson the approach was somewhat quieter: 'The site of the villa soon appeared before us marked by scattered remains of walls and columns showing the vastness of the original buildings. Various sheds have been put up recently to roof over the mosaics.' It was just as well the sheds had been erected as his first visit coincided with heavy rain and muddy conditions.

Today's visitor will still see a plethora of covered glass structures, although of a more permanent nature. He was privileged to meet the overseer of works, a certain Cavaliere Veneziani, who postulated the idea that the whole complex had once been owned by the Roman Emperor Maximian who was father to Maxentius, Constantine's big rival. Berenson's description of the hunting scene captures the whirl of fauna and humanity in this bloody spectacle:

> In the vast composition representing a chase, the most important of the whole lot, we see riders dashing forward and backward, beaters, carts drawn by oxen with cages for wild animals, quantities of tigers, lions, gnus, hippopotamuses, gazelles. The animals done with considerable spirit, the human beings much less so.

Bernard was a little scathing of the quality of draughtsmanship in some of the mosaics, hinted at in the comment, but he was aware of their supreme cultural and historical importance, a wise assumption given they had not completed the excavations at this point, with the villa being a long way from its UNESCO appellation.

In an interesting connection to another Sicilian visitor, Berenson was married to Mary Smith, the sister of Bertrand Russell's first wife, although this did not stop his long-term relationship with Belle da Costa Greene, librarian to J. P. Morgan – a liaison reluctantly tolerated by Mary, as his biographer, Ernest Samuels, indicates. This occasionally complicated private life was not echoed in the clear direction of his professional studies, although his Italian research proved uncomfortable during the war when he felt the heat of the Fascist regime.

Throughout, he maintained his love of the Renaissance and, in turn, its interest in a classical antiquity he also found fascinating. His wistful diary comment on leaving Villa Casale shows the sensitive nature of his imagination and leaves us all wondering what other Casales once existed:

> As we drive back in the sunset light I am pursued by the nostalgic vision of so many country seats and elegant villas, that must have existed in these and other regions of the classical world from the British Isles to the Sahara Desert, of which no trace is left.

Robert D. Kaplan came to the villa in the 1970s and, rarely for Sicily, he experienced the same downpour that Berenson had to suffer. His thoughts on Casale form part of *Mediterranean Winter* – his nostaligic look back at the European travels he undertook as a youth. It is the most personal of Robert's travel books as it is not only a hymn to an off-season Mediterranean world infused with the building blocks of our society, but also a delve into the roots of his wanderlust.

It has been said many times that the Greeks and Romans knew how to choose the best sites for their theatres, palaces and baths. As Kaplan says, 'True affluence is a matter of owning fine vistas, so as to appropriate for yourself nothing less than the beauty of the earth.' The Roman who built this villa surely had the wherewithal to capture that slice of earthly pleasure as the location is perfect – Robert certainly agrees. Like Berenson, Kaplan quotes Maximian as the owner, a former Balkan warrior from the Yugoslav frontiers of the empire. Fresh from Agrigento, the American writer seems less impressed with the architectural endeavours promoted by this Roman man of war.

Contrary to the central provinces' role as Rome's bread basket, the island actually has a paucity of remains from this era. Rather than start from scratch, the Romans often appropriated Greek structures and adapted them – the Taormina theatre being a classic example: the Romans altered the structure to allow for their more gruesome forms of public entertainment, including gladiatorial combat. Casale, therefore, stands out both here and in a worldwide context, for its sheer spread of mosaic artwork, a fact Kaplan is happy to acknowledge.

Having previously travelled to Tunisia, where he was able to view other artefacts created by Roman mosaicists, he is rather scathing of the iconic gymnasts and hunting images in the villa: 'Even with their flesh exposed, the girls had the antiseptic look of cheerleaders, while the scenes of hunting, banqueting, and chariot racing exhibited a cold and overwhelming pomposity.' The pomposity may be due to the rich warrior, Maximian, trying to stamp his credentials and flaunt his wealth before other more cultured visitors who must have visited him in his new country seat – an upstart Roman desperate for some of the intellectual kudos that Gibbon and others have reported he lacked.

Through the lens of Berenson and Kaplan, two writers with quite different lives, the visitor to Casale can look beyond the sheer impressive extent of Roman craftsmanship and focus on the detail. As a casual observer, it is difficult to deny the impact of such Roman endeavour and the images shout their power and wealth, although possibly without a subtlety more akin to that of the Greeks. Kaplan even goes as far as to say, 'There was no soul to any of it.'

## The Mountain Towns

There appears to be a gulf of insuperable proportions between the rolling hills of Armerina, with its evidence of an opulent, decadent past, and the stony crags of Sicily's interior hill villages and small towns. The observation of Theresa Maggio's grandmother regarding the emptiness of the interior may have been the comment of someone whose life had been turned upside down by emigration, but it was evidently a challenge that Maggio could not resist, as she set out to explore the region for herself. The charm of the villages lies precisely in their quiet, understated, timeless existence and Theresa is their greatest champion.

*The Stone Boudoir*, her biographical tour through these out-of-the-way settlements, does not only focus on her ancestral home and the villages around Etna, but widens its net to encompass the likes of Polizzi Generosa and Geraci Siculo on the borders of the Madonie Regional Park. The Madonie are a range of mountains that rise behind the northern coast at Cefalù and spread inland to the heights of the interior. From the pinnacle of Ceres' Rock in Enna, the peaks can be seen in the distance.

Polizzi Generosa is about 40 minutes from the coast and was known by Italians as a centre for tailoring. This trade spawned the Dolces, particularly Domenico, who famously teamed up with Stefano Gabbana. Despite Dolce's somewhat love–hate relationship with the island, the glamorous duo have recently issued a collection, *Sicilianità*, inspired by the very stones of his birth. Martin Scorsese's father was also born here. The town has a vertiginous outlook that Theresa took full advantage of when she rented an apartment on the very edge of a precipice: 'The earth dropped away in tiers; my knees went weak at the view. On tiny natural terraces on the V-shaped walls of the canyon, celery-green pastures clung to the outcroppings like rags blown about by the wind.' Owing to the geography, anyone approaching in a car is likely to find themselves boxed in by one-way streets that curve up ridiculously steep inclines, requiring the manoeuvring skills of a rally driver.

All the roads will eventually meet in Piazza Umberto, where Via Cardinale Rampolla heads uphill past two churches of note: the Chiesa Madre and San Gandolfo la Povera, both of which have surprising artworks. The Mother Church houses a triptych of the *Madonna Enthroned* painted by Rogier Van der Weyden and La Povera boasts an altar piece by Giuseppe Salerno. This artistic heritage mirrors the town's unexpected royal connection, its roots belonging to the Norman conqueror, Roger I.

The epithet Generosa is bound to spark interest as it is an unusual addition to Polizzi's name. Maggio was so taken by the originality she researched the settlement's early development in the town's library. Polizzi, itself, is attributed to varying origins, be they Castor and Pollux or Isis, whose statue was found in a well in 1650. Generosa, though, has no such dispute as the Holy Roman Emperor Frederick II conferred the title on the generous populace when they gave him more than the usual quantity of fighting men and supplies.

When Marlena di Blasi thought of writing her book on inland Sicily she was partially put off by the warning that nobody would speak in any depth to a passing foreigner. Her Ragusan adventures proved this wrong and Theresa's experiences in Polizzi fully endorse the magnanimous name. She came to the town as a complete stranger and a single woman, both of which would have been enough to isolate her from the inhabitants, but the opposite was true: 'I walked around in Polizzi, instead of suspicious looks people spontaneously offered me fruit, a calendar, a cookbook, a cup of coffee, vegetables from a wheelbarrow, three-course meals, and a place to warm myself out of the rain.'

In an interview for the magazine *Nebula*, Maggio is candid about her Sicilian-American background. When asked about her interest in the art of storytelling – the oral tradition of passing on folklore through the generations – she is quick to dismiss the idea that this was a tradition passed through her own family line, where, in fact, the immigrant experience was a closed door to the grandchildren. Sicily was a mysterious presence on the periphery of the family's horizon – that sad nostalgia mentioned in the Catania chapter. Despite, or perhaps because of this, she was keen to see beyond the veil. A trained journalist, she applies these skills to her other writing. *The Stone Boudoir* is spiced with the histories of individuals – tales that enliven the silent stones of her beloved villages.

In Polizzi, one of the few occasions when the town dropped its big-hearted moniker was when Theresa met a female store owner whose story flew in the face of the normal male-dominated society: 'Most Sicilian country girls grow up in patriarchal families, learn to clean, go to grammar school and high school, fill their hope chests with cutwork linens, marry suitably, have children, attend Sunday Mass, keep house, and stay at home.' Things are slowly changing and an increasing number go on to higher education or work outside the home, but even then, as Maggio is at pains to note, they will have patriarchal protection in some form.

Theresa's friend had to put up with the loose tongues and spiteful actions of a few of her fellow townspeople as she tried to keep her little business afloat. Her car tyres were slashed when parking beside her shop and verbal abuse extended to 20-minute tirades in full-on dialect, including threats of a distinctly physical nature. Maggio was also subjected to the supposed rights of male entitlement, albeit away from Polizzi. Back in her ancestral town of Santa Margherita, she had stopped by a watering trough in a park to rest and eat her picnic. Already wary of communication with stray men after a mattress seller had followed her home, she was reluctant to engage a passing mule-driver in conversation. The toothless old man decided to stop for a chat and said he would bring her some fava beans on his return. Strangely, almost immediately, he reappeared and in the politest terms possible, asked her if she wanted to make love. When recounting the story to a distant relative, she was told that the watering hole was the haunt of the local prostitute.

Geraci Siculo rides a saddle of land between the peaks of the Madonie. Sometimes prone to snow in the winter and exposed to summer sun, it is a place of contrasts. A favourite of Theresa's, she loved the small rose gardens and blue-stone walls. On one visit, she intended to stay in the Benedictine convent. After being given the third degree by the nun at the entrance grille, she was told to make her way to the Collegiana sisters at the Collegio di Maria who would be able to rent her a room as the Benedictines were a closed order. Both convents were suffering the familiar decline in a vocational life seen throughout the western world. The Collegianas had fewer than the Benedictines, with just three sisters remaining.

Religion in Sicily is part of the very fabric of society and is largely taken for granted. In many small towns, the main church square is the heart of the community where celebrations are held and the evening stroll passes under the grandiose façades of the ecclesiastical buildings. Despite the deference paid to the Catholic tradition, the birth rate is dropping steadily and the number attending church likewise. As Sicily draws closer to the secular train hurtling through the twenty-first century, the situation for religious institutions, such as those visited by Maggio, is only going to worsen. The confrontation between a conservative religion and an increasingly liberal society has still yet to find much common ground in Sicily.

The influence of foreign thought in the hill villages is not always welcomed with open arms. In Geraci, Theresa met a fellow American who had married a Sicilian whilst he was running a restaurant in London. Neither had connections with the little town but had bought some land with the idea of opening an *agriturismo,* a small holiday accommodation development in the countryside. Despite initial resistance from the locals, the couple brought with them a whirlwind of ideas, leading the ex-restauranteur's wife to be christened 'Tornado'.

The use of nicknames is far more prevalent in Sicily than in many other countries. Very often, the nickname, which usually springs from a character trait, profession or some long-forgotten reason, can be handed down the generations; at the very least, it sticks for a lifetime – once a *Rosso Malpelo,* always a *Malpelo.* This is one of the most pernicious of nicknames and applies to anyone with red hair, as Sicilians used to believe that redheads had a particularly maladjusted disposition owing to their Judas-like flaming locks. People with a reddish tinge are not as uncommon on the island as may be imagined, thanks to the Norman and Swabian genes that have filtered down through the generations.

Giovanni Verga famously wrote the story of 'The Nasty Redhead', a boy labelled with this unfortunate title who goes on to inhabit the role that a harsh mining society has created for him – rather like a self-fulfilling prophecy. The tale is, essentially, a social commentary that examines the way in which society brutalises those who come from the position of underdog. Maggio's own relatives had the less-offensive name of 'little spoon', a recognisable pet-name to most people in their home town of Santa Margherita, including the toothless lothario intent on bedding her.

From Geraci Siculo and Generous Polizzi we move to the town of Roccacolomba. If you have a Sicilian map and are intent on tracing these literary locations, you would now do well to lay it to one side. Roccacolomba is in the Madonie mountains, but no amount of searching will help you find it, even if you were to purchase the Italian equivalent of an Ordnance Survey map. There is a Roccapalumba, further to the west behind Caccamo and a Rocca di Capri Leone near to Capo d'Orlando, but no Roccacolomba.

To all intents and purposes, it is a composite of the Madonie, a fictional location drawing elements from all surrounding settlements. Simonetta Agnello Hornby created it as a location for her book *The Almond Picker* and in the author's own words it is 'a rocky little town'. The waters are muddied somewhat by the title, as almonds are traditionally picked further south, especially in Agrigento Province. However, her lucid descriptions of Roccacolomba clearly place it among the peaks. One of the characters, Pietro Fatta, sits on his terrace, his 'box at the opera', and admires the sweep of grandiose countryside surrounding him: 'he contemplated this backdrop of hills, whose tops had been levelled by the peasants. Behind him, to the north, the mountains were ranked one behind another, undulating and majestic, clad with dappled woods.'

The book, set in 1963, starts with the death of La Mennulara, the maid-turned-family-administrator, and therein lies the story – just how did this woman from humble origins rise to control the destiny of the Alfallipe estate? Agnello Hornby's origins were rather different: a Palermitan with a great love of her city's monumental icon, Monte Pellegrino, she spread her wings, first to London, then America and Zambia. These days, she is firmly based in London with occasional trips back to her roots. *The Almond Picker* has one of the most unusual dedications of any book – to British Airways. We know that the story came to her in a 'vision' at the airport, but if her flight from Palermo to London had not been delayed, it may never have existed.

If you have read the chapter on Messina, you will remember that Agnello Hornby is a lawyer. In an interview with one of the authors of this book she clearly demonstrated her dedication and pride in that side of her working life. Writing is very much a subsidiary activity, despite the many prizes she has garnered and countries in which she has been published. Whilst discussing translation, she made the interesting point that her one experiment with writing in English turned out differently when she verbalised the text and put it into Italian. The clouds over St James' Park in London did not fit the images conveyed by her more luminous Italian phrasing. It is interesting to muse on how different the text for *La mennulara* would have been had she written it in English, although perhaps it is so rooted in the soil of her homeland such a thing would have been impossible.

As the book progresses, a complex portrait of the Alfallipes' maid emerges; at turns contradictory, her path through life left few indifferent to her character. Small-town life is laid bare, as gossip and opinion rumble under a more benign surface. Her story seeps through the lives and loves of others. Are we truly a sum of our own parts or a reflection of what others see in us? If the novel begs this question of our own personalities, it could equally ask it of rural Sicily. The patchwork effect serves to build a verbal mosaic more rooted in the stones than Villa Casale.

Agnello Hornby's Roccacolomba is just awakening to the seams of 1960s modernisation and in an interesting twist at the end Simonetta provides the reader with an epilogue detailing the futures of her characters. To best understand the town's future, we suggest you find your own Roccacolomba and see if its reality is mirrored or distorted by the weight of psychological expectation Sicily carries for so many foreign visitors.

# ❧ 8 ❧

# Trapani and the West

## Salt, Wine and the Misty Goddess

### *Selinunte*

Selinunte is on the south-western coastal strip of the island, some 52 kilometres (32 miles) from the westernmost point of the Sicilian triangle at Marsala. The relatively low-lying land attracts fearsome summer temperatures and its fair share of insect life. The main draw is the temple complex and settlement which was founded in the seventh century BC, although the temples themselves only began to make an appearance from the sixth century. Instead of the evocative names given to the Agrigentine buildings – Concord, Demeter, Juno and Vulcan, homages to the gods – the remains at Selinunte have archaeologically anodine alphabetical epithets so that the shrine dedicated to Hera is more commonly known as Temple E.

The complex is more widespread than that at Agrigento with much less reconstruction. The easiest access is along the Strada dei Templi from Marinella. Lawrence Durrell, dictated to as he was by the constrictions of his guided bus tour, found the itinerary took in the sites of Selinunte. He re-read the letters sent to him by his friend from Cyprus, Martine, who had implored him to visit the island; among them were reminiscences of the site. Sadly for Durrell, he only managed to sign up for his 'carousel' after Martine had died; as such, the whole enterprise became something of a tribute. She told him that his first impressions would be of, 'great loneliness and melancholy; but in a moment you will reflect that what is really wrong with the site is the fact that the headland is not really high enough over the sea'.

To some extent he concurred, but his main preoccupation on arrival was the searing heat and lack of shade, aggravating his bad temper. However, shaking off the sloth, he took advantage of another passenger's knowledge and ex-army binoculars. Durrell and Deeds, the former Raj officer, soon realised a complete tour would involve a two-mile hike amongst the 'blackish dunes'. On her visit, Martine had talked herself into a far more poetic frame of mind and the temperature simply became one more factor in her imaginary recreation: 'The heat throbbed away, it was the pulse of the ancient world still beating somewhere, far away.'

Selinunte may not have had the over-zealous attentions of too many archaeologists intent on rebuilding the past – preservation being the priority – but it has seen its fair share of decorations whisked away to museums, notably that of Palermo: 'a most irritating habit this, common to the archaeologists of all nations' was Durrell's dry comment on the matter. There is, however, plenty that still remains, albeit jumbled, fragmentary and widespread. This slide into ruin has a long history, although not always through the gradual decay of time. Selinunte had been scattered to the four corners of its sandy arena back in the third century BC when the Carthaginians wholeheartedly sacked the place. This may also account for some of the sadly lost dedicatory titles that were surely appended to each and every temple.

The writer Jorge Luis Borges found the whole alphabetical classification amusing and decided to create his own literary system – 'C for Conrad'. His visit in 1984, along with the Magnum photographer Ferdinando Scianna, produced some of the most iconic images of the Argentinian. When his party suggested Temple B could stand for 'Borges', his response was to suggest 'Buster Keaton' instead. No doubt the ageing Borges was ferried around the site in one of the little electric carts that enable the less active tourist to negotiate the distances. Alejandro Luque, on his Borgesian pilgrimage in search of Scianna's photographs of the writer, spent far less time contemplating the architecture than he did frantically searching for the exact locations of each image, including one of Jorge Luis in front of a bare branching tree – a seemingly Sisyphean task given that Borges had visited the site 20 years previously. Alejandro had to make do with a poor substitute.

The most elegiac of the photographer's images of Borges on that day in the early 1980s is that of the aged author, famous for referencing the labyrinth in his work, looking up to a jumble of criss-crossing stone fragments with a crumbling temple in the background. Luque captures the atmosphere of this scene very lucidly: 'Setting aside my Borgesian passion, the shot looks very attractive, very poetic: the aged man, who perhaps feels the proximity of death, scrutinizes the remains of a distant civilization. The ruined architecture still whispers the splendour of its people.'

If it whispered for Luque, it sighed for Durrell as he felt the very sound of the name resembled a poignant exhalation. Unlike the strident cries of a resurgent Agrigento, Selinunte's charms are buried in the shifting sands of time and place. There was once an all-encompassing central acropolis, long since gone, overtaken by the lentisk, berry-bearing shrubs, which the blind Borges likened to the smell of lychees, and the wild celery, a plant that morphed into the name of the location itself, as Durrell tells us.

## Mazara del Vallo

Following the coast westwards from Selinunte, you soon come to Mazara, the most Arabic in look and feel of all Sicilian towns. The centre of town even has a Kasbah district that contains a significant Tunisian population. A walk through its twisting lanes will take you past halal butchers, the Tunisian Social Club and shops selling North African pottery and tagines. You're as likely to hear the throaty tones of Arabic as you are to hear the more open vowels of Italian. Great effort has been made to smarten the area with colourful pots and a series of embedded ceramic tiles on the walls, bearing quotes from enlightened world figures such as Gandhi and Martin Luther King.

The author Andrea Camilleri uses this multicultural connection in his book, *The Terracotta Dog*. Inspector Montalbano is confronted with the mystery of two entwined skeletons found in a cave and watched over by a full-size terracotta hound. His research into the symbolism that this arrangement suggests leads to a Qur'anic story that tells of a cave, sleeping youngsters and a guard dog. Of course, the place he visits to uncover these details is Mazara del Vallo. Talking to Farid Rahman, a friend of the Police Commissioner, he asks about race relations in the town and is pleased to find that confrontational incidents are few. Rahman describes the reason in these terms:

> I think we're sort of a historical memory for the Mazarese, almost a genetic fact. We're family. Al-Imam al-Mazari, the founder of the Maghrebin juridical school, was born in Mazara, as was the philologist Ibn al-Birr, who was expelled from the city in 1068 because he liked wine too much.

Mazara is also one of Sicily's biggest and most important fishing ports. Our fictional hero, Montalbano, learns the true fact that many of the port's boats are crewed by Sicilians and Tunisians together.

A tour of the district uncovers more of Little Tunis as he witnesses life at the public baths and a café with hookah-pipes. The sura from the Qur'an is revealed when he asks Rahman what an imam is recounting to a small group of children. Although all the details do not fit exactly, this amazing coincidence leaves the Inspector reeling. Further literary connection is made by Rahman's friend who ties the story to an old Christian legend – the *Seven Sleepers of Ephesus*, thus leading to a modern Egyptian drama: *The People of the Cave* (*Ahl al-kahf*) by Taufik al-Hakim. Intertextuality is typical of Camilleri, who delights in playing literary games with his main character. Other books in the series, including his short stories, revel in referencing plots from centuries of literature: popular detective fiction such as Maigret or obscure texts, notably *The Manuscript Found in Saragossa* by Jan Potocki, all find their way into his work.

At the end of *The Terracotta Dog*, Camilleri has added an author's note thanking two Arab students who gave him the inspiration for this novel when he was teaching stage direction at the Silvio d'Amico Academy for Dramatic Arts. They were studying al-Hakim's play. Andrea has imbued his detective with some of the values that he holds dear and his humanity manifests itself in Montalbano's attitude to the underdog, which extends to the deep concern he feels for an endangered Tunisian mother and her young son in *The Snack Thief* (*Il ladro di merendine*).

If Palermo contains the remains of a splendid Arab–Norman past, then Mazara is the best face of Sicily's modern-day relations with North Africa – which is not to say that problems do not exist. With the emergence of new governments on the southern side of the Mediterranean shores and the inherent upheaval this has created, Sicily has become one of the first destinations for those intent on escaping the harsh realities at home. The most obvious demonstration of these events has been the refugee centre on the Sicilian island of Lampedusa, one of the nearest landfalls to Tunisia. Many have risked life and limb, often falling prey in the process to unscrupulous people-traffickers whose last priority is their victims' safety, as evidenced by the tragic drownings in 2013.

## *Marsala*

Marsala is the next town of any size if you follow the coastal road north from Mazara del Vallo. It is the westernmost point of Sicily, excepting the Egadi Islands off the coast. The rocky, low-lying coastline juts its nose into the sea, forming part of the harbour, whilst the dusty, sand-coloured town spreads back into the vineyard-covered hinterland. Marsala gets its name from the North African invaders who named it 'the Harbour of Allah', Mars-Allah. To the Romans, it was Lilybaeum and the capital of the administrative region of western Sicily.

One of Lilybaeum's quaestors (regional administrators/accountants) was none other than Marcus Tullius Cicero. He fulfilled his job with integrity and intelligence to such an extent that when Caius Verres, the praetor or governor of Sicily, was indicted for what amounted to the crime of lining his pockets at the expense of the Sicilian people, Cicero was asked to make the case for the prosecution.

Verres used his ill-gotten gains to appoint the best defence money could buy. On the face of it, Cicero had his work cut out but he was a renowned orator and the pleadings which were set down in writing have come down to us as one of the greatest examples of Roman legal articulacy. In 1812, Charles Kelsall decided to translate the work specifically appertaining to Verres. He had already written *A Letter from Athens* and originally intended to produce a travelogue in the style of Brydone and Swinburne. He came to the conclusion that, as there was nothing more that could be reasonably added to these accounts so soon after their publication, it would be a better idea to concentrate on the translation of Cicero, to which he appended some notes of his own investigations. In the introduction he describes why Marcus Tullius' orations were so important:

> The pleadings against Caius Verres, praetor of Sicily, must be enumerated among the most valuable monuments of the eloquence of Cicero. The variety of entertaining anecdotes with which they abound, the works of art which are commemorated, the topographical descriptions, the glaring guilt of the accused, the insight afforded into the laws and manners of the ancient Sicilians, conspire to dazzle the imagination, and rivet the attention of the reader.

Cicero did his homework. He spent a long time travelling around Sicily from Syracuse to Marsala gathering evidence for the case. He was on home ground in Lilybaeum and records the witness testimony of one Pamphilus who had been stripped of his valuables by the voracious praetor: 'I remember that Pamphilus, a gentleman of Lilybaeum, who received me in his house and was my friend, told me, that when he was compelled to deliver up a large water-flagon, exquisitely carved by the hand of Boethus, he returned to his house with sorrow and regret.' It seems that the vessel had been handed down the generations and was a source of pride to Pamphilus, who would produce it on feast days. The story did not end there, for this unfortunate friend of Cicero's was subsequently also asked to produce the cups he owned, which were embossed in high relief.

Extremely upset by this second imposition, Pamphilus decided to accompany the cups to Verres' palace where the governor's henchmen,

Tlepolemus and Hiero, were waiting for him. The greedy praetor was fast asleep taking a siesta and his two lapdogs took the opportunity for some freelance bribery of their own. If Pamphilus agreed to pay them, they would make up a story to tell their boss that the cups were worthless, thereby enabling the man from Lilybaeum to keep something of his heritage. As Cicero explains, 'It was then that I discovered that these Cibyratic brothers were kept in his service, that he might employ their hands and their eyes in his system of plunder.'

As noted, Kelsall the translator did some investigation of his own on the ground in Marsala and was very impressed with the Sicilians themselves, 'naturally a fine people'. However, he laments the government of the day and a certain sense of what he calls 'waggery'. In Marsala, he employed a guide who convinced him that he could see the actual house where Marcus Tullius Cicero had lived whilst acting as quaestor in Lilybaeum.

With awe and reverence, 'this the translator was preparing to approach with nearly as much veneration, as if he was going to tread the site of the Cuman, or Tusculan villas'. The actuality was something of a disappointment; he was presented with the sight of a house 'sprucely white-washed', a property he was sure did not pre-date the sixteenth century. The guide persisted – 'questa fu la casa dove dimorava il signor Cicerone quando fu in Marsala' – honestly, it was the actual house, repeated the Sicilian. One wonders how many less-informed tourists have been taken in by similarly nondescript piles of stones. The deception was not completely dishonest as it transpired that the house belonged to the guide's father – also a *cicerone*. This play on words is effective, as a *cicerone* is both the name for a guide and the Italian name for Cicero.

Marcus Tullius was a discerning lawyer; his interests ranged from philosophy to art and politics. His letters were considered a model in the art of person-to-person communication and his influence on the Latin language was substantial. In part of the Verres orations, he expounded upon the former abundance of beautifully designed artefacts in Sicily, so sadly plundered by its avaricious governor: 'I am of opinion, that when Sicily abounded with wealth and resources, art was carried to a high state of perfection in that island.' His research, witness testimony and evident affection for Sicily shone through and he was to win the court case in the face of the overtly ostentatious displays put on by the defence lawyer, the renowned Hortalus.

The Romans were not averse to the pleasures of the grape, and they owed a debt to the Phoenicians for the viticultural activities already in place at Lilybaeum. However, it is indirectly thanks to Napoleon that Marsala developed a significant wine-producing industry. During the Napoleonic Wars in the early 1800s, British access to madeira, port and sherry was considerably restricted owing to blockades and the danger from French attack. By this time, the British forces and population in general had already developed a taste for fortified wine and were not ready to relinquish its delights.

Step forward the Woodhouses, Benjamin Ingham, Nelson and Ingham's relatives, the Whitakers. In 1798, Nelson first placed an order for Marsalan fortified wine with John Woodhouse – the significance of which only really became apparent when Sicily acted as a key destination in Britain's Mediterranean efforts to avoid Napoleonic attack. During these restricted times, the endorsement of Nelson was enough to set the hare running. Suddenly, the Woodhouses and Benjamin Ingham, who first visited Marsala in 1806, found they were inundated with orders. The Inzolia grape was ideally suited to the fortification process and the hardy conditions it had to endure during a western Sicilian summer.

Ingham was that most Victorian of Englishmen – an entrepreneur with wide horizons. He set up in direct competition to the Woodhouses and was determined to ride the wave of Sicilian investment, which not only included wine but also sulphur, shipping and banking. He threw himself into Sicilian life, living with the Duchess of Santa Rosalia, to whom he may or may not have been married. His supposed hard-heartedness can be glimpsed by the possibly apocryphal story of the arrival in Sicily of Ingham's nephew, Joseph Whitaker. Ingham liked to employ his nephews in the family business and when Joseph Whitaker's elder brother died, it is said he wrote to their mother saying, 'Your son is dead, send me another.' So starts the Whitakers' significant involvement in Sicilian affairs.

Consequently, Marsala is synonymous with the wine trade, but for most Italians it is forever linked to the year 1860, one of history's 'year zeros'. In May of that year, Garibaldi and his Mille (Thousand) landed at the port of Marsala. The Red Shirts were intent on the unification of Italy and the dismantling of the old Bourbon regime which ruled over Sicily from Naples. Expecting resistance, they were fortunate on two counts: firstly, a suicidal crew member had thrown himself overboard, twice forcing Garibaldi's ship to delay whilst waiting for Nino Bixio's crew to fish the half-drowned man from the sea. This delay meant that the floating army missed the attentions of the Bourbon warships that had been previously stationed in Marsala harbour. Secondly, on reaching Marsala, Garibaldi was greeted by the sight of two British boats. The British were supposedly neutral, but there was a certain leaning towards the unification enterprise and a definite emphasis on protecting their considerable economic interests on the island, which extended further than the Whitaker fortune.

Unlike at Milazzo, Alexandre Dumas was not a first-hand witness to the landings. However, he received accounts, chapter and verse, when he met up with Garibaldi and his entourage in Palermo. His description of the scene in Marsala appeared in his book, *On Board the Emma, Adventures with Garibaldi's Thousand in Sicily* (based on *Les Garibaldiens: révolution de Sicile et de Naples*). Not everything went the way of the revolutionaries: Bixio's ship ran aground on a rock and the absent Neapolitans made a late reappearance at the harbour mouth. Dumas picks up the story and recounts the British involvement:

> As soon as the *Stromboli* arrived, she opened the attack, but the first gun missed fire. Seeing what was taking place, the captain of an English warship which was on the spot went on board the *Stromboli* and in-formed the commander of that vessel that some English officers and part of his crew were ashore, and that he would hold the Neapolitan commander responsible if anything happened to them.

The threat of intervention and a misfiring gun were enough to persuade the Bourbon captain to await other vessels. Garibaldi had already disembarked most of his men and munitions when firing resumed. Dumas is scathing of the Neapolitans' ability with their cannons: 'Meanwhile, the fire from the vessels continued, but it was so badly directed that nobody was hit. The only casualty was the death of a poor dog, which had joined the expedition.'

A small vignette in *The Leopard* recalls some British officers overlooking events unfolding in Palermo. The Prince of Salina describes their reactions and his own comments when relaying the story to Chevalley, a representative from Turin:

> They were ecstatic about the view, the light; they confessed, though, that they had been horrified at the squalor and filth of the streets around. I didn't explain to them that one thing was derived from the other, as I have tried to with you. Then one of them asked me what those Italian volunteers were really coming to do in Sicily. 'They're coming to teach us good manners!' I replied in English, 'But they won't succeed because we think we are Gods.'

In the face of such a time-worn response from an aristocrat who knows that Sicilians have seen this all before, one cannot help bringing to mind the British reaction of the uncomprehending English warship captains moored in Marsala harbour.

Dumas is much more effusive in his praise for the response of the Marsalan populace: 'The General now gave the order to march on the town; and this they did, to the great astonishment of the towns-people, who cheered lustily. Assembled in the streets, or at their doors and windows, they could not believe their own eyes.' The ships' guns turned on the town, but with little effect. Garibaldi made a rousingly patriotic exhortation to join the cause and the town council responded with a plea for him to assume the 'dictatorship' – a word used by Dumas and the municipality in a far less pejorative way than we would today.

One of the most fascinating eye-witness accounts comes from Cesare Abba, a Ligurian from Cairo Montenotte. During the campaign he kept copious diaries which he later turned into an ordered written account that he sent to the poet Giosuè Carducci. Carducci was so taken with the memoir he abandoned his own project to write a biography of Garibaldi and insisted that Abba's account be published. After an initial first edition, it was edited and released in 1891 as *Noterelle di uno dei Mille edite dopo vent'anni*, appearing in English as *The Diary of one of Garibaldi's Thousand*. In truth, the expedition never really consisted of just one thousand men; many were drawn to fight from the Sicilian countryside, but that does not detract from Abba's own story.

Retiring to a quiet life of letters and education after the Risorgimento, Cesare also tried his hand at fiction and poetry, most of which hit the buffers at the planning stage. He aborted his own attempt at a Manzonian novel based on past adventure, although versions do exist. His talent lay in conveying the lives of those who had committed to the cause of uniting Italy. For many years, Abba was required reading in Italian schools. Some modern historians have taken a fresh look at unification and have posited new perspectives, not all of them flattering. Abba and Dumas, both keepers of the Garibaldian flame, would have been shocked by some of the opinions. It is quite telling that during the recent celebrations of the Italian state's 150th anniversary, RAI Radio 3 ran a series of 150 documentaries looking at its short history and each one was introduced by disintegrating martial music.

Cesare was in Marsala on that day in May. His account, dated 11 May, remembers the closing Neapolitan ships, the British contingent and the hectic disembarkation, but, most poignant of all, it records the chaos and relief at the taking of the town. His initial reaction on sighting Marsala could have come straight from a travelogue: 'There's Marsala! Its walls, its white houses, its green gardens, and the lovely slope on which it lies.' The realisation soon dawns that battle is to be joined – 'There are bursts of cannon-fire from the port, directed at the city. Many of the houses are flying foreign flags, most of them English. Whatever does this mean?' Abba was obviously ignorant of the influence British merchants had on the wine trade, although not of the wine itself, which he calls 'treacherous'. The foreign residents were intent on proclaiming their neutrality by flying the national standard in an attempt to avoid any shells being aimed at their luxurious villas.

He entered the town through an arched gate, the one that now bears Garibaldi's name. He compares it to an Arabic arch, but one that also resembled the entrance to his own Ligurian village. Once inside, Cesare and his party set up camp in one of the town's many squares, confident, at least, in the securing of their piece of Sicilian soil – 'I am sitting on a stone in front of the piled arms of my company in this squalid, solitary, rather frightening little square. Captain Ciaccio of Palermo is weeping like a child from pure happiness. I pretend not to see him.' More heartache would follow, but for the time being Abba is happy to ride out of Marsala with the Mille, into the vineyards, to sit under an olive tree and eat bread with slices of cheese.

In fact, the British community already had some forewarning of the likely turn of events. The whole build-up to May 1860 was spiced with unrest. Raleigh Trevelyan, in his monumental history of the British in Sicily, *Princes under the Volcano*, quotes from Commander Winnington-Ingram's diary. Winnington-Ingram was appointed by the British government to keep a weather eye on the United Kingdom's interests in Palermo and the west. He lists house searches, police raids during the night, gun shots and burning buildings. Some English residents decided to steal away to the homeland, including another of Benjamin's nephews, Ben and his wife, Emily Ingham, along with Joseph Whitaker's son, Willie. Ben's absence was particularly significant as he was the vice-consul in Marsala. A post, as Trevelyan says, he left in the hands of his warehouse manager Richard Cossins.

The British involvement in the wine trade would continue after the Risorgimento, although it inevitably waned as time passed. The town's role in the unification struggle was bound to last longer in the memory, especially thanks to its literary chroniclers. Marsala was fortunate, though, to escape the fate of Calatafimi and Milazzo – those towns were to become synonymous with decisive and bloody battles.

During the struggle, the Anglo-Sicilian families tried to keep a low profile and the Whitakers were no exception. Trevelyan includes two letters from Joseph Whitaker during this period in his comprehensive book. Both complain of the instability of the situation and implicitly the potential effect on business. At this time, Joseph's son and namesake was only ten years old. We have already met Joseph junior (known as 'Pip') and his wife Tina in subsequent years when living at the Villa Malfitano in Palermo. Pip will be our literary and cultural connection to this part of the island.

He spoke Italian with a Sicilian accent, enthused about the ancient cultures of Sicily and loved to indulge his passion for ornithology, about which he wrote a considerable number of respected tracts in both English and Italian. It was his duty as the other Joseph's heir to join the family business, which he did with little interest or passion. Despite being a keen scholar, he was not suited to the rigours of commerce. Along with his bird watching and specimen collection, Pip is best remembered for the archaeological discoveries on the island of Mozia just off the coast of Marsala.

### *Mozia*

Mozia, or Motya as it is commonly referred to in English, was the subject of Pip's book *Motya: A Phoenician Colony in Sicily*, published in 1921, and also of an interesting piece of historico-geographical biography written by Gaia Servadio in 2000. Gaia came to be known as something of a Sicilian specialist in the 1970s when she wrote three books with Mafia themes: *A Profile of a Mafia Boss: Angelo la Barbera*, *Mafioso: A History of the Mafia as a Social Phenomenon* and *To a Different World*. Her first book, a novel entitled *Melinda*, was a great success and a springboard for her writing career. Gaia's grandfather was Sicilian but she grew up in Padua. Initially pursuing a career as an artist, she studied at St Martin's College in London, becoming disheartened when she felt her art was not going the way of current trends.

She started writing articles for the left-wing Palermitan newspaper, *L'Ora*, a publication which took an anti-Mafia stance. She was also fortunate enough to pick up work with the BBC World Service and subsequently *The Times* and the *Daily Telegraph*. Capable of writing in both English and Italian, she was the perfect guide for a BBC film crew who came to make a documentary in western Sicily in the

1970s – the outcome of which helped her to write the aforementioned *To a Different World*.

Her book on the little island, *Motya: Unearthing a Lost Civilisation*, contains all the ingredients that make up the complex mixture of western Sicily: Phoenician influence, British trade and dilettante archaeology, convoluted bureaucracy and the Mafia. At the heart of the true story is Pip Whitaker, a shy, studious individual who shunned the aristocratic glamour that his wife so enjoyed. He was fortunate enough to be able to follow his interests and, over a period of years, managed to buy up the entirety of Mozia, otherwise known as San Pantaleo, which he did with one sole purpose – that of digging in its sun-baked soil for the remains of the fabled ancient Punic city.

Whitaker was not the first to consider San Pantaleo as the home of Motya. Gaia Servadio details the previous explorations undertaken by Heinrich Schliemann, the German who had used Homer's *Illiad* to guide him to the location of Troy. Fortunately for Pip, Schliemann was unsuccessful and left after a spat with the then head of Sicilian Antiquities, Prince Trabia. Samuel Butler, whose story we will pick up in Trapani, was similarly intent on following Homer, albeit in the footsteps of Odysseus. He too made a cursory visit to Mozia, but was disappointed to find nothing significant on the surface of the soil.

Pip took years to persuade enough people to sell up before he could claim complete ownership and he then used his own money in the excavation of the site. His heartfelt desire to uncover a lost civilisation is evident in the introduction to his own book *Motya: A Phoenician Colony in Sicily*, 'The idea of excavating the buried remains of Motya first occurred to me some forty years or more ago, but it was not until many years later and after overcoming innumerable obstacles and difficulties that I became sole proprietor of the little island, and was finally enabled to give effect to the project that I had for so long cherished *in pectore*, and commence the work of exploration.'

Servadio talks of Motya fever, that desire to hear the stones speak, the desire to listen to their story, which was obviously something at the very core of Whitaker's being. It seems she was also touched by this archaeological infection. She first visited the little island back in 1966 but returned years later with the idea of writing an article. It is easy to see that she was so overcome by the evocative nature of the site, she could not resist turning it into a book:

> While I walked, I inhaled the smell of the sea and the scorched vegetation; a pungent mix which evoked in my imagination scenes I had never witnessed. Sitting on those ochre stones cut some 2,500 years earlier, I watched my mind's eye and I saw shadows; I fantasized. There was so much conjecture about this ghostly island and about Motya, the fallen Punic city, the walls, the steps, the remains of the temples, the Necropolis, the sacred area for human sacrifice; they all evoked a power which I remembered experiencing during my very first visit thirty years earlier.

Drawn back time and again for research, she rented a house in 1997 further to the north near Castellammare. The road down to Motya is an oleander-lined motorway which heads to Trapani then changes into a coastal road that meanders past a distinctive landscape of salt pans that have existed since the antiquity Gaia so evocatively describes. This flat landscape, backed by Motya in the distance, is punctuated by piles of salt and Quixotesque windmills – an idiosyncratic and picturesque scene as the early evening sun tinges the salt crystals with a warm glow. It is easy to eulogise the panorama, sitting by the roadside, sipping a coffee or savouring an ice-cream, but the reality of obtaining the salt from these pans was a back-breaking job. Leonardo Sciascia writes of salt extraction in his book, *Salt in the Wound*, albeit at sites further to the south-east. The vision he conjures is far from romantic: 'The salt is piled up shiny and white at the station; salt, fog, and poverty – salt on the wound, on the red ulcer of poverty.'

Samuel Butler, the hunter of Homer, travelled with another writer, Henry Festing Jones, who was happy to write of his broader experiences whilst Butler got lost in the minutiae of Homerian scholarship. In 1909, his book *Diversions in Sicily* was published. The itinerary it covers essentially bows to the dictats of Samuel's schedule in western Sicily, but provides its own insight. He was fascinated by the spectacle of the windmills and the method by which the salt was obtained.

The placing of mills here dates back to the Middle Ages and Jones describes one with a fan-like structure with 'six dummy ships' forming the arc of the wheel. He attributes Trapani's wealth at that time to the salt industry, which exported its product as far as Newfoundland and Norway, where it would eventually find its way back to Sicily as *baccalà* or salt cod. He also explains the process by which some of the salt was mined: 'the sea water is collected in large, open pans, being raised by means of the screw which has been used all over the island for nearly twenty-two centuries, ever since Archimedes invented it to remove the water from the hold of one of Hiero's ships at Siracusa.' Jones refers to Motya as San Pantaleo, but points out it 'is not a prominent object, being low and near the land'. He is, however, gracious enough to observe that in antiquity it was the most important of the Egadi Islands.

Today, Joseph Whitaker's legacy is a foundation that administers the island along with the Soprintendenza di Trapani, the government department responsible for the supervision of the environment and archaeology. Gaia Servadio has a great deal of affection and respect for Joseph: 'He was interested in the culture, that's why I like him so much and he educated himself; he was very sensitive, intelligent and misunderstood. I think he deserves much more honour really.' She is also an admirer of modern methods of archaeology, through which 'you learn history'. Not that Motya is lacking in the spectacular find so beloved of early Egyptologists: the *Kouros* or 'Young Man' of Motya was discovered in 1979 in the Cappiddazzu Sanctuary area and is now resplendent in the Whitaker Museum.

From the chiselled salt pans with their history of hardship to the Motyan ruins so reluctant to give up their secrets, there is a poignancy to the whole area that demands self-reflection, a spirit Servadio captures on one of her last boat trips rowing across the lagoon: 'Years had passed since I had first come to Motya, knowing nothing about the Punics or about the years ahead of me. Since then four decades had vanished, gliding away like those little waves which reflected the golds and crimsons of the setting sun.'

It is impossible to leave here without giving the last word to Joseph Whitaker. Even before significant excavation it was clear that he loved every aspect of the little island. This withdrawn, introspective man found his real passion away from the spectacular parties and Palermitan limelight. From the low-lying land of Pantaleo where he gazed 'over the clumps of olive and almond trees, with isolated carobs' which 'lend a picturesque and varied colouring to the landscape', he could observe the birdlife and dream.

### Trapani and Erice

At the other end of the salt road lies Trapani, formerly known by the Greeks as Drepanon, meaning sickle, owing to the shape of its harbour. Various myths and legends are attributed to its foundation, including one referring to Ceres, who supposedly dropped her scythe when desperately searching for her daughter. As Mary Taylor Simeti astutely entitles her book, Sicily really is Persephone's Island.

Modern-day Trapani has been built around its port. The thin spit of land forming the sickle's blade has two edges. The concave side of the arc is lined with a higgledy-piggledy collection of dwellings that would have been home to tuna fishermen. Before the seafront broadens out into a modern esplanade, access is via a winding path running by the front doors that give out onto the sea. The outer bow of the blade is home to the industrial port, the ferry dock and a more upmarket marina. Viale Regina Elena is still bordered by palazzi, fading elegantly from their belle époque splendour. The streets between the two are a mixture of boulevards and alleyways that are free from the more frantic aspects of other major cities in Sicily.

The port has long been a staging post. As part of the Spanish fleet after the Battle of Lepanto, Miguel de Cervantes was blown to harbour at Trapani. Despite the aggravations of enforced mooring, Cervantes revisited the city in one of his *Exemplary Novels* (*Novelas ejemplares*), 'The Generous Lover', entitled 'El amante liberal' in its original Spanish. The protagonist Ricardo is taken by Turkish corsairs 'who had captured him in a garden on the coast near Trapani, and along with him a damsel'. The young lady in question is Leonisa and the garden, no less than the coastal 'salt pits'. Overcoming all difficulties, Ricardo makes a getaway with Leonisa in tow. The generousness of the title makes an appearance when Ricardo falls on his metaphorical sword and acquiesces in returning his lover to her former beau. Needless to say, she settles for him instead. Cervantes also refers to Ulysses in this work – no doubt a mention Samuel Butler would have appreciated.

It is to Trapani that the Victorian Butler came in search of evidence for his theories on the origin of the *Odyssey*. Samuel's speculations on the real identity of Homer have been dismissed by the majority of scholars – on occasion, scornfully. This aspect to Butler's writing career is one of his more interesting avenues of thought, but is far less well known than his novels *The Way of All Flesh* and *Erewhon*. The former title was only published after the author had died owing to its controversial content. It is partially autobiographical and focuses on the Pontifex family, notably Ernest Pontifex, who is portrayed as having a troubled and complex relationship with his relatives. It is seen as a reaction against some of the values prevalent in the Victorian era. Alternatively, *Erewhon* pictures the discovery of a fictional utopia which Butler gradually satirises. The title is an anagram of 'nowhere'.

In 1892 Samuel was putting the finishing touches to his translation of the *Odyssey*. It was a passage dealing with Neptune's turning of the Phaeacian ship into a rock at Scheria harbour that set a train of thought in motion. Henry Festing Jones describes this as the moment when his friend 'felt sure that, if an actual place was being described anywhere in the poem, this was the passage'. Butler ran to the atlas and searched for locations that would fit the detail in the text. Rifling through his extensive library, he looked at a work by Mure, who had placed this episode near Cape Boeo, Marsala. Festing Jones picks up the story: 'he went to the British Museum and searched that neighbourhood on the Admiralty charts, whereon he found that Trapani and Mount Eryx supplied everything'.

To broaden our understanding of Butler, it is important to note that he was focusing on a part of the story where King Alcinous witnesses the petrification of the Phaeacians. Such alchemy must have left behind a rock of suitable proportions near to shore. With this in mind, he was delighted to discover such a stone, known as Lo Scoglio di Malconsiglio, near to Trapani. So begins his long association with the city, as this prompted him to write to the mayor, who supplied him with a Christian legend suggesting that the Madonna di Trapani had turned a Turkish ship full of corsairs into the said outcrop. Butler was convinced this was just a Christian interpretation of a more ancient myth, namely the 'Wrath of Neptune'.

After a series of lectures and published letters on the subject, Samuel was ready to place Odysseus' final destination of Ithaca – a Greek island to the more traditionally focused Homerian scholar – within the realms of the Egadi Islands. By May 1892 he had written a pamphlet on the subject, notice of which had actually reached the Trapanese mayor with whom he had already been in contact. He received a letter from Emanuele Biaggini of Trapani requesting a copy be sent out to him. Some Sicilian academics were fascinated with the locational detail but also with the fact that Samuel had suggested a local woman was responsible for the work, rather than the blind Greek.

In a subsequent letter sent to Avvocato Francesco Negri, Butler outlines his intended trip to Sicily and developments so far: 'They are translating my pamphlet about Homer at Trapani, and are evidently a good deal surprised and interested at having the Odyssey thrust upon them. Here (England) the pamphlet has met with a very bad reception, and I have been very angrily or even savagely attacked for it.' The critics' main concern was that he had 'vulgarised Homer'.

By a very circuitous route taking in Genoa, Pisa, Rome and Naples, he arrived in Trapani, subsequently making the acquaintance of the correspondent who had requested his pamphlet, Biaggini. Festing Jones tells us that Emanuele enthusiastically agreed with Butler's theories. Lest we should think him an academic crackpot, he also notes that the man had fought alongside Garibaldi and was with him when he was wounded. Biaggini acted as Butler's *cicerone*, taking him to the now famous rock in the harbour. He also pointed out the islands of Favignana and Levanzo, as well as Mount Eryx behind Trapani.

Biaggini was kind enough to invite the English Homer hunter to stay in his summer retreat on the flanks of Eryx – then, as now, known

*16 The view from Erice to Trapani and the Egadi Islands*

as Mount Erice. Confronted with the sight of the island of Marettimo, floating near Levanzo, Butler knew he had found his Ithaca. The gestation period for his theory was a long one, but now he was more confident than ever of his understanding. Initially, he had fought his ideas, especially any indications that the writer was a woman, but he could not ignore the fact that he had uncovered a missing clue, 'I felt that here was the reading of the riddle that had so long baffled me. I tried to divest myself of it, but it would not go.'

It was in the town of Erice, atop the singular peak to the north of Trapani, that Samuel met a charismatic old priest who indulged in a game of Latin wordplay with his Trapanese guide. The upshot of such encounters, which the padre was apt to indulge in, often resulted in the acceptance of not one but at least three glasses of the local vino in respect for the Trinity. Seemingly, the old curate was a healer as well, asking the sick to disappear under his cloak whilst he said a few prayers. Failures were blamed on their wickedness. This small act of priestly spirituality is dwarfed by Erice's reputation for mysticism of an altogether more classical kind. The goddess Venus Erycina (Aphrodite to the Greeks) was worshipped here but the temple has been thoroughly covered by the Norman castle. Visitors to the shrine used to indulge in what can only be described as divine prostitution – the pilgrims sleeping with Venus' handmaidens. Diodorus, the historian, tells us that Eryx owes its name to a king who was beaten in a wrestling match by Hercules, Erycina being the adjectival derivative applied to Venus.

The modern town cannot have changed significantly since Butler's day, confined as it is to the mountain top. Many of the streets are cobbled and the buildings appear to grow out of the very rock. The living museum captures vistas at every turn. Adding to Erice's association with the enigmatic is the presence of the Ettore Majorana Foundation and Centre for Scientific Culture. It honours the Sicilian physicist of the same name, who was working on neutrinos when he mysteriously disappeared whilst travelling by ship to Palermo in 1938. The vanishing scientist has left behind a goldmine for conspiracy theorists. Among the most popular are theories that he committed suicide, was kidnapped, escaped to South America or, according to Leonardo Sciascia in his book *The Mystery of Majorana* (*La scomparsa di Majorana*), that he entered a monastery. Most seem to revolve around his participation in the development of nuclear science and the research that could have opened the door to potential weaponry, something that his conscience may have found too hard to handle.

Butler's fascination with Eryx was too early to focus on disappearing academics, but his search was fruitful, nonetheless. Contrary to the popular belief that Polyphemus threw his stones into the sea off Aci Trezza, in *Authoress of the Odyssey* Samuel muses on his young writer being disturbed in her thoughts by a rough, hulking shepherd whom she transforms into the 'local giant that exists on Mt Eryx now under the name of Conturràno'. Butler persuaded himself he had found the origins of the Polyphemus myth. Although there are no giants left in Erice today, it still has the capacity to make a human feel small with its geographical aloofness casting a long shadow over the flatter surrounding landscape. Even sailors thought it was a bad omen if Venus' mountain top was shrouded in mist. It would be a long way down without the aid of motorised transport, especially if you had an injured leg, as was the case for Samuel, who had fallen over in the street. Today, there is a cable car that links the lofty town with Trapani spread out at its feet.

Butler's Sicilian journeys were a pure confirmation of everything he believed – however potentially misguided. Wherever he looked in the Trapani area, he found places that he could associate with his hypothesis. The *Authoress* comes complete with maps and sketches that are determined to shoehorn the locations into his theory. He started to savour the idea like the first taste of a good wine, 'I let it stay with me,' but the addiction took longer to build, 'I need hardly say that it was a long time before I came to see that the poem was all of it written at Trapani, and that the writer had introduced herself into her work under the name of Nausicaa.'

Nausicaa is the daughter of Arete and King Alcinous. This is the moment when Odysseus (Ulysses to the Romans) first casts his eyes over her. Minerva, planning to awake our warrior from a sleep, creates a noisy distraction which has the desired effect:

> he crept from under his bush, and broke off a bough covered with thick leaves to hide his nakedness. He looked like some lion of the wilderness that stalks about exulting in his strength and defying both wind and rain; his eyes glare as he prowls in quest of oxen, sheep, or deer, for he is famished, and will dare break even into a well fenced homestead, trying to get at the sheep – even such did Ulysses seem to the young women, as he drew to them all naked as he was, for he was in great want. On seeing one so unkempt and so begrimed with salt water, the others scampered off along the spits that jutted out into the sea, but the daughter of Alcinous stayed firm.

This is Butler's translation and it crosses the years with a sexual tension, taken out of context, that would be worthy of any romantic novel.

Butler was well received in Trapani among the wealthier families such as the Adragna and the Burgarella, admitting that 'they treat me like a Royal Personage.' He stayed in the Albergo delle Cinque Torri, named after the five towers of Trapani, in a room that Festing Jones claimed was once occupied by the Holy Roman Emperor Charles V. When Henry came to write his memoir of Butler's life – *Samuel Butler: Author of Erewhon* – the hotel had been converted to a private residence.

The nearby church of the Annunziata, where the sanctuary of the Madonna di Trapani is located, was the scene of another Butler story. He was witness to a supposed demonic possession that Festing Jones was sensible enough to call 'a nervous disorder'. The people who had brought the poor woman to the church were intent on getting her to shout 'Viva Maria!', thereby summoning the devil from her. Bystanders were advised to shut their mouth and form the cross with their fingers lest the malevolent spirit should take a dive down the nearest accommodating throat. As Henry wryly notes, it would be 'no end of a job to get him up again'.

The ever-faithful Biaggini took Samuel to the Grotta del Toro, one of the many sea caves out in the Egadi archipelago. It was so named after the lone rock that guards its entrance which, to the imaginative, resembles the shape of a bull. The reason for Butler's visit was to sail in the footsteps of Odysseus who hid his treasure in such a location. As we know, he also paid his respects at the site of Motya but his disappointment and lack of Joseph's vision can be seen by his comments which focused on the plundering of Motyan stone to build nearby Marsala.

If Butler found it straightforward enough to reference local landmarks in his historical quest, the other side of his theory was less easy to pin down. Why did he claim that the Homerian legend was written by a woman, specifically Nausicaa? Samuel introduces his idea in these terms:

> We have to find a woman of Trapani, young, fearless, self-willed, and exceedingly jealous of the honour of her sex. She seems to have moved in the best society of her age and country, for we can imagine none more polished on the West coast of Sicily in Odyssean times than the one with which the writer shows herself familiar.

To find this woman and his rationale, he went through the writings of Homer with a fine-tooth comb. Some of his arguments for placing a scribe's tools in the hands of a woman seem surprisingly modern and others, positively antediluvian – 'no other episode is written with the same, or nearly the same, buoyancy of spirits and resiliency of pulse and movement, or brings the scene before us with anything approaching the same freshness, as that in which Nausicaa takes the family linen to the washing cisterns.' Who could possibly know about washing except a female?

It is true that the majority of scholars felt that the theory trivialised Homer in some form or another, but there is no doubt that parts of the *Odyssey* sit well in a Sicilian context. However, Samuel was determined to see connections where others clearly felt there were none – to quote Luigi Pirandello, 'Right you are, if you think you are.' On the other hand, Robert Graves pursued the notion further down the track in writing his novel, *Homer's Daughter*, a recreation of the *Odyssey*. Graves' text centres on a feisty Sicilian girl who is able to protect her father's throne, avoid a bad marriage and save her brothers from a dismal end.

## Castellammare and Scopello

The Gulf of Castellammare was rich tuna-fishing territory. It is one of those god-like bites into the coastline between the Cape of San Vito, north of Trapani and Frank Viviano's Terrasini to the east. At the base of the gulf lies Castellammare and climbing the western arm is Scopello, famed for its *mattanza*. The word is of Spanish origin and, minus the double consonant, literally means slaughter. It is an apt description for the tuna catch which used to take place in the bay at the height of the fishing season (May/June) and is said to have turned the sea red. Due to fishing restrictions and the hard-working seasonal nature of the occupation, the *mattanza* is now, to all intents and purposes, a thing of the past. In this age-old tradition, tuna were corralled into a series of net chambers – the last, the chamber of death, bringing them to the surface where they were killed with spear-like implements as they made a frenzied attempt to escape.

Two writers have found the tuna catch an ideal way of studying a dying Sicily with its own specific traditions and lifestyle. Prior to her search for *The Stone Boudoir*, Theresa Maggio wrote a book entitled *Mattanza: Love and Death in the Sea of Sicily*. Her fishing community was located in the aforementioned Egadi, specifically the island of Favignana where she returned year after year to experience the capture of bluefin tuna as they swam up the Mediterranean from the Straits of Gibraltar. Theresa was able to infiltrate this male-dominated world and gain insight into a way of life that was being threatened by far easier and potentially more destructive fishing methods further afield.

Gavin Maxwell wrote from a similar perspective decades earlier, and was in time to catch the last disappearing *tonnara* (tuna fishing station) in the Castellammare Gulf. Having just completed his biography on the intrigues of the Salvatore Giuliano case, Maxwell was in search of ideas for a new book. He had set his sights on the marsh Arabs in Iraq, but the project was delayed and he persuaded his publishers that there was ample material for a further book on western Sicily that he would call *The Ten Pains of Death*. The book starts with a quote from the *Second Fruits* of Giovanni Florio, who lists all ten pains, including these dark maxims:

> To be a prisoner without hope,
> To lose the way when you would journey,
> To stand at a door that none will open [. . .]

Florio's tribulations reflect the stories that Gavin uncovered amongst the tuna fishermen and their kin in Scopello. He admits in the prologue that Sicilians can be hard to breach; their wall of silence being a protection rather than rudeness or arrogance. It should be borne in mind that he was writing in the late 1950s, at a time when Danilo Dolci was investigating ingrained poverty and the whole island was still recovering from massive postwar austerity. Maxwell was sure the best way to break down the barrier would be to isolate himself amongst a group of people with a common goal. He chose this particular fishing community and went to stay in the coastal building which he calls a barracks, where the off-duty fishermen would eat their meals and spend their time talking about four topics, which he lists in this specific order: sex, money, politics and religion.

In fact, the content of the tales he relates were so liberally spiced with ribald anecdote, he felt compelled to abridge the sexual content of his translations for the supposedly prudish Anglo-Saxon audience of the 1950s. Fluent in Italian, with an ear for dialect, he still had some difficulties in deciphering the thick regional Sicilian of his companions. The book is organised into chapters with titles that reflect the narrated stories within; for example, 'The Killers', 'The Pedlar and the Prostitute', 'The Priest' and 'The Two Old Men'. Essentially, he lets the interviewee speak for him or herself and acknowledges that the real debt he owes is to these downtrodden individuals. Many of the protagonists had been to gaol, but he believed their delinquency was born of necessity rather than malice.

In the chapter entitled 'The Killers', desperate tales of besmirched honour and revenge are laced with the cold hard facts of poverty. A fruitless tuna harvest meant a starving family. When Maxwell quizzed one of the men on the high rate of locals who had seen the inside of a prison cell, he received this frank answer: 'Eighty per cent? Eight men in ten . . . yes, I suppose that is true. What can you expect when people are so poor? When the babies cry for bread and there is none to give them, a man must steal.'

The same person told him of the revenge killing of a man called 'the Fox' involved in a homosexual love affair. This wealthier older man had taken a shine to a local lad from a poor family who, in turn, had placed his affection elsewhere. The young lad went to work for the Fox, but decided to leave and, to his surprise, was presented with a jewel-encrusted watch. There was, however, no altruistic motivation behind this gift and the boy was subsequently convicted of stealing. The double-cross was avenged by his true amour. When Maxwell muses on this rather brutal concept of justice, he is slapped down with pitying peasant wisdom: 'Poor Gavin, you are so educated and so intelligent, and *simpatico* too, but there are things you cannot understand. There are times when it is better not to think too much.'

Another chapter focuses on the olive harvest, 'the third source of life in Sicily'. Fishing families sometimes had enough land to squeeze out a few drops of oil but, as usual, it was the rich farmers who could guarantee a harvest. The Sicilian landscape is covered with olive groves and this was an obvious pilgrimage location for Carol Drinkwater, the English actress-turned-olive-cultivator and author. Her book, *The Olive Tree*, is a sequel to other memoirs focusing more on her farm in the south of France.

Her quest for the secrets of the olive tree, all its mysteries and folklore, took her to the hinterland of Castellammare. She had set up a meeting in Scopello with the granddaughter of a Sicilian-American mobster who once worked for the boss known as the 'Olive Oil King' – a nickname linked to his usage of the industry as a front for more dodgy dealings. The much-cultivated contact went cold but she continued along the byways of rural Sicily, nosing out olive facts as she went. Olive oil is not the front it once was and a few local producers are internationally acclaimed; although Carol does indicate that some Italian-labelled oils are occasionally produced elsewhere, often Spain.

Pootling through the groves, she noticed how Sicily's well-tended cultivation differed from that of its Hispanic cousin. 'All around me were flowering olive groves, exquisitely pruned, each tree a work of art. These groves were clean, cared for but, unlike Spain, the soil had not been denuded. Wild flowers sprouted insouciantly at their bases.' One of the delights of the *primavera siciliana* is the profusion of yellow, red and purple wild flowers that smudge the green canvas of a burgeoning spring. The other speciality of this region is the vine, particularly the white wines of Alcamo.

## Alcamo

Alcamo and its district, just south of Castellammare, produces much wine, often from the Catarratto, Grecanico and Grillo grape varieties. Alcamo has a DOC label, a quality assurance specifying controlled designation of origin. It was not the wine, though, that brought Gaia

Servadio to Alcamo. Years before she turned to the archaeological excavation of Motya, Gaia came to Alcamo with her BBC TV crew. The aim, to observe the problem of organised crime, led to the transformation of her documentary into the book *To a Different World*. Ostensibly an investigation of Mafia influence, it is also a portrait of Alcamo in more troubled times. Servadio was able to meet up with Marcello Cimino, the campaigning journalist who was also close friends with Norman Lewis. He had a place at nearby Tufanio and the pair of them would sit on his terrace and discuss her other project, a history of the Mafia.

Despite the serious nature of the subject matter, the idyllic situation was conducive to contemplation: 'A bottle of wine on the table – Tufanio wine – sitting in the sun, looking towards the bay of Castellammare, one could not possibly imagine a more congenial place for thought.' It was during the time which saw the application of a particular law that banished Mafia bosses in custody to more isolated areas, away from the main island, another attempt from the Italian state to rework its complex difficulties with organised crime.

The nefarious impact of such activity became very evident when Gaia took her BBC producer, Rex, to the local cemetery. She explained that the older headstones had a feature with columns cut into two – a trait designed to show a murder victim, and some stones even expressly detailed the fact. Several of the more modern stones were extravagantly melancholic, a sign of a wealthier incumbent. Sicilian cemeteries are extraordinary places, where the larger tombs appear to be little conservatories; visitors can sit in an easy chair and while away the hours with their departed relative or friend.

Alcamo's central square is much cleaned and spruced up from the days of Servadio's visits in the 1970s. A plaque, centrally placed, refers to the poet Cielo (often known as Ciullo) who wrote *Il Contrasto* – verses of which Gaia remembers trying to commit to memory at school. He was one more of Frederick II's Sicilian School of versifiers. The square is still the focus of town activity she described. It seems she cut a distinctive figure in the days when Sicilian women were still tied to the home – an anglicised Italian with stylish hair and the chic fashions of Chelsea boutiques.

Between Alcamo and nearby Calatafimi is the site of the lonely classical Segesta. This well-preserved roofless temple sits impressively on a hillock. The only other feature of note is the beautifully located theatre atop the neighbouring hill. Gaia traversed the short distance between the two, her memories an intense olfactory experience: 'Walking up the hill, from the temple (actually, driving now, although I still remember climbing among wild scented herbs which put one in a mystical mood), one finds the walls of the city, hardly excavated, and the amphitheatre, perfectly Greek in style, which Goethe did not like.'

Johann Wolfgang passed by Alcamo and Segesta, limiting himself to a few paragraphs on the monument's construction. He seemed just as interested in the stone from which the columns were carved and the interesting geology of the area – references to which are made on signs in the modern town. He was also 'flabbergasted' to find that his groom was watering down the wine, something completely alien to a German used to strong alcohol. It is a practice that has largely fallen out of fashion – the only dilution today being a chilled spritzer in the height of summer.

## Calatafimi

Calatafimi is the town most commonly associated with Segesta. The advertising executive Angus Campbell, retreating from the hectic pace of Rome, semi-retired to the town with his wife, a member of a long-standing local family. Being in the unique position of an outsider with access to an insider's perspective – similar to that of Mary Taylor Simeti – Campbell found Calatafimi interesting enough to devote an entire volume to its historical development and everyday life, entitled *Calatafimi: Behind the Stone Walls of a Sicilian Town*. He dedicated one chapter to *Odyssey*-obsessed Samuel Butler.

Butler wrote much of *The Authoress of the Odyssey* whilst staying in Calatafimi. Angus' research led him to uncover not only a newly formed 'Circolo Culturale Samuel Butler', a local cultural association that was yet to inaugurate its first meeting, but, more profoundly, Butler's links with the defrocked priest, Biagio Ingroia, who was drummed out of the Church for allowing Garibaldi to use the pulpit to preach his unification message. Butler dedicated the book to his heroic friend, who believed in his theory and actively helped him with the manuscript. A street in the town used to be named after Samuel until an anti-British Mussolini swept it away; nearby Sasi, though, still has one.

Campbell's account also follows the others who came in search of Butler's footsteps. The novelist Louis Golding wanted to find the hotel where Samuel slept and ate. Angus tells us it was the Albergo Centrale, renamed in honour of its illustrious guest before disappearing into private obscurity upon the death of the owners. His book reproduces some of Butler's sepia-toned photographs of local families and landscapes. One shows a moustachioed paterfamilias standing behind his family and in front of a memorabilia-clad drawing-room wall. The man in question was Pietro Adamo, Garibaldi's liaison before the Battle of Calatafimi.

In the wider world, the town resonates to the sound of this clash between Bourbon and revolutionary unifier. Alexandre Dumas is once again a good, if propagandistic, source of literary observation. He picks up the story as the Mille, Garibalidi's troops, converge on the town:

> The main body of their army is posted at Calatafimi, and occupies the situation on the slope of a mountain – whilst their advanced posts are about a mile in front of the town. No sooner do the Neapolitans perceive that Garibaldi's troops are at Vita, scarcely have they seen a group of officers reconnoitring on the top of an opposite mountain, than they quit the town, to occupy the valley,

The momentous conflict is set to take place. At the sight of the Neapolitan advance and the sound of Garibaldi's horns, the battle begins. The ever-keen Nino Bixio rushes to engage the enemy. Dumas continues, 'In the midst of the contest, now raging on all sides, some admirable charges are executed. Every officer who can rally round him a hundred, sixty, or even fifty men, charges with vigour at their head.' Such hand-to-hand fighting had extremely bloody consequences. Retreat was considered by the Red Shirts. Garibaldi's famous retort was:

'Here we make Italy or die.' Things were touch and go, but eventually the Bourbons withdrew to Palermo, even Garibaldi acknowledging their 'resistance worthy of a better cause'.

Today, a monument stands at the site of victory, commemorating the occasion and mourning the loss of the fallen. The year was 1860. We have come full circle – geographically and literarily. In Palermo, Don Fabrizio, the Leopard, began by guiding us through the demise of the *ancien régime*, its twilight reflected in the opulent parties of an aristocracy defiantly fiddling whilst Rome burned. Lampedusa's weary insight encapsulated the French refrain, *plus ça change, plus c'est la même chose*. The debate around the notion of changing in order to stay the same has raged ever since; the ever-decreasing circle of this argument is anathema to many who seek a brighter future for Sicily. Whatever the politics of the argument, Calatafimi 1860 was a literary turning point.

The fallout of unification has concerned so many Sicilian authors ever since, shaping their work and their anxieties. The angst-ridden personal malaise of the Pirandellian universe is almost a metaphor for the island, searching for its place in a modern world. Sciascia's cry for enlightened values and decency in a society full of obfuscation and turmoil is another facet of the flawed diamond. Foreign writers could not help but be pulled into this complex web. Those who wanted to write about the society or live and travel amongst its members were bound to mirror a certain sense of disquiet in their work. Few places have received such a plethora of Nobel laureates or produced novelists so capable of writing about the local whilst appealing to the universal.

Letting go of the coat-tails of Sicilian history is no easy feat. Every turn confronts an author with a new scenario or historical connection, but it is also the landscape – pure and unadorned – that has drawn the ink from so many pens. Patrick Brydone and others brought volcanic Sicily to the drawing rooms of eighteenth-century Europe; a rich seam that has led writers to dabble in its classical past, quote its ancient authors, indulge in its food and drink, or turn over the stones found in its more obscure corners, revealing to the world all its brilliance and shadow.

# Author Profiles

**Cesare Abba (1838–1910)**
Abba was from Liguria and fought alongside Garibaldi during the conquest of Sicily in 1860. He took copious notes during the expedition and had a failed attempt at turning them into a novel resembling Manzoni's *The Betrothed.* Instead, he turned to non-fiction and had the notes published in diary-style format thanks to the encouragement of the poet Carducci. The book became known as *Da Quarto al Volturno: Noterelle d'uno dei Mille*, which appeared as *The Diary of One of Garibaldi's Thousand* in English translation. It was a regularly studied text in the Italian school system.

**Harold Acton (1904–94)**
Anglo-Italian writer most known for his poetry and being wrongly attributed as the inspiration for a character in Evelyn Waugh's *Brideshead Revisited*. He wrote two works on the Bourbons of the Kingdom of the Two Sicilies and undertook a road trip through Sicily in 1953. He is famously quoted as saying that Taormina was 'a polite synonym for Sodom'. His autobiographical accounts appear in two volumes, *Memoirs of an Aesthete* and *More Memoirs of an Aesthete.*

**Aeschylus (*c.*525–*c.*455 BC)**
Greek tragedian. He spent part of his adult life at the court of Hiero in Syracuse. He wrote the *Oresteia*, the only Ancient Greek trilogy of plays still extant, whilst in retirement at the Sicilian port of Gela. His tragedies were staged, and still are to this day, in the Syracusan Greek theatre. He was an initiate into the cult of Demeter and some believe that he included clues to these secret rites in his stage works. Both of his sons went on to become poets.

**Howard Agg (1909–77)**
Primarily known as a music journalist and dramatist, Agg was born in the English county of Cheshire. He worked for *The Times* newspaper and the BBC.

In addition to writing his own plays, including *The Little Plays of Sicily*, he also adapted the likes of Dickens, Thackeray and Somerset Maugham. Prompted by a visit to D. H. Lawrence's former home, Fontana Vecchia in Taormina, he took up residence in the same property. His story of the time spent in Lawrence's footsteps is recounted in his book, *A Cypress in Sicily*.

### Simonetta Agnello Hornby (1945–)
Sicilian lawyer and author based in London. In addition to her work as a lawyer dealing with cases concerning children, domestic violence and minority rights, she published her first book in 2000. Her books are mostly located in Sicily, with her most well known being *The Almond Picker*; a story set in the fictional town of Roccacolomba in the Madonie. Her works often look towards the island's past and its inhabitants' historical struggles.

### Roberto Alajmo (1959–)
Italian journalist, broadcaster and playwright. His stories, novels and plays have been translated into numerous European languages. His account of Sicily's capital, *Palermo è una cipolla* (simply titled as *Palermo* in English), reveals the city's multi-layered culture: a history that owes much to its many invaders and influences. Alajmo approaches his native soil with a satirical eye and much affection. He is a frequent collaborator with RAI, the Italian national broadcaster.

### Tariq Ali (1943–)
British Pakistani novelist and political campaigner. He is the author of the Islam Quintet – the fourth of which is *A Sultan in Palermo*. In 1153, Palermo rivalled the Arabic cities of Baghdad and Cordoba despite being taken over by the Normans. He evokes the court of King Roger II and his reliance on Arabic intellectuals. Ali's activism has seen him visit Bolivia at the time of Che Guevara's demise and stand as a British parliamentary candidate for the International Marxist Group.

### Matthew Arnold (1822–88)
Arnold was part of a family of high literary achievers. He attended the sermons of John Henry Newman whilst a student at Oxford, but did not follow in his footsteps. Soon after being appointed as a school inspector, he published *Empedocles on Etna, and Other Poems*. He continued to write poetry throughout his working life, including 'Dover Beach' in 1867. He is also known for his prose work in the fields of social and literary criticism.

**Bernard Berenson (1865–1959)**
American art historian specialising in the Renaissance. He visited Sicily on several occasions, resulting in articles for the newspaper *Corriere della Sera*, which ended up in the volume, *Trip to Sicily*. Bernard's diaries between 1947 and 1956 became a book entitled *The Passionate Sightseer*, a volume that brings the sum of his critical eloquence to many of Sicily's greatest highlights. Berenson spent much of his life in Italy, particularly the Villa I Tatti near Florence.

**Jorge Luis Borges (1899–1986)**
Argentinian writer, usually associated with Palermo in Buenos Aires. Owing to the British side of his family, he learned English before Spanish, but was also fluent in French and German, graduating in Geneva. His voracious appetite for reading resulted in essays, poetry and stories on a wide-ranging series of themes, from the backstreets of Latin America to the classical world. His trip to Sicily in 1984 was recorded in a book by the Magnum photographer Ferdinando Scianna. By this time Borges was already blind and had to dictate his works.

**Vitaliano Brancati (1907–54)**
Sicilian writer born in Pachino. His works *Don Giovanni in Sicilia* and *Il bell'Antonio* (*Beautiful Antonio*) take a satirical look at southern Italian *gallismo* (machismo). Whilst teaching in Caltanissetta, he met and guided the development of future writer Leonardo Sciascia. He also worked in the fields of theatre and cinema, writing screenplays for movies by Roberto Rossellini and Luigi Zampa.

**Patrick Brydone (1736–1818)**
One of the first to include Sicily as part of the Grand Tour. His letters to his friend William Beckford were subsequently collated into the book *A Tour through Sicily and Malta*. He is most famed for his descriptions of Mount Etna. On the strength of his descriptive powers, Brydone was admitted to the Royal Society and contributed papers to the organisation's *Philosophical Transactions*. He also held the post of Comptroller of the Stamp Office, essentially the chief stamp duty administrator.

**Gesualdo Bufalino (1920–96)**
Writer from Comiso. Before being discovered by Leonardo Sciascia, he spent many years as a teacher in his home town. Writing both short stories and novels, he was inspired by the everyday struggles of his fellow citizens in the place he once described as a *città teatro*. His years of frenetic literary activity in the 1980s

gave rise to a book virtually every year, a progression that was tragically cut short when he died in a road accident whilst going to pick up his wife.

### Andrea Camilleri (1925–)

Historical and detective fiction writer from Porto Empedocle. Coming late to the art of novel writing, this former theatre director is the creator of Inspector Montalbano, one of the world's most well-known literary detectives. His fiction is set in Vigàta, the alter ego of his home town, Porto Empedocle. Montalbano's cases reflect a catalogue of Sicily's current problems but the books are also laced with humour and a warmth towards his fellow Sicilians. Camilleri is a notorious smoker, but the habit does not impede the incredible rapidity of his literary output. Andrea also cooperates with the popular television adaptation of his detective.

### Angus Campbell (date unknown)

Campbell is an expatriate resident of the western Sicilian town of Calatafimi. He is married to a woman whose family has deep roots in the town. He was formerly an advertising executive in London and Rome, but has also translated many works from Italian. His book, *Calatafimi: Behind the Stone Walls of a Sicilian Town*, takes a look at life in this district through the lens of an outsider with an insider's perspective. He recounts the area's history, interspersed with anecdote and observation from the everyday life he sees on the streets.

### Robert Camuto (1958–)

Sicilian-American writer specialising in wine. From his home in the south of France, he has frequently travelled to Sicily in search of innovative yet traditional methods of wine production. The resulting book, *Palmento: A Sicilian Wine Odyssey*, reflects his travels around the island exploring new forms of viticulture, a search which becomes a vehicle for investigating Sicily's history, culture and anti-Mafia movement.

### Truman Capote (1924–84)

American author of *Breakfast at Tiffany's* and *In Cold Blood*. No stranger to the Mediterranean, he rented the same villa in Taormina, Fontana Vecchia, as D. H. Lawrence. His account of the villa and his time spent there, is included in the essays published in *Portraits and Observations*. Capote spent most of his childhood with elderly relatives in the deep south of the United States. He enjoyed the limelight in his best years, but was ostracised towards the end when he penned a work that portrayed many friends less than favourably.

**Miguel de Cervantes Saavedra (1547–1616)**

Spanish author of *Don Quixote* and the *Novelas ejemplares* (*Exemplary Novels*). After fighting in the Battle of Lepanto, he spent six months in Messina recuperating from his injuries. Sicilian myth and legend make an appearance in *The Quixote* and one of his *Exemplary Novels* centres around Sicilians from Trapani. Cervantes struggled against debt and hardship for most of his life. On his way home to Spain, he was kidnapped from his ship and held captive in Algiers for five years. His success as a writer only arrived in later years, but his publishing contract still afforded him little profit.

**Marcus Tullius Cicero (106–43 BC)**

Roman philosopher, orator, politician and lawyer, Cicero was a Renaissance man long before the Renaissance. His first political posting was as a quaestor, or public administrator, in western Sicily. He was known for his honest dealing and it was no surprise that the grateful inhabitants invited him to prosecute their corrupt governor, Caius Verres. Cicero spent a great deal of time gathering evidence on the island and his prosecution was successful despite the noble lawyer hired by Verres. His sharp skills and Sicilian investigations are immortalised in *The Verrine Orations*.

**Samuel Taylor Coleridge (1772–1834)**

Romantic poet and literary critic. Between 1804 and 1806, Coleridge travelled to Malta and Sicily. His extensive reading of Italian literature helped develop his critical thought but his notebooks written on the island reflect a mixed view of the society. Treated for his assorted bag of ailments, both mental and physical, with laudanum, the poet inevitably developed an addiction to opium – a habit he could not break. Clouded with depression and an unhappy marriage, Sicily was intended as a break from the norm. It failed in this respect, but gave him time to reflect on his own personality. He is best known for *Kubla Khan* and *The Rime of the Ancient Mariner*, both composed in West Somerset.

**Vincenzo Consolo (1933–2012)**

Sicilian writer born in Sant'Agata di Militello. His historical novel, *Il sorriso dell'ignoto marinaio* (*The Smile of the Unknown Mariner*), takes the reader on a journey to Sicily, as do many of his other works. The portrait of the Unknown Mariner, found in the Mandralisca Museum in Cefalù, plays a key role in the book. Consolo's language was always searching for originality; he once claimed he wrote neither in Italian nor dialect. In the 1960s, he took his literary inspiration from Leonardo Sciascia and Lucio Piccolo. He also collaborated with the left-wing paper *L'Ora*.

**Vincent Cronin (1924–2011)**
British writer on cultural and biographical themes. His diverse and impressive education saw time at Harvard University, the Sorbonne and Oxford. In search of the island's ancient and medieval treasures, Cronin wrote an account of his travels entitled *The Golden Honeycomb*. It is still considered an indispensable guide to the island and is accompanied by the superb black and white photography of Werner Foreman. Cronin divided his time between London, Dragey in Normandy and Marbella, where he died.

**Aleister Crowley (1875–1947)**
English occultist and mystic. He founded the Abbey of Thelema in Cefalù, a hedonistic pseudo-religious cult that resulted in his expulsion from Italy by Mussolini's government. Crowley wrote prolifically on mysticism and magic; his collective works became known as the Holy Books of Thelema. He descended into heroin addiction, but was still able to pen *The Diary of a Drug Fiend*, a fictionalised look at addiction and mysticism that mirrored his own experiments in Cefalù.

**Michael Dibdin (1947–2007)**
British writer of crime fiction, mostly notably the Aurelio Zen mysteries. A former Italian resident, his novels are intricate observations of corruption at high levels. In *Blood Rain*, Zen gets his feared posting to Sicily, specifically Catania and the towns around Mount Etna. Educated at Sussex University in the UK and Edmonton, Canada, Dibdin eventually returned to North America, dying in Seattle after a short illness.

**Carol Drinkwater (1948–)**
English actress and author, famed for her role as the wife of veterinary James Herriot and subsequently as the writer of the Olive Farm books. The work on *The Olive Tree* took her away from her retreat in the south of France in search of olive cultivation and lore throughout the Mediterranean basin. Her travels feature a substantial section on Sicily. She also writes acclaimed books for children.

**Alexandre Dumas, père (1802–70)**
French author. Some of his works are directly inspired by visits to Sicily, including *Le Speronare* (*Impressions of Travel in Sicily*) and *Pascal Bruno* – a story of Sicilian brigandage. He became involved in the struggle for a united Italy, editing a newspaper called *L'indipendente*, penning a biography of Garibaldi in addition to writing a book following in his footsteps. His worldwide fame is

chiefly due to *The Count of Monte Cristo* and *The Three Musketeers*. His profligate spending meant that he had to write rapidly for many publications.

### Lawrence Durrell (1912–90)

Expatriate British author famous for the *Alexandria Quartet* and the *Avignon Quintet*. He referred to himself as an islomane, a lover of islands, and his travel books reflect this description. He undertook a tour of Sicily with fellow tourists in a red bus and his account of the trip, *Sicilian Carousel*, scrutinises both the island and those travelling with him. In addition to writing, Durrell also spent some time working for the British Foreign Office in Athens, Belgrade and Cairo.

### Frances Minto Elliot (1820–98)

English writer of travelogues, historical works and novels. Born in Somerset and married at 18, she divorced, subsequently marrying a vicar 20 years her senior. During the divorce proceedings she became friends with Charles Dickens and Wilkie Collins and acted in Collins' plays. After her second marriage went sour she moved to Italy. The memoirs of her stay in Sicily are recorded in *The Diary of an Idle Woman in Sicily*. Some of her parodies and sketches were published under the nom de plume Florentia.

### Duncan Fallowell (1948–)

English travel writer and novelist. In the 1980s he spent much of his time in Sicily, resulting in the travelogue *To Noto, Or London to Sicily in a Ford*. Immersing himself in the culture, his work demonstrates an understanding of the arts and the wilder aspects at the fringes of society. Oxford educated, with a degree in history, Fallowell has been happy to court the controversial – some of his other works focusing on drugs, trans-sexual issues and madcap English eccentricity.

### Henry Faulkner (1924–81)

American poet and artist from Kentucky. He was known for his eccentricities and colourful lifestyle. He was a close friend of Tennessee Williams, at one point purporting to manage the playwright's affairs. He was given the use of an outbuilding at Daphne Phelps' Casa Cuseni in Taormina, where he pursued his artistic endeavours. Faulkner also spent some time in mental institutions owing to his erratic and unpredictable behaviour. He died in a car accident in 1981.

### Anatole France (1844–1924)

French poet, journalist and novelist. He was a Nobel laureate and supreme documenter of the *fin de siècle*, whose travels in Sicily contributed to works such as *The Crime of Sylvestre Bonnard*, which made him famous, and *The Procurator of Judea*. He was elected to the Académie Française in 1896 and became well respected amongst his fellow authors. His real name was Jacques Anatole François Thibault. Married and divorced, his liaison with Arman de Caillavet inspired the novels *Thaïs* and *Le Lys rouge*.

### Sigmund Freud (1856–1939)

The Viennese father of psychoanalysis. In 1930 he was awarded the Goethe Prize for his contribution to psychology and German literary culture. Despite these accolades, he had to flee via Paris to London when the Nazis took power. He had a life-long fascination with southern Italy and its ancient Greek culture. He was able to indulge his passion for these southern climes before World War I. Sicily even appears in his *Interpretation of Dreams* and *The Psychopathy of Everyday Life*.

### André Gide (1869–1951)

French author and Nobel laureate. Best known in the English-speaking world for his works *Strait is the Gate*, *The Counterfeiters* and *The Immoralist*, this latter work being partly set in Syracuse and Taormina. He had an extended stay in the eastern resort of Taormina, where he mixed with other authors, artists and cinematographers. Married to his own cousin, Gide met Oscar Wilde and Alfred Douglas in North Africa, an encounter that encouraged him to confront his homosexuality. Much of his work is partially autobiographical in nature.

### Johann Wolfgang Goethe (1749–1832)

German polymath. His travels around Italy from 1786 to 1788 were essential in developing his philosophical outlook. In his diaries and letters, subsequently published as *Italian Journey*, he famously described Sicily as the key to understanding the entire Italian peninsula. Goethe's Sicilian itinerary took in the classical sites, famous residents and the new urban architecture of the day. His journey to Italy started with a clandestine flight from the spa town of Carlsbad. During his time on the island he continued to update his account, but also wrote a work that remained unfinished, 'Nausikaa'. He returned, dragging his feet, to Weimar in 1788. The list of his work, including *The Sorrows of Young Werther* and *Faust*, reflects his position in the world literary canon.

### Ernest Hemingway (1899–1961)

American author and journalist famed for his war reporting and *For Whom the Bell Tolls*. He was extremely well travelled, with extended sojourns in Spain, Italy and Africa. He deeply regretted not having spent a year in Taormina when given the opportunity. His letters show affection for this part of Sicily. He left us one short story, 'The Mercenaries', inspired by this period. Few American writers of the twentieth century were so famous; critics and populists alike have agreed on his merits. Erratic, ill and confused, he committed suicide after returning from Cuba and Spain to rural Idaho.

### Robert Hichens (1864–1950)

Novelist, journalist and playwright born in the English county of Kent. He became most well known for his satire on the life of Oscar Wilde and Lord Alfred Douglas, *The Green Carnation*. He also wrote supernatural tales and was one of the first to fictionalise morphine addiction in the book *Felix*. He set his work, *The Call of the Blood*, in Sicily. An early flowering talent, he wrote his first novel when 17. He was happy to spend the majority of his life overseas.

### Homer (*c.*eighth century BC)

Greek poet, author of the *Iliad* and the *Odyssey*. Many of the places and stories in the *Odyssey* refer to real locations in Sicily; for example, the Straits of Messina, Aci Trezza and the Aeolian Islands. Aeneas in Virgil's Roman epic the *Aeneid* also covers much of the same territory as Homer's hero Odysseus. Some scholars see Homer as a composite author, essentially the name attributed to a series of storytellers who have passed the story down the generations using the oral tradition. Alternatively, Samuel Butler was convinced the *Odyssey* was written by a woman.

### Muhammad al-Idrisi (1095–1165)

Moroccan geographer and traveller who adopted Sicily as his home. Owing to political strife in Andalucía, he moved to the court of King Roger II. He became an essential part of the intellectual circle surrounding the King, writing his major work, entitled *Pleasure Excursion of One Eager to Traverse the World's Regions* – better known as the *Book of Roger*. His geographical works, with ample descriptions, were still considered authoritative in the early twentieth century. Idrisi also forms one of the main characters in Tariq Ali's *A Sultan in Palermo*.

### Washington Irving (1783–1859)

American author, essayist and biographer. Famous for his stories *The Legend of Sleepy Hollow*, *Rip Van Winkle* and *Tales of the Alhambra*. He served in the US legation to Spain and travelled extensively throughout Europe. His impressions of Sicily are preserved in his published travel journals. Much of his other work takes a satirical look at society, interlacing fact, fiction and essay. It was his work *The Sketch Book of Geoffrey Crayon, Gent* that eventually persuaded him to turn from a judicial career to focus on writing.

**Edmund John (1883–1917)**

English poet who modelled his work on earlier Victorians such as Algernon Swinburne. He fought in World War I, but was sent home suffering from injury in 1916. He was not considered fashionable in his day due to his stylistic choices inspired by another era. His decadent symbolist works include *The Flute of the Sardonyx* and *The Wind in the Temple*. He died of a drug overdose in the Hotel Timeo, Taormina.

**Tobias Jones (1972–)**

English journalist and writer, married to an Italian. His search for political truths in modern Italy and his later disillusionment with twenty-first-century life, have led to two books that took him to Sicily – *The Dark Heart of Italy* and *Utopian Dreams*. Jones is also a regular contributor to British newspapers. He has recently turned to crime fiction, his second novel in the Castagnetti series came out in 2011. After an extended period in Italy, he now lives in Bristol.

**Ibn Jubayr (1145–1217)**

Traveller, writer and poet from al-Andalus. On a return journey from Mecca he visited Sicily. His observations of the island are tinted with nostalgia for its recent Muslim domination, but also highlight the influence of Islamic culture on the new Norman rulers. His writing is highly detailed and full of vivid portraits. He continued to travel after his Sicilian visit, making it as far as Acre and Baghdad despite inclement weather and a shipwreck. He died in Alexandria, leaving his manuscripts to influence generations of future scholars in the Muslim world and beyond.

**Robert D. Kaplan (1952–)**

American journalist and writer. His writing has often appeared in the *Washington Post* and *New York Times*. His book, *Mediterranean Winter*, retraces the travels of his youth around the Mediterranean, a significant portion of which includes Sicily and the cities of Agrigento, Palermo, Syracuse and Taormina. In addition to his authorial career, Kaplan has taught courses at the US Naval Academy and acted as a consultant to other branches of the United States military.

**Michael Kelly (1762–1826)**

Irish tenor and composer. Sometimes known as O'Kelly (or Ochelli to the Italians). He was one of the first British or Irish singers to become famous in Italy and Austria. His appearance on the Palermo music scene and his visits to the local aristocracy are set down in his *Reminiscences*. He was taken under the wing of

Sir William Hamilton and given the opportunity to train in Italy. His illustrious collection of friends was also able to gain him invitations to the best salons. Whilst in Sicily he was given free tuition by the respected singer Giuseppe Aprile.

### Henry Gally Knight (1786–1846)

British writer, traveller and parliamentarian. Born in Yorkshire, educated at Eton and Cambridge, Knight's writing covers two genres – novelistic tales of oriental folklore and the more serious field of architectural travel. His books on the Normans in Sicily and Italian church architecture were well respected. He was also a fellow of the Royal Society. Knight was the nephew of Frances Jacson, author of *Disobedience*. His folkloric stories were lampooned by Lord Byron.

### Selma Lagerlöf (1858–1940)

Swedish Nobel Prize-winning author, who was the first woman to be awarded the prize. Originally a teacher, she is most well known for her children's book *The Wonderful Adventures of Nils*. She devoted herself completely to writing from 1895 onwards and was able to take an extensive journey to Sicily, taking advantage of grant funding. In situ, she wrote *The Miracles of the Antichrist*, drawing on a local legend that has a Christ-child figure replaced by a false prophet.

### Giuseppe Tomasi di Lampedusa (1896–1957)

Author of *Il Gattopardo* (*The Leopard*), Sicilian literature's most famous novel. Lampedusa died before seeing his work in print. His aristocratic life was divided between Palermo, his country estate in Santa Margherita and the residence of his cousins in Capo d'Orlando. *The Leopard* is a poignant portrait of the island's declining aristocracy and the futility of political change. Lampedusa was a very private and shy man who devoted much time to reading and imparting his considerable knowledge to a select few. He married a Baltic psychoanalyst, Alexandra Wolff von Stomersee, who never felt at home in the Mediterranean. Other memoirs, stories and letters of his have been published since the success of *The Leopard*.

### David Herbert Lawrence (1885–1930)

English writer and critic, Lawrence was married to the aristocratic German, Frieda Weekley, née Richthofen. He left England in 1919, after being suspected of giving signals to the enemy in 1917. Lawrence headed south to Italy and then on to Sicily. He rented the Villa Fontana Vecchia in Taormina. His short story 'Sun', in the book *The Princess*, is set in the villa's garden and some of his poems also contain Sicilian themes. His work *Sea and Sardinia* is an account of his journey from Taormina to this neighbouring island. After leaving Sicily, his wandering existence continued, taking in Ceylon, Australia, New Mexico, Italy again and finally the south of France.

### Halldór Laxness (1902–98)

Icelandic author and Nobel Prize winner. Writer of plays, articles, novels and travelogues. His novel *The Great Weaver from Kashmir* was written in Taormina and caused a sensation in his native Iceland. It saw the end of a religious period during which time he had converted to Catholicism. Laxness was also a talented linguist who translated Ernest Hemingway's *A Farewell to Arms*.

### Edward Lear (1812–88)

English artist, poet and author famed for his nonsense poetry, in particular *The Owl and the Pussycat*, which he wrote for the Earl of Derby's children. Many of his journeys are accompanied by visual accounts illustrated in his own distinctive style. His Sicilian travels are recorded in published sketchbooks and letters. His nonsense verse is still admired today. Not all of his artistic endeavour was whimsical; he was a landscape painter, created ornithological drawings for the naturalist John Gould and worked for the British Museum. Most of his later years were spent abroad.

### James Henry Leigh Hunt (1784–1859)

Poet, writer and critic born in Southgate, London. He was a friend of Keats and Shelley. A founder of newspapers and magazines fomenting liberal opinions, he enjoyed spending time in Italy. Whilst in residence he also dedicated his time to translation. His work, *A Jar of Honey from Mount Hybla*, is an anthology of classical and Renaissance lore, literature and history from the island. His own verses reflect his deep knowledge of Italian verse forms and themes. Ironically, he is best known for his biography of Lord Byron and the poets/writers who moved in his circle.

### Jacopo da Lentini (*c.*1210–*c.*1260)

Born in Lentini, in the province of Syracuse. One of the principal exponents of the Sicilian School of poetry and recognised by Dante as its leading light. He was part of the court of Frederick II (*stupor mundi*), who was himself a poet. He wrote in the Sicilian dialect, taking thematic influences from the courtly troubadours of Provence. Forty of his lyrics survive, including those in sonnet form, a format he is accredited with creating. Little detail remains about his life and loves outside of his poetry.

**Carlo Levi (1902–75)**
Levi's achievements are prodigious: he was a writer, painter, doctor and political campaigner. He wrote two works that brought the problems of southern Italy to the attention of a wider nation: *Cristo si è fermato a Eboli* (*Christ Stopped at Eboli*) and *Le parole sono pietre* (*Words Are Stones*). He was an anti-Fascist campaigner, which caused his exile to the remote south before World War II.

**Norman Lewis (1908–2003)**
British travel writer and novelist. Lewis' first wife, Ernestina, was a Sicilian aristocrat and many of his books have Sicilian themes, including *The Sicilian Specialist*, *The Honoured Society* and *In Sicily*. His deep knowledge of the island was reflected in his writing, which has tackled the issue of Mafia involvement in Sicilian society. Born in the suburbs of north London, he could not wait to get out and explore the world, something he continued to do right up until his death. His home base in old age was rural Essex.

**Eliza Lynn Linton (1822–98)**
Novelist and journalist born in Cumbria, England. In addition to the prodigious output of 20 novels, she was also the first female to be a contracted journalist. She started her writing career under the wing of the Italianophile poet, Walter Savage Landor. Contrary to her ground-breaking work, she was a fierce critic of feminism and actively believed that politics should remain a male-dominated world. A guest of Tina Whitaker, she encouraged the wealthy wife of Pip Whitaker to pick up a pen. Her own works were influenced by trips to Sicily and resulted in articles like 'Some Sicilian Customs', which appeared in *Eclectic Magazine*.

**Alejandro Luque (1972–)**
Spanish writer, critic and journalist. He is the culture editor for *El Correo de Andalucía* and one of the instigators of *M'Sur*, which reports on Mediterranean culture. His love of Sicily and the writings of Jorge Luis Borges prompted a journey in his footsteps, recounted in the book *Viaje a la Sicilia con un guía ciego* (*Journey to Sicily with a Blind Guide*). He has also written a story compilation inspired by the island called *La defensa siciliana* (*The Sicilian Defence*, English translation forthcoming). Luque continues to interview prominent Sicilian cultural figures and report on the island's literary developments.

**Theresa Maggio (1953–)**
American travel writer of Sicilian ancestry. Her visits to relatives and friends have resulted in two books that delve into the customs and traditions of the

coastal towns and hilltop villages of the interior – *Mattanza: Love and Death in the Sea of Sicily* and *The Stone Boudoir: In Search of the Hidden Villages of Sicily*. Theresa's grandparents emigrated to America, but their closed attitude to the island always intrigued her. Following these thoughts, her own travels included a relationship with a Mondello fisherman and a series of encounters with hilltop islanders willing to tell their moving stories.

### Valerio Massimo Manfredi (1943–)

Italian writer and university professor now based in Milan. He specialises in historical novels set in the classical era. Famous for his Alexander trilogy, he has also written a novel, *Tyrant*, set in the Sicily of Dionysius during the fifth century BC. It focuses on his struggle with the Carthaginians and the rise of Syracuse as the most powerful city-state outside of mainland Greece.

### Dacia Maraini (1936–)

Italian writer and daughter of a Sicilian princess. After World War II, her family returned to live in the town of Bagheria. Her memoir of her time spent in Bagheria evokes postwar Sicily. Her novel, *La lunga vita di Marianna Ucrìa* (*The Silent Duchess*), tells the story of the eponymous Duchess and is set in eighteenth-century Palermo. It took Dacia decades before she turned to write about her Sicilian experiences, a time she remembers as bittersweet. Recent years have seen her garlanded with awards, including an honorary doctorate.

### Guy de Maupassant (1850–93)

French writer recognised as master of the short story. His wider travels began in 1880. In 1885 his Sicilian travel memoirs were published in instalments in the newspapers *Le Figaro* and *Gil Blas*, later to be collated as part of the book, *La Vie errante* (*The Wandering Life*). Another lawyer-turned-writer, he was taken under the wing of Gustave Flaubert, whose death deeply affected him. It is the work *Boule de suif* that pushed his writing career in the right direction. After a suicide attempt, a situation not helped by his advanced syphilis, he was committed to an institution in 1892.

### Gavin Maxwell (1914–69)

Scottish naturalist, reporter and travel writer. His most notable work is *Ring of Bright Water*, a touching story of his relationship with an otter. Prior to the success of this story set in Scotland, he lived and travelled in Sicily. A linguist, with a keen ear for Sicilian dialect, his book *God Protect Me from My Friends*, gives an insight into the intrigues surrounding the bandit Salvatore Giuliano.

*The Ten Pains of Death* is a warts-and-all portrait of provincial Sicily. In defiance of his sexuality, Maxwell married and quickly divorced in the 1960s. Famously, his otter book became a much-loved film.

### Giovanni Meli (1740–1815)

Sicilian poet from Palermo. He took inspiration from Cervantes and wrote *Don Chisciotte e Sancio Panza nella Scizia* (*Don Quixote and Sancho Panza in Sicily*), describing the further adventures of the famous pair in a trip around the island. His subsequent *Fiabe morali* (*Moral Fables*) are full of Sicilian humour and disguised satire. Writing in Sicilian, he published a five-volume *Poesi siciliani* in 1787, but was also an avid collector of dialect poetry by other writers. In addition to his literary output, he worked as a medical doctor in the town of Cinisi to the west of Palermo.

### Maria Messina (1887–1944)

Sicilian writer born in Palermo Province. She kept up a detailed correspondence with fellow writer Giovanni Verga, and with his support had her first stories published in the prestigious journal *La Nuova Antologia*. At the age of 20 she was diagnosed with multiple sclerosis, a condition that complicated and shortened her life. She is best remembered for her stories giving an insight into the reality of women's lives in early twentieth-century Sicily. Some of them appear in English translation as *Behind Closed Doors: Her Father's House and Other Stories of Sicily*.

### Arthur Miller (1915–2005)

Pulitzer Prize-winning American playwright and husband of Marilyn Monroe. He is best known for his works *The Crucible*, *Death of a Salesman* and his play based on Sicilian immigrants in the USA, *A View from the Bridge*. Miller was inspired to write *A View* after hearing a story told to him by politician and lawyer Vincent Longhi during their trip to Sicily in 1948. Miller also met the expatriate Mafioso Lucky Luciano: a story which he recounts in his autobiography, *Timebends*. During the 1950s he was investigated by the House Un-American Activities Committee, ending in his failure to obtain a passport to attend the London premiere of *The Crucible*. Further McCarthyesque persecution continued, including an actual committee appearance, which he attended with Marilyn. Ironically, later years saw Miller's plays banned in Soviet Russia, owing to his campaign for dissidents.

### Alan Moorehead (1910–83)

Australian-born war correspondent. He is most well known for his book *Gallipoli* about the Allies' ill-fated campaign during World War I. A friend of Hemingway, he divided his time between England and Italy from 1937 onwards. He reported from Sicily during the hunt for the bandit Salvatore Giuliano, and his postwar Italian memoirs are compiled in the book *The Villa Diana* – also his base in Italy. In the 1960s, he always tried to return annually to his native Australia.

### Francesco da Mosto (1961–)

Half-Venetian, half-Sicilian architect, author and documentary presenter. In his book *Francesco's Italy*, and his DVD *Italy: Top to Toe*, he gives an overview of Sicilian life, past and present. His mother's family, who still have a palazzo in Palermo, are descended from the dukes of Archirafi. Francesco has also contributed a foreword to the recently published English version of Giuseppe Tomasi di Lampedusa's letters.

### John Henry Newman (1801–90)

Born in London, Newman became a fellow of Oriel College, Oxford. His ordination led to involvement with the Oxford Movement (High Church Anglicanism), which was influenced by Catholic tradition. His theological writing was widely read in religious circles. During a sojourn in Sicily, he caught a fever that nearly led to his death. Time and the kindness of strangers enabled a full recovery. His convalescence in Palermo gave him time to think and write poetry. Much of *Lyra Apostolica* was written in the Mediterranean. His illness is also recorded in letters home. In 1845 he converted to Catholicism, giving his reasons in *Apologia pro Vita Sua*, the autobiographical explanation of his religious life. Pope Benedict beatified him in 2010.

### Friedrich Nietzsche (1844–1900)

German philosopher and poet. He started as a professor of classical philology in Basel before moving into the field of philosophy. In search of warmer climes for his health and stability, he travelled Europe, including a stay in Taormina. It was here that he wrote part of *Thus Spake Zarathustra*, his philosophical novel composed in four parts between 1883 and 1885. After collapsing in Turin, the last 11 years of his life were spent battling chronic mental illness.

### John Julius Norwich (1929–)

Historian, travel writer and English peer. A former Foreign Office diplomat, he has written extensively on the history of Italy and the eastern Mediterranean. His works, *The Normans in the South* and *The Kingdom in the Sun*, focus specifically on Norman rule in medieval Sicily. In his book *The Middle Sea: A History of the Mediterranean*, he also places the island's complex history in a wider context.

### Daphne Phelps (1911–2005)

British writer who lived in the Casa Cuseni in Taormina. An Oxford graduate, she looked after the property following the death of her uncle, Robert Kitson. She never went back to her nascent career in psychiatric social work. In 1999 she published the tale of her time on the island in *A House in Sicily*. She describes the visits of illustrious colleagues such as Tennessee Williams, Ezra Pound and Henry Faulkner.

### Lucio Piccolo (1901–69)

Sicilian aristocrat and poet. He was born in Palermo, but spent much of his life in Capo d'Orlando. Along with his cousin, Giuseppe Tomasi di Lampedusa, he had a life-long love of literature. In 1954 his work containing nine lyrics was first presented to the Italian literary world by Eugenio Montale, spurring his cousin to write *Il Gattopardo* (*The Leopard*). He went on to pen three books of poetry. The family villa echoes its eccentric inhabitants; Lucio's dogs even had their own pet cemetery.

### Pindar (*c.*522–443 BC)

Ancient Greek lyric poet who became involved in the world of Greek politics. Pan-Hellenic festivals took him across Magna Graecia, often to Sicily. His victory odes celebrate the town of Akragas, now known as Agrigento. He was the first Greek poet to reflect upon the nature of poetry and his role in this field of cultural endeavour. If it suited his purpose, he was happy to swim against the tide of literary fashion, at times extolling forms that were no longer in vogue. Longer stanzas with irregular verses have become known as Pindarics.

### Luigi Pirandello (1867–1936)

Native of Caos, a suburb of Agrigento. Writer, dramatist and Nobel laureate. His life was full of personal tragedy, often reflected in his ground-breaking theatre, novels and short stories. *Il fu Mattia Pascal* (*The Late Mattia Pascal*) and *Sei personaggi in cerca d'autore* (*Six Characters in Search of an Author*) are his most well-known translated works. His father wanted him to enter the commercial sector, but fortunately he had another string to his bow when the family business went bankrupt. An alumnus of Bonn University, where he wrote a thesis on Agrigentine dialect, Pirandello wrote some of his works in Sicilian rather than standard Italian. He won the Nobel Prize for Literature in 1934.

**Ezra Pound (1885–1972)**
American poet. His controversial life was largely spent overseas. With a view to settling in Sicily, he travelled to the island in 1924/5, accompanied by his wife and W. B. Yeats. After his notorious support of Mussolini during World War II, he was deported to the United States, where he spent time in a psychiatric hospital. His *Pisan Cantos* were published in 1948 and include references to the island.

**Mario Puzo (1920–99)**
Italian-American author famed for his fictional accounts of the Corleone Sicilian-American crime family. His novel *The Sicilian*, considered the literary sequel to *The Godfather*, is set in and around Palermo and represents a fictionalised account of Salvatore Giuliano's life, interspersed with the fictional exploits of Michael Corleone. Puzo grew up in New York's infamous Hell's Kitchen. He was already a mature student when he went to Columbia University after the war. A desire to create something that would sell in numbers led to a change of tack and the writing of *The Godfather*.

**Salvatore Quasimodo (1901–68)**
Nobel Prize-winning poet born in Modica, Sicily. His father's railway job led to his early relocation and subsequent study in Messina. He was considered to be one of the foremost poets in twentieth-century Italy. His poetry is suffused with imagery from his native island. Throughout his writing life, he also translated authors from Roman and Greek antiquity. He trained as an engineer, but gave up this career to teach in Milan. After World War II his poetry took on a clearer social edge, shocked at the nightmare of Fascism.

**Peter Robb (1946–)**
Australian author of *Midnight in Sicily*. The book uses the trial of the former prime minister, Giulio Andreotti, as a starting point for investigating the history, literature, painting and politics of Sicily. His subsequent book, *M*, is a biography of the artist Caravaggio, who escaped to Sicily after an argument on the island of Malta. Robb has also taught courses at universities in his native Australia, Finland and at the Istituto Universitario Orientale in Naples, a city that plays a key role in his latest book – appropriately titled *Street Fight in Naples*.

**Federico De Roberto (1861–1927)**
Born in Naples but an adopted son of Catania. He is most famous for his novel *I vicerè* (*The Viceroys*), the story of a noble Catanese family of Spanish origins.

The book depicts Sicily at the time of decline in the Bourbon monarchy which reigned over the Kingdom of the Two Sicilies. He started writing professionally as a journalist, a career that introduced him to the older Giovanni Verga. Time has judged *The Viceroys* a classic, but its lack of success disillusioned De Roberto. He left a sequel unfinished.

### Dante Gabriel Rossetti (1828–82)

Anglicised son of an Italian émigré, Rossetti is perhaps more famously known as a pre-Raphaelite painter. In addition to his work as an artist, he also wrote poetry and translated the Italian classics; his first collection was published in 1872. His writing often focuses on the same themes contained within his paintings and other artistic endeavours, as he regularly wrote sonnets in conjunction with his pictures. His later life was plagued with drug addiction and mental instability.

### Raymond Roussel (1877–1933)

Surrealist author and poet born in Paris. He used a method based on homonymic puns to write some of his material, a system that was only revealed after his death. Unsurprisingly, he was not a popular writer during his lifetime. He influenced the New York School of poets with his most well-known translated work *Locus Solus*. He struggled in later years with mental health issues and a drug problem, which he never conquered, dying in the Hotel des Palmes in Palermo of a suspected barbiturate overdose.

### Bertrand Russell (1872–1970)

Nobel Prize-winning philosopher and social critic. One of the founders of analytical philosophy and one of the twentieth century's leading logicians; this Briton from an aristocratic family enjoyed stays in Taormina, particularly with the writer Daphne Phelps who played host to many literary figures. Russell's complex private life was, in part, due to his role in defying the moral norms of the day. His second wife Dora had two children with another man and raised the children in the Russell household with her and Bertrand's children. The experiment ended in acrimonious divorce. He then married Patricia Spence, who went by the nickname of Peter. The wider public know him for his *History of Western Philosophy*.

### Siegfried Sassoon (1886–1967)

English poet and author renowned for his war poetry. He was decorated for bravery during World War I, but was sufficiently troubled by his experiences to proclaim pacifism whilst still enlisted. Whilst recovering in a sanatorium he met Wilfred Owen, publishing his works after Wilfred died during the war. At the beginning of the 1930s he undertook a journey to Sicily which led to the poem 'In Sicily'. It was illustrated by his friend Stephen Tennant. He also wrote autobiographically in texts such as *Memoirs of a Fox-Hunting Man* – his early years masked as a novel.

### Leonardo Sciascia (1921–89)

Sicilian writer, essayist and politician born in Racalmuto. His story *Il giorno della civetta* (*The Day of the Owl*) was one of the first works to confront the theme of Mafia corruption. He has written extensively on Sicilian history, culture and politics. Often wrongly categorised as a crime novelist, his fiction uses the vehicle of the detective story to expose underlying problems in society. Sciascia himself dabbled in politics, spending time in both the Italian Parliament, as an MP for the Radical Party, and subsequently in the European Parliament.

### Gaia Servadio (1938–)

Born in Padua, Gaia has lived in the United Kingdom since 1956. She trained as a graphic designer, but segued into journalism. She has written books in both English and Italian on a variety of subjects, from the Mafia to the ancient civilisation of Motya on the west coast of Sicily. Her work also includes novels, a travelogue, an autobiography and numerous contributions to magazines and newspapers in both countries. Her frequent trips to Italy have included a great deal of research in Sicily. Her credits also include BBC documentary work.

### William Shakespeare (1564–1616)

Although it is thought he never visited the island, plays such as *The Winter's Tale* and *Much Ado About Nothing* are based in Sicily. *Much Ado* is set in Messina and relies upon Italian sources such as Ariosto and Bandello for some of its subplot. Andrea Camilleri has translated *Much Ado* into Sicilian dialect, jokingly attributing its authorship to a Messinese called Michele Crollalanza. This story has some basis, even forming the heart of a book by Martino Juvara, who claimed Shakespeare for Messina. The real Bard retired to Stratford, dying on the same day and year as Miguel de Cervantes. This is now World Book Night.

### William Sharp, aka Fiona Macleod (1855–1905)

Scottish author who often wrote under the pseudonym Fiona Macleod. He was part of the noteworthy Rossetti literary group, where he mixed with Dante Gabriel and Algernon Charles Swinburne. His works include novels, biography and poetry. He was a member of the Hermetic Order of the Golden Dawn along with W. B. Yeats and Aleister Crowley. He suffered from a heart condition and was also diabetic. These weaknesses led to his death in Sicily, where he was buried in the Castello di Maniace cemetery – part of the dukedom belonging to the Nelson Hood family.

### Mary Shelley (1797–1851)

Mary was the daughter of Mary Wollstonecraft, a fervent advocate of gender equality. She eloped with Shelley to France and Geneva, where she had the idea of writing *Frankenstein* after a night of ghostly storytelling with Lord Byron. Mary and Percy Bysshe were able to marry after the suicide of Shelley's first wife. Her play *Proserpine* is based on the Greco-Roman myth set in the heart of Sicily.

### Percy Bysshe Shelley (1792–1822)

Romantic poet and liberal thinker whose complicated life was cut short in a boating accident off the coast of Livorno, northern Italy. In the dark summer of 1816, Shelley, his wife-to-be Mary and Claire Clairmont met with Byron at Lake Geneva. Shelley would return to Byron's side during subsequent stays at various Italian destinations, penning verses that cut to the heart of the human moral condition. In addition to translating classical poetry, he often looked to the ancients for inspiration in his own work. His poem 'Prometheus' reworked Aeschylus. He contributed 'Arethusa' and the 'Song of Proserpine' to Mary Shelley's play *Proserpine*.

### Diodorus Siculus (*c*.90–*c*.27 BC)

A Greco-Sicilian historian and writer known for his comprehensive 40-volume work, the *Bibliotheca historica* or *Library of History*. Only volumes 1–5 and 11–20 have survived intact, with fragments preserved in the works of others. He was from Agira near Enna in central Sicily, formerly known as Agyrium. His work can be segmented into mythic history, the period from the Trojan Wars to Alexander the Great and finally from Alexander to approximately 60 BC. He used and often acknowledged many other sources, including Timaeus and Polybius, but also utilised first-hand personal accounts, including things that he himself witnessed.

### Mary Taylor Simeti (1941–)

American author married to a Sicilian. She has written an account of her life entitled *On Persephone's Island*, in addition to *Pomp and Sustenance: Twenty-Five Centuries of Sicilian Food* and *Travels with a Medieval Queen*, the history of Norman Queen Constance of Sicily. Her biographical work details the pattern of her year, buying cannoli from a Palermo convent, harvesting olives on the farm or attending the local *festa*.

**Douglas Wheelton Sladen (1856–1947)**

English author who wrote on Sicilian subjects. He spent many months staying with friends such as the Whitakers, whose family founded a large Marsala wine business. He was an editor of *Who's Who*, novelist, poet and biographer. In addition to his southern Italian travels he also spent a period as the first modern-history lecturer at Sydney University. He carefully collated a personal library of correspondence with over 70 people who were famous in his day.

**John Steinbeck (1902–68)**

Pulitzer Prize-winning American writer of *The Grapes of Wrath*. Steinbeck spent part of World War II as a correspondent from the front; in particular he followed the commando raids of Douglas Fairbanks Jr's 'Beach Jumpers' during the invasion of Sicily. His war reports appear in the book *Once There Was a War*. His modern-day reputation is built on his earlier works which looked at American hardship. He never quite regained the same prestige in later years. He also adapted some of his own books for the cinema.

**Henry Swinburne (1743–1803)**

English travel writer who spent two years travelling around the Kingdom of the Two Sicilies (Naples and Sicily). Later editions of the book based on his journey, *Travels in the Two Sicilies*, included drawings by the writer himself. His oft-quoted work has frequently been confused with the observations of his great-nephew Algernon Charles Swinburne. His peripatetic existence included further travels to Austria and France, where he was content to cultivate royalty and the literary set. An English Catholic, he seemed happier on the continent. His later years saw financial difficulties and the loss of his West Indian properties.

**Caitlin Thomas (1913–94)**

Caitlin Thomas is perhaps best known as the wife of the Welsh poet Dylan Thomas. Their relationship was punctuated with infidelity and fuelled by alcohol. After Dylan died in 1953, Caitlin moved to Italy, staying for a period with Daphne Phelps in Taormina. She was driven to write a memoir, *Leftover Life to Kill,* which documents this time in her life. She formed a relationship with a Sicilian director's assistant from Catania.

**Gioia Timpanelli (1936–)**

An American broadcaster, storyteller and writer. She has been credited with reinvigorating the oral storytelling tradition for the American public and was presented with the Women's National Book Award. Her work *Sometimes the Soul: Two Novellas of Sicily* draws on Sicilian fairy-tale conventions, but uses a modern sensibility in its portrayal of life on the island.

### Raleigh Trevelyan (1923–)

Trevelyan was born in the Andaman Islands, but moved to England when he was eight. Part of the illustrious Trevelyan family, including the historian G. M. Trevelyan, he made a career as an editor and author. His book *The Fortress*, on the Battle of Anzio, has been claimed as one of the most insightful works on close combat to have been written. It was based on his diary entries. He has penned two works on Sicily, a companion guide to the island and a comprehensive study of the British in Sicily, *Princes under the Volcano*. His research utilised many unpublished letters and papers from the Whitaker family archives.

### Henry Theodore Tuckerman (1817–71)

Writer and critic born in Boston, Massachusetts. He wrote in both prose and verse, often taking inspiration from his extensive travels through Italy and Sicily. In 1839 his book *Isabel, or Sicily: A Pilgrimage* was published. A travelogue disguised as a novel, it follows in the footsteps of the young Isabel Otley on her travels around the island. A keen essayist and poet, his work in these fields also echoes Sicily's influence.

### Barry Unsworth (1930–2012)

British writer of historical novels and former Booker Prize winner. The last part of his life was spent in Italy and he set his novel *The Ruby in her Navel* in Norman Sicily. The book evokes life at the time when the island was a melting pot of Greek, Arab, native Sicilian and Norman cultures. The central character witnesses the construction of Palermo's golden Palatine Chapel. Unsworth approached historical fiction by trying to capture a sense of place and time rather than getting bogged down in particulars.

### Fulco de Verdura (1898–1978)

Designer, jeweller and Sicilian aristocrat. His career started when he was introduced to Coco Chanel by Cole Porter. He began working for her as a textile designer and then moved into jewellery. He collaborated on designs with the likes of Paul Flato and Salvador Dalí. A cousin of Giuseppe Tomasi di Lampedusa, he fondly remembered his Sicilian childhood in his memoir, *Happy Summer Days*. The family villa still stands on the outskirts of Palermo.

### Giovanni Verga (1840–1922)

Born in Catania. Whilst studying at university, he gave up law to pursue a literary career. His early work had a historical, sentimental perspective, but he moved to a *verismo* (realist) style which detailed the language and culture of everyday Sicilian life. He is best known for *I malavoglia* (*The House of the Medlar Tree*) and *Mastro don Gesualdo*. Some of his works, including *Novelle siciliane* (*Little Novels of Sicily*) were translated by D. H. Lawrence. The neo-realist cinematic movement in postwar Italy found his writing a natural fit. Luchino Visconti brought the *Medlar Tree* to the screen as *La terra trema*.

### Elio Vittorini (1908–66)

Siracusan writer who formed part of the anti-Fascist resistance movement; he joined the clandestine communist faction during the war. His novel *Conversazione in Sicilia* (*Conversations in Sicily*) sees the return of an emigrant worker to his native island after working in the north of Italy. Vittorini was the son of an itinerant railway worker and part of the novel is set on the train network. In Milan after the conflict, he worked for the publishing house Einaudi.

### Frank Viviano (1947–)

Sicilian-American writer and journalist. In the book *Blood Washes Blood* he tells the story of the assassination of his namesake Francesco Viviano in nineteenth-century Sicily. Frank visited the island in an attempt to piece together this old family mystery which his grandfather recounted to him on his deathbed. Whilst researching his family tree, he was also still working as a foreign correspondent for the *San Francisco Chronicle*, a newspaper that carried his reports from the Yugoslav conflict and Tiananmen Square.

### Booker T. Washington (1856–1915)

American educator, author and political leader. After emancipation from slavery, he went on to become a spokesman for African-American citizens. In 1912 he wrote *The Man Farthest Down*, a book which looked at the enslavement of people in Europe. His research took him to the sulphur mines of Sicily. Part of his philosophy espoused the virtue of economic well-being, financial security acting as the bridge to political and social acceptance. He also wrote an autobiography entitled *Up from Slavery*.

### Evelyn Waugh (1903–66)

English novelist, journalist and reviewer. He travelled extensively as a newspaper correspondent during the 1930s, converting to Catholicism in the same decade.

He wrote about his visit to Sicily in the travelogue *Labels*. He was posted to the Mediterranean during World War II and returned in 1953, touring through Sicily as his mental health declined. He was accompanied by Harold Acton, who noted his mercurial moods. Often called a social satirist, he is best known for *Brideshead Revisited* and his World War II trilogy, *Sword of Honour*.

### Alan Whicker (1925–2013)

British broadcaster and journalist. He was stationed in Sicily during World War II with the British Army's film and photo unit. The account of his time spent at the forefront of the Allied invasion of Sicily and Italy appears in his book *Whicker's War*. The book was also made into a BBC documentary, the name a play on his long-running programme, *Whicker's World*. His distinctive delivery to camera has spawned hundreds of impersonations, most notably by Monty Python.

### Joseph Whitaker (1850–1936)

Although ostensibly a businessman, the Anglo-Sicilian Whitaker is better known for his work as a proto-archaeologist and ornithologist. Married to Tina Whitaker, the couple set up home at the luxurious Villa Malfitano in Palermo. His inherited wealth allowed him to follow his twin passions and he was the first to dig for Phoenician remains on the island of Motya. He wrote over 30 tracts on ornithology in both Italian and English, but is most remembered for his work detailing the archaeological excavations.

### Tina Whitaker (1858–1957)

Tina Whitaker, neé Scalia, married into the Whitaker family, which was heavily involved in the Marsala wine trade. Her home, the Villa Malfitano, was the venue for extravagant parties that often had royal or celebrity connections, notably Richard Wagner and Queen Mary. Her unsuccessful attempt at fiction writing was supplanted by a more worthwhile memoir which focuses on the connection between England and Sicily. Her ebullient personality was in distinct contrast to that of her husband Joseph, who went on to excavate the Phoenician island of Motya.

### Oscar Wilde (1854–1900)

Irish writer and poet. After studying Classics at Oxford, some of his early poetry is based on Italian themes. Witty and colourful, Wilde was at home in the Aesthetic movement. His work extended to novels, essays, plays and verse. He conducted lecture tours on both sides of the Atlantic. Wilde's downfall was his relationship with Lord Alfred Douglas, known as Bosie. Douglas' father accused Oscar of sodomy – unwisely Wilde sued him for libel. The ploy backfired and he was gaoled for gross indecency. Having completed *De Profundis* whilst incarcerated in Reading gaol, Wilde then moved to the continent. During his subsequent stay in Taormina (1897), he befriended the Prussian Baron von Gloeden, renowned for his pastoral nude photography.

**Tennessee Williams (1911–83)**
American playwright and author. Williams visited Sicily with his partner Frank Merlo, a Sicilian-American whose family lived just outside Palermo. His play *The Rose Tattoo* is set in an immigrant Sicilian community in Louisiana. The playwright also spent a lot of time in Taormina, famously observing the tourists and locals from his seat at the Caffè Wunderbar. Addiction to sleeping pills and alcohol took over his life in the 1960s, leading to a breakdown at the end of the decade. He dreamed of retiring to the Sicilian hills.

**William Butler Yeats (1865–1939)**
Irish poet, playwright and politician. He travelled to Sicily under doctor's orders in the early 1920s. He was accompanied to the classical sites by Ezra Pound. The ancient Sicilian coins he saw in Syracuse inspired his choice of design for the new coinage of the Irish Free State. Shunning Protestantism and Catholicism, Yeats followed his own spiritual and mythical path. He dabbled with the Theosophical Society and the Order of the Golden Dawn. The work *Celtic Twilight* also mirrors this shift to the artistic, mythological and esoteric. He corresponded with a similarly minded Lucio Piccolo.

**Adam Zagajewski (1945–)**
Polish poet, novelist and translator. He left home to live in Paris in 1982 whilst Poland was under Communist rule. After the fall of the Iron Curtain, he returned in 2002 and now lives in Krakow. His poetry has been inspired by the sights and sounds of Sicily and includes some beautiful verses on Syracuse and the island's ancient sites. In 2004, he was awarded the Neustadt International Prize for Literature.

# CHRONOLOGY

|  | *Literary and Cultural Events* | *Political Events* |
|---|---|---|
| *c.*800 BC | Homer composes the *Odyssey.* | |
| 735 BC | | Naxos near Taormina founded as Sicily's first Greek city. |
| *c.*700 BC | | Island of Mozia settled by the Phoenicians. |
| 581 BC | | Akragas (Agrigento) founded by a group of Greek colonists from Gela. |
| 470 BC | Pindar composes his first ode to the tyrant Hiero. | |
| 458 BC | Aeschylus writes the *Oresteia.* | |
| 413 BC | | Syracusans defeat the Athenians in the Peloponnesian War. |
| 264 BC | | Start of the First Punic War between Carthage and Rome. |
| 70 BC | Cicero delivers the *Verrine Orations* against the crooked Governor of Sicily, Caius Verres. | |
| *c.*AD 303 | | The martyrdom of Santa Lucia in Syracuse. |
| *c.*330 | | The construction and expansion of Villa Casale, Piazza Armerina. |
| 827 | | Asad ibn al-Furat and his troops come from Tunisia to invade Sicily. |
| 1061 | | The Norman, Roger de Hauteville, crosses the Straits of Messina with his army. |

| | Literary and Cultural Events | Political Events |
|---|---|---|
| 1071 | | Palermo falls to the Normans. |
| 1154 | al-Idrisi produces his world map, the *Book of Roger*. | |
| 1160 | | Influential politician, Maio of Bari, is stabbed to death by conspirators. |
| c.1174 | | Construction begins on the Cathedral of Monreale. |
| 1184 | Ibn Jubayr starts his visit to Sicily. | |
| 1198 | | Frederick II (*Stupor Mundi*) crowned King of Sicily. |
| 1282 | | The war of the Sicilian Vespers and the arrival of the Spanish Aragonese. |
| 1347 | | Plague arrives in Western Europe via the port of Messina. |
| 1487 | | The Spanish Inquisition is established in Sicily. |
| 1519 | | Charles V becomes Holy Roman Emperor. |
| 1571 | | The Battle of Lepanto. |
| 1572 | Cervantes released from hospital in Messina. | |
| 1608 | Caravaggio paints the *Burial of Santa Lucia* in Syracuse. | |
| 1624 | | Palermo struck by plague and the bones of Santa Rosalia found on Monte Pellegrino. |
| 1693 | | Massive earthquake, prompting the reconstruction of Noto in Baroque style. |
| 1713 | | Direct Spanish rule comes to an end. |
| 1720 | | Austria takes the throne. |
| 1734 | | The Spanish Bourbons return. |
| 1759 | | The Bourbon throne separates from Spain. |

|      | *Literary and Cultural Events* | *Political Events* |
|------|--------------------------------|--------------------|
| 1770 | Patrick Brydone makes Sicily a Grand Tour destination. | |
| 1786 | Goethe embarks on his Italian journey. | |
| 1798 | | King Ferdinand flees from Naples to Palermo in Nelson's ship. |
| 1804 | Coleridge leaves Malta for Syracuse. | |
| 1806 | | Britain takes over the island's defence. |
| 1809 | Lord Byron's ship docks at Porto Empedocle. | |
| 1812 | | A constitution is established and feudalism abolished. |
| 1832 | John Henry Newman falls dangerously ill in Enna. | |
| 1840 | Giovanni Verga born. | |
| 1847 | Edward Lear visits Sicily. | |
| 1848 | | Start of a failed revolution to overthrow the Bourbons. |
| 1860 | Alexandre Dumas follows in Garibaldi's footsteps. | The arrival of Garibaldi and the Thousand. Sicily votes to join a united Italy. |
| 1882 | Richard Wagner stays at the Hotel des Palmes in Palermo. | |
| 1889 | | Foundation of the Fasci movement – Sicilian workers' leagues fighting for land reform. |
| 1892 | Samuel Butler announces his theory on the origins of Homer's *Odyssey*. | |
| 1897 | Oscar Wilde visits Taormina. | |
| 1908 | | The Messina earthquake destroys the city. |
| 1918 | Hemingway visits Taormina. | |

| | Literary and Cultural Events | Political Events |
|------|------------------------------|------------------|
| 1920 | D. H. Lawrence goes house-hunting in Taormina and stays until 1922. | |
| 1922 | | Mussolini comes to power. |
| 1923 | Aleister Crowley expelled from Cefalù. | |
| 1925 | Ezra Pound and his wife tour Sicily with W. B. Yeats. | |
| 1929 | Siegfried Sassoon and Stephen Tennant arrive in Sicily. | |
| 1930 | | Cesare Mori, Mussolini's prefect, sent to combat the Mafia. |
| 1934 | Luigi Pirandello receives the Nobel Prize for Literature. | |
| 1939 | The Fascist censors close the magazine *Omnibus*, which had regular contributions from Vitaliano Brancati. | |
| 1943 | John Steinbeck becomes a war reporter and Alan Whicker takes part in the Sicilian invasion. | The Allies land on Sicilian soil during World War II and Mussolini is overthrown. |
| 1947 | | Salvatore Giuliano and his band kill 11 people at Piana degli Albanesi. |
| 1949 | Pirandello's birthplace declared a national monument. | |
| 1950 | Truman Capote stays in D. H. Lawrence's old house in Taormina. | Giuliano is betrayed and shot dead. |
| 1953 | Gavin Maxwell arrives in Sicily. | |
| 1958 | Lampedusa's book, *The Leopard*, published posthumously. | |
| 1959 | Salvatore Quasimodo receives the Nobel Prize for Literature. | |
| 1961 | Leonardo Sciascia publishes his ground-breaking novel, *The Day of the Owl*. | |

| | *Literary and Cultural Events* | *Political Events* |
| --- | --- | --- |
| 1968 | | Large earthquake in western Sicily destroys many areas including Santa Margherita di Belice. |
| 1972 | | Mafia boss Tommaso Buscetta is arrested and cooperates with the justice system. |
| 1982 | | General Dalla Chiesa is assassinated. |
| 1984 | Jorge Luis Borges visits Sicily. | |
| 1987 | | Tommaso Buscetta's confessions aid the judicial proceedings against hundreds of Mafiosi. |
| 1992 | | Judges Falcone and Borsellino are assassinated. |
| 1994 | Andrea Camilleri publishes the first book in his Inspector Montalbano series. | Silvio Berlusconi becomes the Italian prime minister, aided by winning all the Sicilian seats. |
| 1996 | Gesualdo Bufalino dies in a car accident. | |
| 1999 | Inspector Montalbano makes his first TV appearance. | |
| 2003 | Tobias Jones publishes his book, *The Dark Heart of Italy*. | |
| 2012 | | Sicily elects its first openly gay president, Rosario Crocetta. |
| 2013 | | Beppe Grillo's populist Five Star Movement makes significant inroads in Sicily during the general election. |

# SELECT BIBLIOGRAPHY

Abba, C., *The Diary of One of Garibaldi's Thousand*, trans. E. R. Vincent (Oxford: Oxford University Press, 1962).

Acton, H., *More Memoirs of an Aesthete* (London: Faber and Faber, 2008).

Adams, C., *Memoir of Washington Irving* (New York: Carlton and Lanahan, 1870).

Aeschylus, *English Specimens of the Greek Dramatic Poets: Aeschylus* (London: John Murray, 1831).

Agg, H., *A Cypress in Sicily* (Edinburgh: Blackwood, 1967).

Agnello Hornby, S., *The Almond Picker*, trans. A. McEwen (London: Penguin, 2006).

—— *The Nun*, trans. A. Shugaar (New York: Europa Editions, 2012).

Alajmo, R., *Palermo*, trans. G. Waldman (London: The Armchair Traveller, Haus, 2010).

—— *L'arte di annacarsi. Un viaggio in Sicilia* (Rome: Laterza, 2012).

Alexander, A. (ed.), *Stories of Sicily* (New York: Schocken Books, 1975).

Ali, T., *A Sultan in Palermo* (London: Verso Books, 2005).

Arcara, S., *Oscar Wilde e la Sicilia: temi mediterranei nell'estetismo inglese* (Catania: Cavallotto, 1998).

Arnold, M., *Empedocles on Etna and Other Poems* (London: B. Fellowes, 1852).

Barański, Z. and Pertile, L. (eds), *The New Italian Novel* (Edinburgh: Edinburgh University Press, 1997).

Berenson, B., *The Passionate Sightseer: From the Diaries 1947–1956* (London: Thames & Hudson, 1988).

Blasi, M. di, *That Summer in Sicily: A Love Story* (New York, Ballantine, 2009).

Blyth, C. (ed.), *Decadent Verse: An Anthology of Late-Victorian Poetry, 1872–1900* (London: Anthem Press, 2009).

Booth, M., *A Magick Life: The Biography of Aleister Crowley* (London: Hodder & Stoughton, 2000).

Borges, J. L., *Selected Poems* (London: Penguin, 2000).

—— *Labyrinths: Selected Stories and Other Writings* (Harmondsworth: Penguin, 1970).

Botting, D., *Gavin Maxwell: A Life* (London: HarperCollins, 1993).

Boulton, J. T. and Robertson, A. (eds), *The Letters of D. H. Lawrence: Volume III, Part 1, 1916–1921* (Cambridge: Cambridge University Press, 2002).

Brancati, V., *Don Giovanni in Sicily*, trans. C. Biazzo Curry (Leicester: Troubador Storia, 2009).

Brydone, P., *Travels in Sicily and Malta* (Aberdeen: George Clark & Son, 1843).

Bufalino, G., *Blind Argus*, trans. P. Kreagh (London: HarperCollins, 1992).

—— *The Keeper of Ruins*, trans. P. Kreagh (London: Harvill, 1994).

Butler, S., *On the Trapanese Origin of the Odyssey* (Cambridge: Metcalfe, 1893).

—— *The Authoress of the Odyssey* (London: A. C. Fifield, 1897).

Byron, G. G., *The Works of Lord Byron. Poetry: Volume VII* (London: John Murray, 1905).

—— *Childe Harold* (London: John Long, 1923).

Byron, W., *Cervantes: A Biography* (London: Cassell, 1979).

Camilleri, A., *The Shape of Water,* trans. S. Sartarelli (London, Picador, 2005).

—— *The Terracotta Dog*, trans. S. Sartarelli (London, Picador, 2005).

—— *Excursion to Tindari*, trans. S. Sartarelli (London, Picador, 2006).

—— *The Scent of the Night*, trans. S. Sartarelli (London, Picador, 2007).

—— *The Patience of the Spider*, trans. S. Sartarelli (London, Picador, 2008).

Campbell, A., *Calatafimi: Behind the Stone Walls of a Sicilian Town* (London: Giles de la Mare, 2008).

Camuto, R., *Palmento: A Sicilian Wine Odyssey* (Lincoln: University of Nebraska Press, 2010).

Capote, T., *Portraits and Observations: The Essays of Truman Capote* (New York: Random House, 2007).

Caputi, A., *Pirandello and the Crisis of Modern Consciousness* (Urbana: University of Illinois Press, 1988).

Cervantes, M., *The Exemplary Novels*, trans. W. K. Kelly (London: Henry G. Bohn, 1855).

—— *The Ingenious Gentleman Don Quixote of La Mancha*, trans. J. Ormsby (New York: Thomas Y. Crowell, 1885).

Cicero, M. T., *The Two Last Pleadings of Marcus Tullius Cicero Against Caius Verres*, trans. C. Kelsall (London: White, Cochrane & Co., 1812).

Clarke, G., *Capote: A Biography* (New York: Simon & Schuster, 1988).

—— (ed.), *Too Brief a Treat: The Letters of Truman Capote* (New York: Vintage Books, 2007).

Clausi, M. et al., *I luoghi di Montalbano: una guida* (Palermo: Sellerio, 2007).

Coleridge, E. H. (ed.), *Anima Poetae: From the Unpublished Notebooks of Samuel Taylor Coleridge* (London: Heinemann, 1895).

Coleridge, S. T., *Specimens of the Table Talk of the Late Samuel Taylor Coleridge: Volume II* (London: John Murray, 1835).

—— *Samuel Taylor Coleridge: Selected by James Fenton* (London: Faber and Faber, 2006).

Consolo, V., *The Smile of the Unknown Mariner*, trans. J. Farrell (Manchester: Carcanet Press, 1994).

Cronin, V., *The Golden Honeycomb* (London: Harvill, 1992).

Crowley, A., *The Diary of a Drug Fiend* (York Beach: Samuel Weiser, 1970).

Dibdin, M., *Blood Rain* (London: Faber and Faber, 2004).

Drinkwater, C., *The Olive Tree: A Personal Journey through Mediterranean Olive Groves* (London: Phoenix, 2009).

Dumas, A. (père), *Pascal Bruno* (London: Henry Colburn, 1837).

—— *The Garibaldians in Sicily*, trans. E. Routledge (London: Routledge, Warne & Routledge, 1861).

—— *On Board the Emma, Adventures with Garibaldi's Thousand in Sicily*, trans. R. S. Garnett (New York: D. Appleton & Co., 1929).

Dummett, J., *Syracuse, City of Legends: A Glory of Sicily* (London: I.B.Tauris, 2010).

Durrell, L., *A Sicilian Carousel* (London: Faber and Faber, 2012).

Edwards, A., interview with Simonetta Agnello Hornby, Times of Sicily blog, 2012, www.timesofsicily.com/from-designer-to-journalist-an-interview-with-gaia-servadio, accessed 6 January 2014.

—— interview with Gaia Servadio, Times of Sicily blog, 2012, www.timesofsicily.com/interview-with-frank-viviano-author-of-blood-washes-blood, accessed 6 January 2014.

—— interview with Frank Viviano, Times of Sicily blog, 2012, www.timesofsicily.com/interview-with-simonetta-agnello-hornby-author-of-la-monaca, accessed 6 January 2014.

Evans, J., *The Semi-Invisible Man: the Life of Norman Lewis* (London: Picador, 2009).

Fallowell, D., *To Noto, Or London to Sicily in a Ford* (London: Bloomsbury, 1991).

Farinella, E., 'Ireland and Sicily: Two Islands', from *Feile-Festa, Literary Arts Journal of the Mediterranean Celtic Cultural Association*, www.medcelt.org /feile-festa/v001-n001/prose/farinella.html.

Festing Jones, H., *Diversions in Sicily* (London: A. C. Fifield, 1909).

—— *Samuel Butler: Author of Erewhon (1835–1902), A Memoir* (London: Macmillan, 1920).

France, A., *The Crime of Sylvestre Bonnard*, trans. L. Hearn (London: Folio Society, 1948).

Galvagno, R., 'Freud and Greater Greece: Metamorphoses of the 'Exotic' Journey between Ancient and Modern Imaginary', *Between*, 1:2 (2011), http://ojs. unica.it/index.php/between/article/view/312/295.

Geisthövel, W., *Homer's Mediterranean: A Travel Companion*, trans. A. Bell (London: Haus, 2008).

Gide, A., *The Immoralist*, trans. D. Watson (London: Penguin, 2000).

Gilmour, D., *The Last Leopard* (London: Eland, 2007).

Goethe, J. W., *Italian Journey, 1786–1788*, trans. E. Mayer and W. H. Auden (London: Penguin, 1982).

Graham-Dixon, A., *Caravaggio: A Life Sacred and Profane* (London: Penguin, 2010).

Graves, R., *Homer's Daughter* (London: Penguin, 2012).

Griffin, N., *The Selected Letters of Bertrand Russell, Volume 2: The Public Years, 1914–1970* (London: Routledge, 2002).

Griffin, P., *Along with Youth: Hemingway The Early Years* (Oxford: Oxford University Press, 1985).

Gudmundsson, H., *The Islander*, trans. P. Roughton (London: Maclehose, 2008).

Hart Davis, R. (ed.), *Selected Letters of Oscar Wilde* (Oxford: Oxford University Press, 1979).

Hichens, R., *The Call of the Blood* (Toronto: William Briggs, 1905).

Homer, *The Odyssey*, trans. S. Butler (London: A. C. Fifield, 1900).

House, C., *The Outrageous Life of Henry Faulkner* (Knoxville: University of Tennessee Press, 1988).

Irving, P. M., *The Life and Letters of Washington Irving* (New York: G. P. Putnam and Son, 1869).

Irving, W., *Notes and Journal of Travel in Europe, 1804–1805* (New York: Grolier Club, 1920).

John, E., *The Flute of Sardonyx* (Llandogo: Old Stile Press, 1991).

Jones, T., *The Dark Heart of Italy* (London: Faber and Faber, 2007).

Ibn Jubayr, *Travels*, trans. R. Broadhurst (Delhi: Goodword Books, 2001).

Kaplan, R. D., *Mediterranean Winter: A Journey through History* (London: Arrow, 2006).

Kay, G. (ed.), *The Penguin Book of Italian Verse* (Harmondsworth: Penguin, 1958).

Kelly, M., *Reminiscences: Volume 1* (London: Henry Colburn, 1826).

Knight, H. G., *The Normans in Sicily* (London: John Murray, 1838).

Lagerlöf, S., *The Miracles of Antichrist: A Novel*, trans. P. Bancroft Flach (London: Arthur F. Bird, 1909).

Lampedusa, G. T. di, *The Leopard*, trans. A. Colquhoun (London: Collins and Harvill Press, 1960).

—— *The Siren and Selected Writings*, trans. A. Colquhoun (London: Harvill, 1995).

—— *Letters from London and Europe*, trans. J. G. Nichols (Richmond: Alma Books, 2011).

Lawrence, D. H., *Sea and Sardinia* (Harmondsworth: Penguin, 1944).

—— *The Woman who Rode Away and Other Stories* (Cambridge: Cambridge University Press, 1995).

—— *D. H. Lawrence (Poet to Poet): Selected by Tom Paulin* (London: Faber and Faber, 2007).

Laxness, H., *The Great Weaver from Kashmir*, trans. P. Roughton (New York: Archipelago Books, 2008).

Layard, G. S., *Mrs Lynn Linton: Her Life, Letters, and Opinions* (London: Methuen, 1901).

Lear, E. and Proby, G., *Lear in Sicily* (London: Duckworth, 1938).

Lefebure, M., *Samuel Taylor Coleridge: A Bondage of Opium* (London: Quartet Books, 1977).

Leigh Hunt, J., *Byron and Some of his Contemporaries* (London: Henry Colburn, 1828).

—— *A Jar of Honey from Mount Hybla* (London: Smith, Elder & Company, 1870).

Levi, C., *Words Are Stones: Impressions of Sicily*, trans. A. Shugaar (London: Hesperus Press, 2005).

Lewis, N., *The Sicilian Specialist* (London: Penguin, 1985).

—— *The March of the Long Shadows* (London: Secker & Warburg, 1987).

—— *In Sicily* (London: Picador, 2001).

—— *The Honoured Society: The Sicilian Mafia Observed* (London: Eland, 2003).

Luque, A., *La defensa siciliana* (Seville: Algaida, 2006).

—— *Viaje a la sicilia con un guía ciego* (Cordoba: Almuzara, 2007).

Lynn Linton, E., 'Some Sicilian Customs', *Eclectic Magazine*, 41 (1885).

Maggio, T., *Mattanza: Love and Death in the Sea of Sicily* (Cambridge: Perseus, 2000).

—— *The Stone Boudoir: In Search of the Hidden Villages of Sicily* (London: Headline Review, 2002).

Manfredi, V. M., *Tyrant: A Novel*, trans. C. Feddersen-Manfredi (London: Pan Books, 2006).

Maraini, D., *Bagheria*, trans. D. Kitto and E. Spottiswood (London: Peter Owen, 1994).

—— *The Silent Duchess*, trans. D. Kitto and E. Spottiswood (London: Arcadia Books, 2010).

Marino, E., 'Beyond Ethnicity: An Interview with Teresa Maggio', *Nebula*, 2:3 (2005), www.academia.edu/793115/Beyond_Ethnicity_An_ Interview_with_ Theresa_Maggio.

Maupassant, G. de, *Sicily*, trans. R. W. Berger (New York: Italica Press, 2008).

Maxwell, G., *God Protect Me from my Friends* (London: Pan Books, 1958).

—— *The Ten Pains of Death* (Gloucester: Sutton Publishing, 1986).

Meli, G., *Don Chisciotti and Sanciu Panza*, trans. G. Cipolla (Ottawa: Legas, 2002).

Messina, M., *Behind Closed Doors: Her Father's House and Other Stories of Sicily*, trans. E. Magistro (New York: The Feminist Press, CUNY, 2007).

Miller, A., *Timebends: A Life* (London: Methuen, 1988).

—— *A View from the Bridge* (London: Penguin, 2010).

Milton, J., *Paradise Lost, A Poem in Twelve Books* (Paris: Theophilus Barrois, 1803).

Minto Elliot, F., *The Diary of an Idle Woman in Sicily* (Leipzig: Bernhard Tauchnitz, 1882).

Moorcroft Wilson, J., *Siegfried Sassoon: The Journey from the Trenches. A Biography, 1918–1967* (London: Routledge, 2003).

Moorehead, A., *The Villa Diana: Travels through Post-war Italy* (Chichester: Summersdale, 2008).

Mosto, F. da, *Francesco's Italy* (London: BBC Books, 2006).

Mozley, A. (ed.), *Letters and Correspondence of John Henry Newman during his Life in the English Church* (London: Longmans, Green & Co., 1903).

Newman, J. H., *The Poems* (London: John Lane, 1905).

Nietzsche, F., *Thus Spoke Zarathustra*, trans. R. J. Hollingdale (London: Penguin, 1974).

Norwich, J. J., *The Kingdom in the Sun: 1130–1194* (London: Longman, 1970).

O'Faolain, S., *South to Sicily* (London: Collins, 1953).

Perrone, D. (ed.), *Los lugares de los escritores: guía literaria de Sicilia* (Seville: Editorial Doble, 2010).

Phelps, D., *A House in Sicily* (London: Virago, 2000).

Piccolo, L., *Collected Poems of Lucio Piccolo*, trans. B. Swann and R. Feldman (Princeton: Princeton University Press, 1972).

Pindar, *The Odes of Pindar*, trans. G. West (London: Munday and Slatter, 1824).

Pirandello, L., *The Old and the Young*, trans. C. K. Scott-Moncrieff (London: Chatto and Windus, 1928).

—— *The Late Mattia Pascal*, trans. N. Simborowski (Sawtry: Dedalus, 1990).

—— *Six Characters in Search of an Author*, trans. S. Mulrine (London: Nick Hern Books, 2002).

—— *The Turn*, trans. H. Curtis (London: Hesperus Press, 2007).

Pound, E., *Selected Poems, 1908–1969* (London: Faber and Faber, 1975).

Pound Shakespear, D., 'Pound Family Postcards', Hamilton Pound Family Postcard Archive, http://elib.hamilton.edu/pound-family-postcards.

Puzo, M., *The Sicilian* (London: Arrow, 2000).

—— *The Godfather* (London: Arrow, 2009).

Quasimodo, S., *Selected Poems*, trans. J. Bevan (Harmondsworth: Penguin, 1965).

—— *The Night Fountain: Selected Early Poems*, trans. M. Sonzogni and G. Dawe (Todmorden: Arc Publications, 2008).

Robb, P., *Midnight in Sicily* (London: Harvill Press, 1999).

—— *M: The Caravaggio Enigma* (London: Bloomsbury, 2000).

Roberto, F. De, *The Viceroys*, trans. A. Colquhoun (London: Harvill, 1989).

Roe, R. P., *The Shakespeare Guide to Italy: Then and Now* (London: Harper Perennial, 2011).

Samuels, E., *Bernard Berenson: The Making of a Connoisseur* (Cambridge, MA: Harvard University Press, 1979).

Sassoon, S., *Collected Poems 1908–1956* (London: Faber and Faber, 1984).

Scianna, F., *Jorge Luis Borges fotografato da Ferdinando Scianna* (Milan: Sciardelli, 1999).

Sciascia, L., *Salt in the Wound followed by Death of the Inquisitor*, trans. J. Green (New York: Orion Press, 1969).

—— *The Wine Dark Sea*, trans. A. Bardoni (London: Paladin Grafton Books, 1987).

—— *Sicilian Uncles*, trans. N. S. Thompson (London: Paladin Grafton Books, 1988).

—— *The Moro Affair and The Mystery of Majorana*, trans. S. Rabinovitch (London: Paladin Grafton Books, 1991).

—— *Candido, or a Dream Dreamed in Sicily*, trans. A. Foulke (London: Harvill Press, 1995).

—— *Pirandello e la Sicilia* (Milan: Adelphi, 2001).

—— *The Day of the Owl*, trans. A. Colquhoun and A. Oliver (New York: New York Review of Books, 2003).

Servadio, G., *To a Different World* (London: Hamish Hamilton, 1979).

—— *Motya: Unearthing a Lost Civilization* (London: Phoenix, 2000).

Shakespeare, W., *Much Ado About Nothing* (Ware: Wordsworth Editions, 1995).

Sharp, E., *William Sharp (Fiona Macleod): A Memoir, Volume 1* (London: William Heinemann, 1910).

Sharp, W., 'Through Nelson's Duchy', *Pall Mall Magazine*, October 1903.

—— 'Sicilian Highlands', *Atlantic Magazine*, vol. unknown, 1904.

—— The William Sharp 'Fiona Macleod' Archive (University of London), 2013, www.ies.sas.ac.uk/research/current-projects/william-sharp-fiona-macleod-archive, accessed 6 January 2014.

Shelley, M. and Shelley, P. B., *Proserpine and Midas* (London: Milford, 1922).

Sheridan, A., *André Gide: A Life in the Present* (London: Penguin, 2000).

Siculus, D., *The Library of History: Volume 3*, trans. C. H. Oldfather (Cambridge, MA: Loeb, 1989).

Sladen, D., *In Sicily, 1896–1898–1900: Volume I* (New York: E. P. Dutton, 1901).

—— *In Sicily, 1896–1898–1900: Volume II* (New York: E. P. Dutton, 1901).

—— *Sicilian Lovers* (London: Clear Type Press, 1905).

—— *Sicily, the New Winter Resort* (New York: E. P. Dutton, 1907).

—— *Twenty Years of my Life* (New York: E. P. Dutton, 1913).

Steinbeck, J., *Once There Was a War* (London: Penguin, 2001).

Sugg, J., *John Henry Newman: Snapdragon in the Wall* (Leominster: Grecewing, 2001).

Swinburne, H., *Travels in the Two Sicilies: Volume III* (London: Cadell and Elmsly, 1790).

—— *Travels in the Two Sicilies: Volume IV* (London: Cadell and Elmsly, 1790).

Taylor Simeti, M., *On Persephone's Island* (London: Bantam Books, 2001).

Tempio, D., *Domenico Tempio: Poems and Fables*, trans. G. Cipolla (Ottawa: Legas, 2009).

Thomas, C., *Leftover Life to Kill* (London: Putnam, 1957).

Thornton, M. B. (ed.), *Notebooks: Tennessee Williams* (New Haven: Yale University Press, 2007).

Timpanelli, G., *Sometimes the Soul* (New York: Vintage Books, 1999).

Trevelyan, R., *Princes under the Volcano* (London: Phoenix, 2002).

Tuckerman, H., *Isabel, Or Sicily: A Pilgrimage* (Philadelphia: Lea and Blanchard, 1839).

Unsworth, B., *The Ruby in her Navel* (London: Penguin, 2007).

Various, *Poems from Italy* (London: George G. Harrap, 1945).

Velez-Giraldo, J., 'Newman's Mediterranean "Verses"', *Newman Studies Journal* 3:2 (2006).

Verdura, F. de, *The Happy Summer Days* (London: Phoenix, 2000).

Verga, G., *The House by the Medlar Tree*, trans. M. Craig (New York: Harper & Brothers, 1890).

—— *Little Novels of Sicily*, trans. D. H. Lawrence (New York: Thomas Seltzer, 1925).

—— *Sparrow, Temptation and Cavalleria Rusticana*, trans. D. H. Lawrence (Sawtry: Dedalus, 2002).

—— *Sicilian Stories: A Dual-Language Book*, trans. S. Appelbaum (New York: Dover Publications, 2003).

Vittorini, E., *The Women of Messina*, trans. F. Frenaye and F. Keene (New York: New Directions Publishing, 1973).

—— *Conversations in Sicily*, trans. A. Salierno Mason (Edinburgh: Canongate Books, 2004).

Viviano, F., *Blood Washes Blood* (London: Arrow, 2002).

Washington, B. T., *The Man Farthest Down* (New York: Doubleday, Page & Company, 1912).

Waugh, E., *Labels: A Mediterranean Journal* (London: Penguin, 1985).

Weatherby, H. L., *Cardinal Newman in his Age: His Place in English Theology and Literature* (Nashville: Vanderbilt University Press, 2008).

Whicker, A., *Whicker's War* (London: HarperCollins, 2006).

Whitaker, J., *Motya: A Phoenician Colony in Sicily* (London: G. Bell and Sons, 1921).

Whitaker, T., *Sicily and England: Social and Political Reminiscences 1848–1870* (London: Constable & Company, 1907).

Williams, T., *The Rose Tattoo* (New York: New Directions Publishing, 2010).

Yeats, W. B., *Sailing to Byzantium* (London: Weidenfeld and Nicolson, 1995).

Zagajewski, A., *Eternal Enemies*, trans. C. Cavanagh (New York: Farrar Straus Giroux, 2009).

## Useful Resources

Dummett, J., *Syracuse: City of Legends* (London: I.B.Tauris, 2010).

Jones, T., *Florence and Tuscany: A Literary Guide for Travellers* (London: I.B.Tauris, 2013).

Keahey, J., *Seeking Sicily* (New York: Thomas Dunne Books, 2011).

Malta, J.G., *The Books*, the Official Mario Puzo Library, www.mariopuzo.com, Mario Puzo Library, 2008.

# INDEX